颐和园长廊彩画故事

STORIES BEHIND THE LONG CORRIDOR PAINTINGS IN THE SUMMER PALACE

五洲传播出版社

前　言

颐和园位于北京市西北郊，是中国著名的古典皇家园林，总面积达290多万平方米，主要由万寿山和昆明湖组成。

颐和园的前身为金代行宫。清乾隆十五年（1750年），乾隆皇帝在此大兴土木，修建清漪园，前后用时15年。完工后的清漪园不仅继承了中国北方园林的恢宏大气，又兼具江南园林的秀美多姿，更将京城西北郊的皇家园林连接成片，构成一组完整的园林体系。咸丰十年（1860年），英法联军攻入北京，清漪园内木结构建筑均被付之一炬。光绪十一年（1885年），垂帘听政的慈禧太后，挪用海军经费开始动工修复清漪园，并将其改名为“颐和园”。

1900年，颐和园再次遭到八国联军的破坏和洗劫。后因清廷没落，慈禧只是对前山和园内东部进行了再次修缮。1924年，颐和园被辟为公园。新中国成立后，政府多次拨款修葺，再现了这座皇家园林辉煌的景观布局。1998年，颐和园被联合国教科文组织列入《世界遗产名录》。

颐和园是北京现存规模最大，保存最完整的清代园林。昆明湖水域辽阔，约占全园面积的四分之三；万寿山上层层叠间了以佛香阁为主的重重高大雄伟的建筑，构成全园景观的中心。万寿山南麓的建筑因地构筑，设计巧妙。一条长廊沿岸而设，与佛香阁建筑群垂直相交。

长廊东起邀月门，西止石丈亭，全长728米，共273间。长廊以排云门为中心，左右对称，布局严谨，两侧建有四座亭重檐八角和两座水榭。四座亭子，自东而西依次为“留佳”、“寄澜”、“秋水”、“清遥”，象征一年四季。

长廊形式独特，布局完整，将以仁寿殿为代表的政治活动区、以乐寿堂、玉澜堂等庭院为代表的生活区和以长廊沿线、后山、西区组成的苑园游览区三个区域联为一体；长廊建筑构思巧妙，它将以万寿山为中心的山景和以昆明湖为中心的水景相隔，而漫步长廊时，游人既能北眺万寿山，又能南望昆明湖，长廊又将山与水无形地连为一个整体。除了连接景点，引导行人的旅游路线之外，长廊还为游人遮风避雨、抵骄阳挡暴雪，即使在恶劣的天气下，游人依然可以绕亭而坐，歇息之时，又可以仰望、欣赏廊上幅幅精美的彩画。

长廊蜿蜒曲折，移步换景，每根梁枋上都绘有精美的彩画。长廊彩绘属于“苏式彩画”，是中国木结构建筑上的装饰艺术。它的特点是主要画面被括在大半圆的括线内（称为“包袱”）。由于建筑形式不同，画师在颐和园长廊四周的

梁枋等处绘制了大小不同、题材广泛、形式多样的14000多幅彩画，主要有花木虫鸟，人物故事，山水风景等。其中，最引人入胜的是人物故事彩画，故事大多出自中国古典文学名著《红楼梦》、《西游记》、《三国演义》、《水浒传》、《封神演义》、《聊斋志异》等。彩画上没有任何文字说明，人们只能依据画上人物的容貌神情、衣着装扮、动作造型和场景等猜测故事的内容。无论是人物画，还是花鸟画，都有深刻的寓意。1990年，长廊以建筑形式独特、绘画丰富精美，被评为世界上最长的画廊，被载入“吉尼斯世界大全”。

PREFACE

The Summer Palace, a famous classic royal garden in China, is located in a northwest suburbs of Beijing, China. Covering an area of more than 290 hectares, it is made up of two major sections: the Longevity Hill and Kunming Lake.

The origin of the Palace is something of a Xanadu from the Jin Dynasty (1115-1234). In 1750, Emperor Qianlong in the Qing Dynasty (1644-1911) started a huge project, Qingyi Garden, in this area, which took 15 years to complete. The garden not only inherited the mighty style of the northern Chinese garden, but also absorbed the delicate beauty of the southern Chinese garden; moreover, it connected all the royal gardens in the northwest suburbs of Beijing, which constituted a series of garden complex. In the 10th year of Emperor Xianfeng's reign (1860), the British and French troops seized Beijing; Qingyi Garden was looted by the foreign troops, and all of its wooden architecture was burnt to the ground. In the 11th year of Emperor Guangxu's reign (1885), Empress Dowager Cixi, who was actually running the country, re-allocated funds meant for the country's marine force to restore Qingyi Garden, and then renamed it the Summer Palace.

In 1900, the Summer Palace was again looted and destroyed by foreign invaders consisting of troops from eight countries. The Qing court, by this time, reduced to such financial shortage that it was unable to allocate any money for restoration. In 1902, Cixi

had only the front of Longevity Hill and the eastern part of the Summer Palace rebuilt. In 1924, the Summer Palace was opened to public as a park. Since the founding of the People's Republic of China, the government has repaired it many times, eventually restoring the general landscape of this grand royal garden. In 1998, the Summer Palace was listed by UNESCO on the list of World Heritage Sites.

The Summer Palace is, by far, the largest and most complete garden preserved from the Qing Dynasty.The broad Kunming Lake occupies threequaters of the entire imperial garden. With its unique structure, ingenious layout, towering terrace and convincing grandeur, the Buddhist Incense Tower was artfully set out by the imperial garden and beautiful scenery surrounding it, making it the very center of the whole garden. The structures on the southern side of the Longevity Hill are wonderfully designed according to the topography. They are connected by a long corridor, which vertically converges with the complex of the Buddhist Incense Tower.

The long corridor, 728-meter long, stretches from the Yaoyue Gate (Gate of Inviting the Moon) to the Shizhang Pavilion (Stone-old-man Pavilion), and is divided into 273 sections. The Paiyuan Gate (Gate of Dispelling Clouds) is its center; the symmetrical beauty of the entire corridor is delicately designed. Around the Gate of Dispelling Clouds, there are four pavilions and two waterside pavilions, and each of the four pavilions is decorated with multiple eaves and eight roof angles. From the east to the west, the four pavilions are named "Liu Jia (Mesmerizing Scenery)", "Ji Lan (Harmonizing with the Lake)", "Qiu Shui (Autumn Water)", and "Qing Yao (Clear and Carefree)", respectively, which symbolize the four seasons of a year.

The unique artistic corridor is almost perfect in design. It links the political business area which features the Hall of Benevolence and Longevity, the living area featuring the Hall of Happiness and Longevity and the Hall of Jade Ripples, as well as the garden area highlighted by the various landscapes running along the corridor, mountainous area, and the western area, and gives the entire Summer Palace a sense of unity. Its location is also appreciative; it serves as a division between the mountainous landscape centered around the Longevity Hill and the water settings centered around the Kunming Lake; tourists can appreciate the entirety of the Longevity Hill and Kunming Lake at the same time

while strolling in the corridor; thus, it also acts as an medium between the mountain and water. In addition to linking the different scenic spots and setting a reasonable traveling route for the tourists, the corridor also functions as a shelter so tourists can avoid the harsh wind, rain, scorching sunlight, and severe snow; when the weather suddenly becomes unfavorable, tourists can sit in the corridor and take a rest, and during the time, the paintings on its balks become another wonderful sort of appreciative scenery.

The long corridor is meandering, and the views inside change as the viewer's vantage point shifts. On each of its balks, there are exquisite colorful paintings. They embody the wonderful decorative art of Chinese wooden buildings, whose genre belongs to the colorful Suzhou-styled painting school. The main feature of which is that each of these paintings is painted within a large semicircle wrapper. Artists have painted more than 14,000 paintings of different sizes, relevance and patterns on the balks of the corridor according to the shapes of the relevant architectural parts. These paintings feature flowers, birds, insects, plants, legendary or historic stories, as well as landscapes, among which the most outstanding are the figural stories; those stories mostly originate from Chinese classic fiction, such as *A Dream of Red Mansions*, *Pilgrimage to the West*, *The Romance of the Three Kingdoms*, *Outlaws of the Marsh*, *The Creation of the Gods*, and *Strange Tales from Make-Do Studio*. Since there are no literary illustrations available, visitors have to guess the content of the painted stories according to the appearance, countenance, dressing and postures of the painted figures and the backgrounds. -In fact, each of those paintings, whether about humans or about flowers and birds, carries profound cultural significance. In 1990, the corridor was ranked as the longest gallery in the world, as listed in the *Guinness Book of World Records*, for its unique artistic pattern, exquisite style and rich content.

目录CONTENTS

目录CONTENTS

目录CONTENTS

目录CONTENTS

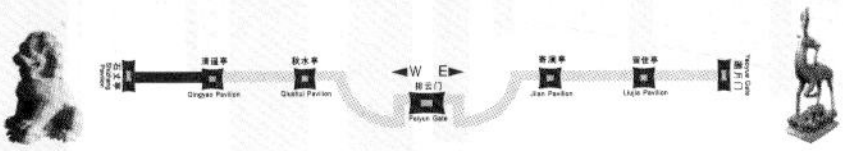

颐和园长廊 LONG CORRIDOR

STORIES BEHIND THE LONG CORRIDOR PAINTINGS IN THE SUMMER PALACE

《颐和园长廊彩画故事》

东汉末年，西凉刺史董卓统军攻打都城洛阳，废少帝刘辩，立陈留王刘协为献帝，自封为相国。西凉兵在城中烧杀抢掠，无恶不作。曹操多权谋、善机变，一心想除掉董卓，便假意屈身事董卓，深得董卓信任。一日，曹操随身暗藏一把宝刀，来到相府。董卓问他为何来迟，曹操答道，马走太慢。董卓听了，命义子吕布去选一匹西凉好马送给曹操，吕布领令而出。董卓体态肥胖，不能久坐，倒身向内而卧。此时，曹操拔刀即欲行刺，不料被董从镜中看见。曹操急中生智，忙跪在地上，谎称献刀。董卓一看，果然是宝刀，大喜之下，带曹操看马。曹操急忙翻身上马，加鞭逃走。等到董卓、吕布醒悟过来，派人捉拿曹操时，曹操早已逃出城外。

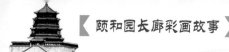

谋董贼曹操献刀

Cao Cao Presenting a Sword to Dong Zhuo

Dong Zhuo, a brutal unmerciful general of the Eastern Han Dynasty who took advantage of an internal conflict between the eunuchs and relatives of the royal family members, led his army and marched into Luoyang (in today's Henan Province), the capital city of the Han Dynasty. Then he dethroned Liu Bian and placed the puppet Emperor Xian, Liu Xie, in the throne, and appointed himself Prime Minister. His soldiers did every conceivable evil in Luoyang, burning, killing and robbing. Many righteous officials tried desperately to get rid of Dong, but failed miserably. What's worse, some were captured and killed by Dong. Cao Cao (155-220), a resourceful and flexible general, had been longing to do away with Dong for a long time. He pretended to make concessions to serve Dong and won Dong's trust, thus freely circulating around Dong.

One day, Cao visited Dong with a hidden but valuable sword when Dong sat on the bed with Lü Bu, Dong's adoptive son, in attendance. Seeing Cao, Dong inquired why he was late. Cao complained that his horse moved too slowly. Having heard this, Dong ordered Lü Bu to select an excellent horse to bestow on Cao. Subsequently Lü left to do so. Dong was too fat to sit for long so he lay down on his side, having his back toward Cao. Cao took the chance and drew his sword, but Dong caught a glimpse of it in a mirror. Cao hurriedly knelt down, holding the sword and saying, "I came here especially for presenting this valuable sword to you." Seeing that the sword hilt was encrusted with precious stones, Dong accepted it and led Cao out to see the horse. "Can I have a try?" asked Cao. Being permitted, Cao mounted the horse and left. Before Dong and Lü Bu came to their senses, Cao had escaped out of the city and vanished without a trace.

本故事与《三顾茅庐》相连。诸葛亮上通天文，下晓地理。刘备两次与关羽、张飞去隆中拜访诸葛亮，均未遇到。刘备求贤若渴，又第三次拜访。正遇诸葛亮在家，两人相见，谈得十分投机。诸葛亮为刘备分析了天下形势：如今曹操统率百万大军，挟天子以令诸侯，难以与其争锋；孙权占据江东，历三世之治，根基已稳。曹操占有天时，孙权占有地利，刘备欲成霸业，就要占据人和。荆州（今湖北境）为交通重镇，益州（今四川和云贵部分地区）乃天府之国。刘备可先攻荆州，后取西川，建立基业；外结孙权，内修政理，则大业可成、汉室可兴。刘备茅塞顿开，对诸葛亮心悦诚服。后来，诸葛亮辅助刘备，三足鼎立的局面形成。

定三分隆中决策

Making Decisions in Longzhong

The stories follows "Liu Bei Visiting the Grass-Roof Farmhouse Three Times". The two talked happily. Zhuge Liang offered an analysis of the current situation:

A portrait of Zhuge Liang

Cao Cao occupied the North China Plain. He seized the favorable moment and ruled an immense army, which helped him to control the court, the various feudal lord as well. You should not think of opposing him. Then Sun Quan held the Yangtze River region known as Jiangdong, where the Suns ruled for three generations. Maybe you could gain support there but hard to win at last. In view of this, a move to occupy Jing (today's Hubei) and Yi (today's Sichuan and parts of Yunnan and Guizhou) was vital for success. The region of Jing had been a strategic place, while the region of Yi fertile and extensive. Cao won by an excellent opportunity, while Sun by a strategic place, thus you could win by support from the people. You should seize Jing and Yi, and then encourage economic development, strengthen the legal system, as well as developing cordial relations with the non-Han people located in the west and south. It was necessary to effectively manage inside the zone of influence and to make an ally of Sun Quan as an external strategy. Such a policy would reduce resistance and increase manpower and economic resources. These done, you could occupy the North China Plain easily and then reestablish the Han Dynasty.

Hearing these words, Liu Bei was convinced wholeheartedly. In 221, Liu Bei finally established the State of Shu, and a tripartite confrontation as Zhuge described took shape.

周敦颐，北宋时期道州营道（今湖南道县）人。他是中国理学的创始人，其学术思想的特点在于援佛、道入儒，发挥了天人合一的思想，代表作为《太极图说》。

周敦颐为官不畏权贵，深得民心；晚年积劳成疾，辞官归家，在庐山莲花峰下养病。画中的情景就是周敦颐在莲花峰下的生活情景。他的住所周围，莲塘相连，山青水秀，因此写下脍炙人口的名篇《爱莲说》。篇中“出淤泥而不染，濯清涟而不妖”的词句表达了诗人洁身自好的高尚品德；而“中通外直，不蔓不枝，香远益清，亭亭净植”表明了诗人不甘同流合污、耿直正派的人格。

周敦颐爱莲

Zhou Dunyi Loving the Lotus

Zhou Dunyi (1017-1073), a famous thinker and philosopher during the Northern Song Dynasty, was born in present-day Daoxian, Hunan. He was the founder of Neo-Confucianism, and his academic thought was characterized by his intro-duction of the doctrines of Buddhism and Taoism into Confucianism and further development of the thought of “the unity of heaven and human beings”. His representative work was *Explanation of the Diagram of the Supreme Ultimate*, in which some basic doctrines of Neo-Confucianism, including cosmogenesis, the relationship between human beings and nature, ways for self-cultivation, etc., were illustrated with the help of the diagram of the Supreme Ultimate (*Taiji*).

A portrait of Zhou Dunyi

He defied the dignitary when he was a governmental officer, thus was deeply supported by the people. Later, he became sick, resigned and went back home to recuperate at the foot of the Lotus Peak, Lushan Mountain, in Jiangxi Province. This picture draws its material from Zhou’s daily life. His residence was surrounded by lotus ponds and green mountains. His article *Ode to the Lotus* was very popular. In the article, the sentences, like “Though growing in the mud, the lotus is never contaminated by it; floating on the water, yet it isn’t seductive” indicate the author’s noble character of preserving his purity. The sentences “The branchless stem is hollow inside yet straight outside; it stands in water gracefully, with the fragrance suffusing all around.” reveal the author’s upright personality of never associating with evil.

徐庶为刘备的军师，他多次出谋划策，帮助刘备大败曹军，深受刘备倚重。曹操惊其才，有心将其召至麾下。曹操得知徐庶是个孝子后，派人把徐庶的母亲接到许昌，又模仿徐母笔迹给徐庶修了一封家书，让他速来许昌救母。徐庶见信后泪如泉涌，向刘备辞行。

第二日，刘备送徐庶出城，送了一程又一程，久久不肯离去。忽然徐庶拍马回来，向刘备说道："险些忘了一件大事。距襄阳城外二十里处，有一位奇人，叫诸葛亮。他上知天文，下晓地理。如能得他辅佐，您就可以稳坐天下了。"刘备急忙请徐庶引见。徐庶告诉刘备，这样的奇人非得他亲自去请，才显诚意。说完，便策马离去。

徐庶走马荐诸葛

Xu Shu Recommending Zhuge Liang on the Horseback

Xu Shu was one of Liu Bei's military advisors during the Three Kingdoms Period. He helped to provide strategies against Cao Cao, and had successfully defeated Cao several times. Thus surprised by his talent, Cao Cao had long admired the man, wishing to lure Xu into his service. Knowing that Xu Shu was noted for his affection for his mother, Cao captured his mother and took her to the capital, Xuchang, and treated her exceedingly well. Then Cao Cao's advisor wrote a forged letter in the lady's handwriting to Xu Shu, and told him that her life hung by a thread and she looked to him to save her. Xu Shu was full of fear when he read the letter. He asked Liu Bei for an immediate departure, and promised never to serve Cao.

The next day, as Liu Bei was seeing Xu Shu off he couldn't bring himself to let Xu Shu go completely so he accompanied over a rather long distance. Staring at Xu Shu's obscure figure farther and farther, Liu Bei was still reluctant to leave. Suddenly, they saw Xu Shu galloping back. Xu Shu said, "In the turmoil of my feelings, I forgot an important thing. There is a person of wonderful skill named Zhuge Liang, who live about 10 kilometers from the city of Xiangyang, and styled himself Master Sleeping Dragon. He is a veritable genius, and could tell configurations of stars and recognize everything on the earth. If he will help you, you need feel no more anxiety about peace in the empire. You ought really to visit him."

Liu Bei asked Xu Shu to visit Zhuge Liang on his behalf, but Xu shook his head and said, "You must go and offer your invitation personally, and his acceptance depends entirely on your sincerity." After finishing these words, Xu Shu turned his horse and left.

隋朝末年，隋炀帝暴虐淫逸，大臣杨素助纣为虐，隋朝危在旦夕。李靖心怀大志，却无人赏识。一天，他到杨素府上，一个手持红拂的歌女见李靖是个英雄豪杰，便起了爱慕之心，投奔李靖，二人结为夫妻。为了躲避杨素的追查，他们随即收拾行装，逃往太原。途中结识了一个满脸卷曲胡子的虬髯客。虬髯客听说太原李世民准备起兵反隋，便和李靖相约去太原见李世民。说完，起身向李靖夫妇告别。画中便是此情景。到了太原，三人相会，见李世民果真是一代英豪，虬髯客把自己的全部钱财交与李靖助李世民打天下，自己去东南方开创事业。

风尘三侠

Three Travel-Stained Knight-Errants

At the end of the Sui Dynasty, Emperor Yang (the last emperor of Sui, reigned 604-618) was extravagant and tyrannical; and Yang Su, his prime minister, helped him carry out his wicked deeds. Thus the whole dynasty was submerged in crises and many people prepared to overturn the Sui Reign. Li Jing (571-649), a courtier with great ambitions and extraordinary intelligence, could not get any recognition. One day at Yang Su's mansion, Li Jing met a female singer who was commonly referred to as "Hongfu" (literally Red Server because she held a red scarf in hand while she waited on Yang Su). Hongfu was filled with admiration the first time she met Li Jing and the next day resolutely switched her allegiance to him. Attracted by her frankness and beauty, Li married her and both fled to Taiyuan in fear of Yang Su.

One day on their trip they encountered a man called Dragon-Beard Man, known for his long curly red beard. Li Jing and the man chatted happily. Having promised to meet in Taiyuan where Li Shimin (the later Emperor Taizong of Tang, reigned 626-649) was mobilizing forces to overthrow the rule of the Sui Dynasty, the Dragon-Beard Man bade farewell to the couple and left. This is just the scene shown in the painting. The two together met Li Shimin after they arrived at Taiyuan. Several days later, the Dragon-Beard Man entrusted all his jewels to Li Jing who would then use them to support Li Shimin to gain the throne and he himself left to pursue his cause in the southeast. Later, Li Jing became famous, being one of the most prominent generals in the early Tang Dynasty.

A portrait of Li Jing

一日，唐僧师徒来到一座深山，悟空安顿师父下马休息后，便去化缘求斋。临走前，他施展法术，用金箍棒在地上画了个圆圈，并嘱咐师父、师弟不可走出圆圈。山里有个白骨精，听说吃了唐僧肉能长生不老，便伺机抓唐僧。第一次她变成一美丽女子，以斋饭诱惑唐僧师徒。不料被悟空识破。悟空举棒就打，白骨精只得扔下假尸离去。白骨精不甘心，故伎重演，变成一老太婆和一老头，但两次均未得逞。唐僧不识妖怪，训斥悟空误杀三条生命，赶走了悟空。没有悟空的保护，没走多远，唐僧便被妖怪抓去。猪八戒跑到花果山说尽好话、将孙悟空请回，才把唐僧救出。

The Monkey King Subduing White-Bone Demon Three Times

One day, Tang Seng and his disciples went deep into a mountain, desolate and uninhabited. After settling down for a rest, the Monkey King set out to probe the way ahead and beg food. Before taking his leave, he drew a circle on the ground with his magic cudgel, and exhorted Tang Seng not to go outside the circle. There was, indeed, a White-Bone Demon lurking in the mountain. Learning that eating a piece of flesh of Tang Seng would help her become immortal, she was planning to catch him. First she changed into a girl and headed towards Tang Seng, trying to lure them out of the circle. At just moment the Monkey King returned and gave her a blow. The White-Bone Demon had to run away, leaving a false corpse lying dead on the ground. The demon, using her old tactics, then turned into an old lady and a white-bearded man for the second and third time. But the time she came near Tang Seng and his disples, she was hit by the Monkey King and had to escape. Tang Seng could not distinguish the demon from the human beings, blamed the Monkey King for killing three lives, and drove him away. Shortly after that, Tang Seng was seized by the demon. Finally, it was the Monkey King who returned to save him.

东汉末年，天下大乱。朝廷发布文告，招兵买马。刘备看榜文时，长叹一声，忽听背后有人说："男子汉大丈夫不思为国出力，在这里叹什么气？"并自报姓名说，他叫张飞，靠卖酒杀猪为生。刘备言，想为国出力，但力量不够。张飞说愿意拿出家产，招兵买马，创建大业。刘备听后非常高兴。二人来到一个小店，边喝酒边谈，正说得投机，门外突然来了一个红脸大汉，威风凛凛，相貌堂堂。刘备、张飞请他一同饮酒。交谈中得知，此人名叫关羽，因仗义除霸有家不能归。他们各自抒发自己的志向，谈得十分投机。隔日，三人来到一个桃园，点燃香烛，叩拜天地，结为兄弟，并发誓同心协力，报效国家。

桃园结义

Forging a Brotherhood in the Peach Garden

Toward the end of the Eastern Han Dynasty (25-220), a large-scale Yellow-turban Uprising broke out and landed a heavy blow against the royal court, which immediately issued royal edicts to raise forces around the country. Utilizing this chance, three men Liu Bei (161-223), Zhang Fei (167?-221) and Guan Yu (162?-220) surfaced.

Liu Bei was a royal descendant. One day on the street Liu could not help sighing after reading the edict. At the same moment a voice from behind demanded, "Without devotion to your country, what use is your trouble?" Liu Bei turned around, saw an extraordinary man and hurriedly asked his name. The man was called Zhang Fei, a butcher selling meat. While the two sat drinking and chatting, a martial-looking and handsome man with a powerful frame came in. Immediately Liu and Zhang invited him to join them. Through talking, they learned that this man was named Guan Yu. As he had killed a local tyrant several years before, he had been forced to flee his home and lived on hauling goods on a cart. When he heard the edict, he wanted to get involved.

During the amiable conversation, they found they shared the same ambition, and on the next day in a peach garden they lit some sticks of incense and knelt down to swear brotherhood to heaven and earth: Liu Bei the eldest, Guan Yu the second oldest and Zhang Fei the youngest all vowed to devote themselves to the country. Thereafter, the three sworn brothers went on to achieve significant careers culminating with Liu Bei ascending the throne of the Shu State in 221 in present-day Sichuan. And this story has since been known as "forging a brotherhood in the peach garden".

蔡文姬，东汉末年人，是文学家、书法家蔡邕的女儿。她自幼聪慧博学，擅长诗歌音律。但是，她的命运却很悲惨：父亲因为得罪了权臣，被杀死；她自己出嫁后不到两年，丈夫又死去。在一次南匈奴入侵中原时，蔡文姬被劫到匈奴，被迫作了匈奴左贤王的妻子。从此，她就在匈奴住了整整12年。曹操为汉丞相时，对北部的匈奴等少数民族采取了亲善政策。他尊重蔡邕，想让蔡文姬整理蔡邕的文稿，于是就派了蔡文姬的亲戚董祀带着许多金银财宝到匈奴去，和匈奴单于商谈，把蔡文姬赎了回来。这幅画就是描绘蔡文姬从匈奴回来的路上，路过长安城郊外，拜谒父亲坟墓时的情景。她在墓旁想到父亲的惨死和自己坎坷的半生，不禁仰天叹息，操琴吟唱，来抒发自己的悲凉与哀思。蔡文姬归汉以后，整理了蔡邕遗留下的400多篇书稿，后与董祀结婚，偕老而终。

文姬谒墓

Wenji Paying Homage at Her Father's Grave

Cai Wenji (177-?), also know as Cai Yan, was a Han Dynasty poet and composer. From childhood, she was smart and knowledgeable, especially excelling in poetry and music. Nevertheless she had a miserable fate. Her father Cai Yong (133-192), a writer and a calligrapher, had offended a powerful courtier and was eventually persecuted to death. And her husband died less than two years after they married.

What's worse, when the Huns invaded the Central Plains she was taken as prisoner to the norterlands, and later was forced to be the wife of Prince Zuoxian. She spent 12 years there. During her captivity, Cao Cao became the prime minister of Han; he implemented a united and friendly policy towards the Huns and other minorities. As Cao respected Cai Yong for his work, he wanted someone to sort it out and organize it. There was no doubt that Wenji was the best person, so Cao dispatched Dong Si, a relative of Wenji, as an envoy, to negotiate with the Huns with a large sum of treasure as the ransom. Thus Wenji had the chance to return to Han. Most of her father's works were lost in the ravages of war; fortunately, Cai Wenji was able to recite from her memory up to 400 pieces of poem and article.

This picture depicts the moment when Wenji reached her father's grave when they hit the outskirts of Chang'an. Recalling her father's tragic death and the first half of her life of frustration, she could not but look up to the sky and sigh deeply, expressing her grief through a chord.

“文人三才”是民间对宋代大文豪苏轼、秦观和佛印的美称。苏轼，号东坡居士，博经通史，文思敏捷，行文如飞云流水，走笔似蛟龙腾空。一世文章，雄视百代。秦观，性格豪放慷慨，文辞盖世。他与苏东坡邂逅于徐州，一见如故，结为密友。佛印是位出家人。这三位才子不但才华出众，而且友谊也超凡脱俗。相传三位朋友聚会时，东坡与秦观经常合伙灌醉佛印，这里面还有一段有趣的故事。

佛印原名谢端卿，通古博今，东坡与他是莫逆之交。这一年天下大旱，宋神宗（1048~1085年）设坛祈雨，命苏东坡主持斋戒仪式。谢端卿听说消息后，想趁此机缘面见皇帝，便让东坡带他前去。这

文人三才

Three Talented Literary Men

The Three Talented Literary Men refer to Su Shi, Qin Guan and Fo Yin. Among them, Su Shi, popular known as Su Dongpo, was well-informed on classics and history and sharp-minded, and excelled in writing various genres of literature. Qin Guan, a generous and open-minded man, was also brilliant at writing lyrical poems and essays. He and Su Shi felt kindred spirits at their first meeting and became fast friends. Fo Yin was a monk. Not only were the three prominent in literary circles, but also their friendship was extraordinarily legendary. It was said that Su Shi and Qin Guan used to collaborate to trick Fo Yin into being drunk when they met. The following is a story about that.

Fo Yin, whose original name was Xie Duanqing, was knowledgeable and brilliant in both history and literature. He and Su Shi were intimate friends. During a drought year, Emperor Shenzong of Song (reigned 1067-1085) planned to hold a sacrificial ceremony to pray for rain, and Su Shi was decreed to be the host. In order to seize the chance to see the emperor, Xie Duanqing asked Su Shi to take him to the ceremony. At the ceremony, Su Shi asked Xie Duanqing to disguise himself as a servant in order to get into the main hall. After the ceremony, it was Su Shi's duty to

日，东坡让端卿化装成杂役，来到殿堂。斋仪完毕，东坡命谢端卿献茶。神宗见端卿眉目清秀，身材伟岸，应对明敏，遂赐号佛印，于御前披剃为僧。谢端卿本指望来京一举成名，建立功业，却不想出此意外，被皇帝恩赐出家。出家后，他整日在寺中研究佛理，渐渐地反倒把功名富贵之想化作清静无为之业。东坡以为是自己害了佛印，便力劝其还俗出官，佛印不依。东坡没有办法，只好约来秦观。二人在花园中摆下酒席，欲灌醉佛印，使其破戒还俗。这幅画画的即是此情景。左边是东坡，居中者佛印，右边是秦观。无奈佛印德性清高，东坡的计策最终落空。从此，东坡、秦观更加敬重佛印。

send a servant (usually a low-ranking monk since the ceremony was held in a temple) to offer a cup of tea to the emperor. The servant was none other than Xie Duanqing. Seeing Xie Duanqing handsome and smart, the emperor liked him very much and endowed him with a Buddhist name, Fo Yin, and baptized him right away. Although it was a great benefit at that time, being appointed as a monk by the emperor, the result was really contrast to Xie Duanqing's original ideal of becoming famous and building his career in the capital city Kaifeng. After being initiated into the temple, however, he immersed himself in the study of Buddhist theories and gradually turned his secular ideal for wealth and fame into a firm commitment to Buddhism.

On Su Shi's part, he thought he had harmed Fo Yin, and tried every means to persuade him to come back to secularity and take a position in the government, but Fo Yin declined. Su Shi then invited Qin Guan to help him. They set a trap, in the name of holding a feast, to get Fo Yin drunk, and then to force him to come back to secularity. This painting reveals that scene. The person on the left is Su Shi, in the middle Fo Yin, and on the right Qin Guan. Unfortunately, their attempt did not succeed due to the noble character of Fo Yin. After that, Su Shi and Qin Guan showed more respect to their monk friend.

唐僧师徒行至火焰山，方圆百里火焰腾腾，孙悟空向铁扇公主借芭蕉扇，欲熄灭火焰，以便师徒继续行路。不料，铁扇公主见到悟空举剑就砍。原来观音收走红孩儿，铁扇公主正在恨处。悟空任她砍了十几下，毫发无损，铁扇公主见奈何不了他，慌忙跑进洞里，关了洞门。悟空变成小虫钻入洞中，飞到茶沫下，被铁扇公主喝下。悟空在铁扇公主肚子里一翻折腾，痛得铁扇公主只好交出扇子。铁扇公主给了悟空假扇子，悟空又气又恼，这次，他变成牛魔王的样子，骗得芭蕉扇。牛魔王获悉后，变成猪八戒的模样，又将芭蕉扇骗回。两人不肯相让，随即展开一场大战，悟空最终擒获牛魔王，在天兵天将的帮助下，得到芭蕉扇。

孙悟空三调芭蕉扇

The Monkey King Borrowing the Plantain Fan Three Times

On their way to the West, Tang Seng and his disciples arrived at the Flaming Mountain, where fires raged for hundreds of miles. The only way to get across the mountain was to borrow a Plantain Fan from the Princess Iron Fan, which could put out the fire. Knowing that the Princess Iron Fan was the wife of Bull Demon King, his sworn brother, the Monkey King volunteered to borrow the magic fan. However, since Kwan-yin caught her only son, the Red Boy, the princess had been longing to get her revenge on the Monkey King, but didn't know where to find him; now the Monkey King was just standing in front of her. Her face went bright red and evil anger flared up in her heart. Without a word, she swung both of her swords and hacked at the Monkey King's head. The Monkey King let her poke a dozen times but remained unhurt. Realizing she would never be able to kill him, she brought out her plantain fan and with a single wave blew the Monkey King right out of sight. The Monkey King borrowed a Wind-fixing Pill from a Bodhisattva and came back. He turned into a fly, and got into the princess' body. He pulled her liver and hit her heart, which brought extreme pain to the her. She rolled all over the ground, and had to give her fan to the Monkey King. The Monkey King took the fan and went to the Flaming Mountain. However, when he flapped the fan, the fire grew fiercer. Apparently, the fan was a fake one. He was furious and resentful, and decided to seek the Princess Iron Fan again. This time, he turned himself into the Bull Demon King and easily got the fan. But the real king came back and played a trick back on the Monkey King: he changed into Bajie, recouping the fan. Then the two had a good fight. Just as they were becoming locked in the struggle, the real Bajie came. He joined in the battle and defeated the bull, who tried to escape but was stopped by heavenly generals dispatched by the Buddha. The couple had to surrender and give the real fan to the Monkey King.

故事与《王司徒巧使连环计》相连。貂蝉被董卓霸占，吕布愤愤不平。他私会貂蝉，却被董卓发现，逐出相府。一天，吕布随董卓上朝，他趁董卓和汉献帝谈话之际，退出宫，溜进相府，来到后花园凤仪亭与貂蝉幽会。貂蝉哭着说道，她忍辱偷生，只为见吕布一面。说着就要投水自尽以表"真心"。吕布大惊，急忙拦腰抱住。董卓在殿上不见吕布，心中生疑，便辞别献帝回府。董卓找到后花园，远远看见吕布、貂蝉在凤仪亭下卿卿我我，不禁大怒，猛吼一声，冲上前去。吕布转身就跑，夺门而逃。董卓体胖，追赶不上，吕布逃脱。

谋士李儒知道此事，劝董卓借此机会，把貂蝉赐给吕布，吕布必感激，以死报恩。董卓不听。后来，连环计果然成功。在一次混战中，董卓最终死在吕布手里。

凤仪亭吕布戏貂蝉

Lü Bu Trysting with Diao Chan in the Fengyi Pavilion

Seeing that Dong Zhuo forcibly occupied Diao Chan, Lü Bu was furious and ruminated on his thoughts of Diao Chan. Accordingly he conducted a liaison with her. Unfortunately, they were discovered by Dong Zhuo and Lü Bu was banished from Dong Zhuo's residence. One day, while Dong Zhuo was holding a conversation with Emperor Xian, Lü Bu slipped into his father's residence, and met his beloved Diao Chan in the Fengyi Pavilion. Diao Chan sobbed out, "I lived in disgrace just to wait for a chance to have a final meeting with you. Fortunately my wish has come true and I would like to die here before you to show you how deep my feelings are for you." Then she stood up and tried to end her life by throwing herself into the pool; this greatly surprised Lü Bu, who stopped her immediately. Diao Chan pled with Lü Bu to rescue her from Dong Zhuo, and Lü held Diao Chan in his arms and comforted her with words. Suddenly aware of Lü Bu's absence at court, Dong Zhuo was suspicious. Then he bade farewell to the emperor and hurried to his residence. When he found the two in the pavilion, Dong Zhuo flew into a rage, roared and dashed up to them. Lü Bu was startled and turned to flee.

After Dong Zhuo had calmed down, Li Ru, one of Dong's councilors, hastened to advise Dong, "Diao Chan is just a girl, yet Lü Bu is your brave general. If you take this opportunity to marry Diao Chan to Lü Bu, he will be grateful, devoting himself whole-heartedly to help you." However, Dong refused. On the other hand, Lü Bu was becoming increasingly displeased with Dong, which was further heightened by Wang Yun, who suggested subtly that Lü take over Dong. Upon hearing this, Lü Bu made up his mind and ultimately, he found a chance and killed Dong Zhuo.

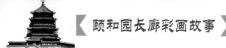

洛神又叫宓妃，传说她是伏羲的女儿，在一次游渡洛水时，不幸坠河淹死，就做了洛水的女神。此后嫁给风流放荡的水神河伯为妻，生活在悲伤忧郁之中。后来她又与后羿相爱。河伯知道后，找后羿算账，被后羿射瞎了一只眼睛。善良的宓妃怜悯河伯，中断了与后羿的往来。

洛神非常美丽，许多文人都用最美丽动听的语言来赞颂她。最富盛名的莫过于三国时期曹植的《洛神赋》。曹植是曹操的儿子，多才多艺，有壮志雄心，由于骨肉间争权夺利的矛盾，使他备受猜忌，最后抑郁而终。他的《洛神赋》以浪漫主义的手法，通过梦幻的境界，描写人神之间的真挚爱情，但终因人神无法结合而分离。然而作者生动细腻地刻画了一位优美的富有艺术感染力的女神的形象。

Goddess of Luoshui River

Lady Mi was the daughter of Fu Xi, the legendary Chinese emperor. When crossing the Luoshui River, she was so fascinated with the beautiful scenery on both sides of the river that fell into the Luoshui River and drowned, and thus was elevated to Goddess. One day when she was playing her sever-string *qin*, the melodious tune was heard by Hebo, who was demigod of the Yellow River. Fascinated by beautiful goddess, Hebo caused a great havoc in the Luoshui River and took her away. Later, they married. However, Hebo turned out to be a dissipated character, cherishing no real love for his wife but loafing abroad all the time. The goddess was therefore extremely disappointed but had to live in sorrow. At this time, she happened to meet Yi, whose wife abandoned him and flew to heaven. The two lonely fell in love. On hearing this, the furious Hebo came to find Yi, trying to kill him. However, Yi shot an arrow into Hebo's left eye, which sent the panicky Hebo fleeing.

The Goddess of Luoshui River was of extreme beauty. Many poets and writers, like Qu Yuan and Cao Zhi, praised her in the most vivid words. Qu Yuan, a native of the Chu Sate during the the Warring States Period, by highly praising the Goddess of Luoshui River, expressed his patriotism in his poems. Cao Zhi, the third son of Cao Cao, was versatile and full of ambition. But because of the struggle for power and wealth between his blood relations, he was suspicious and eventually died from depression. His famous work *Prose about the Goddess of Luoshui River*, in romantic style and imaginable circumstance, revealed a sincere feeling between the goddess and a commoner. Though he poured out his complaint and misery, he portrayed a graceful goddess in an artistic way, which moved generation after generation.

周瑜带兵攻打南郡时，中了毒箭；诸葛亮抢先一步夺取南郡、荆州和襄阳，周瑜一气之下，箭疮迸发。周瑜不甘心，便东吴招亲，想要扣押刘备，以换荆州，却“赔了夫人又折兵”，箭疮再次迸发。周瑜假借攻打西川，绕道夺取荆州，不料中计兵败。周瑜招招输给诸葛亮，怒气填胸，箭疮复裂，仰天长叹“既生瑜，何生亮”，连叫数声而亡，终年仅36岁。诸葛亮得知消息，到柴桑吊丧，设祭物于灵前，奠酒，跪读祭文，哀恸不已。

柴桑口诸葛亮吊丧

Zhuge Liang Mourning Zhou Yu

While Zhou Yu was leading his troops against Nanjun Prefecture, he was unfortunately struck by a poisonous arrow. When he was recovering, he heard that Zhuge Liang had seized Nanjun Prefecture, Jingzhou and Xiangyang (all in present-day Hubei Province) before him, and he was furious, which aggravated his injury. He wanted to continue his competition with Zhuge Liang, so he came up with an idea that the Eastern Wu State married its princess, Sun Quan's younger sister, to Liu Bei so that they could detain Liu and exchange him for Jingzhou, but the result was a loss of soldiers as well as the loss of Lady Sun, which further aggravated his injury. Then he made an excuse that he wanted to pass by Jingzhou so he could attack Xichuan, while in actuality, he besieged Jingzhou, but fell into Zhuge Liang's trap and was defeated.

A portrait of Zhou Yu

Zhou Yu was greatly agitated by his failures. He witnessed Zhuge Liang drinking and having fun, while he was humiliated by his failure, which finally aggravated his injury and took his life. His last words were: "Having born (Zhou) Yu, why also (Zhuge) Liang?" On learning the news, Zhuge Liang went to mourn Zhou Yu. He set up a sacrificial ceremony in front of Zhou Yu's coffin, and offered wine and read his sacrificial prose for the dead – he looked genuinely sad.

这幅画画的是唐朝大将郭子仪的故事。传说郭子仪从军之初，只是个无名的小卒。一次，他在路边一间破屋歇息。夜半时分，一道红光从窗口射入，郭子仪跑出屋子，只见一个仙女乘着彩云飘来。郭子仪忙跪在地上，望仙女拜道："今日正是七月初七，想必是织女娘娘降临世间。请赐我富贵和长寿吧。"仙女听罢，笑着说道："大富贵，亦寿考。"说罢，冉冉升天。郭子仪正要再问，仙女已消失不见。这时候，天已破晓。郭子仪想着织女娘娘对他说的话，骑上马继续前进。

公元755年，安史之乱爆发，郭子仪带领军队，多次以少胜多，击败叛军，先后收复了长安、洛阳等地，对平定叛乱、维持唐朝统治起了重要作用。他活到84岁，八个儿子和七个女婿全都做了高官，真是应了织女娘娘那句"大富贵，亦寿考"。

富贵寿考

The Trial for Wealth and Longevity

This painting is based on a story about Guo Ziyi (697-781), a famous general in the Tang Dynasty. It was said that when Guo Ziyi joined the army, he served as an ordinary soldier. Once, he took shelter in an old house by the road. At midnight, he faintly saw a shoot of red light in his dream. He took a careful look, and found the light was penetrating through a window. He hurried to go out, and saw a luxurious carriage in the sky. A fairy got out of the carriage and rode a piece of colorful cloud, flying over to him. Guo Ziyi knelt down, kowtowed to the fairy, and said, "It is July 7th today. Your Excellence must be the Weaving Queen. I beg for wealth and longevity." The fairy heard his words, smiled and said, "You will be rich and hornorable, as well as long-lived." Then she gradually rose back into the sky. When Guo tried to ask for something more, the fairy disappeared. Then at daybreak Guo Ziyi thought over the fairy's word, and continued his journey.

Later in 755, the An-Shi Rebellion broke out. Guo Ziyi, leading his out-numbered army, defeated the rebels and recovered important cities such as Chang'an and Luoyang for the court, which contributed a crack down on the rebellion. and was credited by many historians to allow the Tang to survied for a longer period. Just as the fairy told him, he gained power and reputation. He died at the age of 84, and all his eight sons and seven sons-in-law became dignitaries.

一日，唐僧师徒来到一座深山，悟空安顿师父下马休息后，便去化缘求斋。临走前，他施展法术，用金箍棒在地上画了个圆圈，并嘱咐师父、师弟不可走出圆圈。山里有个白骨精，听说吃了唐僧肉能长生不老，便伺机抓唐僧。第一次她变成一美丽女子，以斋饭诱惑唐僧师徒。不料被悟空识破。悟空举棒就打，白骨精只得扔下假尸离去。白骨精不甘心，故伎重演，变成一老太婆和一老头，但两次均未得逞。唐僧不识妖怪，训斥悟空误杀三条生命，赶走了悟空。没有悟空的保护，没走多远，唐僧便被妖怪抓去。猪八戒跑到花果山说尽好话、将孙悟空请回，才把唐僧救出。

三打白骨精

The Monkey King Subduing White-Bone Demon Three Times

One day, Tang Seng and his disciples went deep into a mountain, desolate and uninhabited. After settling down for a rest, the Monkey King set out to probe the way ahead and beg food. Before taking his leave, he drew a circle on the ground with his magic cudgel, and exhorted Tang Seng not to go outside the circle. There was, indeed, a White-Bone Demon lurking in the mountain. Learning that eating a piece of flesh of Tang Seng would help her become immortal, she was planning to catch him. First she changed into a girl and headed towards Tang Seng, trying to lure them out of the circle. At just moment the Monkey King returned and gave her a blow. The White-Bone Demon had to run away, leaving a false corpse lying dead on the ground. The demon, using her old tactics, then turned into an old lady and a white-bearded man for the second and third time. But the time she came near Tang Seng and his disples, she was hit by the Monkey King and had to escape. Tang Seng could not distinguish the demon from the human beings, blamed the Monkey King for killing three lives, and drove him away. Shortly after that, Tang Seng was seized by the demon. Finally, it was the Monkey King who returned to save him.

明嘉靖年间，毛朋、田伦、顾读、刘题四个人是非常要好的朋友。他们一起考中了进士，出京为官。临行前，四人盟约赴任后不得违法渎职。画面上即此情景。

田伦的姐姐为谋夺家产，毒死夫弟，又将弟媳杨素贞卖给布商为妻。刘题赴任后嗜酒贪杯，不务政事，根本不过问此案。时毛朋微服私访，杨素贞便倾吐冤屈。毛朋替她写了状子，嘱托她去信阳顾读那里告状。杨素贞辗转来到信阳，住在一个叫宋士杰的老人的店里。得知素贞遭遇，老人领她去官府告状。然顾读早已收到田伦的求情信和银两，将杨素贞收押在监，又把老人鞭打出衙门。老人回到店中，恰巧田伦派来向顾读行贿的衙役投宿在此。老人盗取了田写给顾串供的信件，跑去毛朋的公堂检举赃官、诉说冤情。毛朋判斩了田氏，处罚了违法乱纪的刘、田、顾三人，释放了杨素贞。

四进士

Four *Jinshi*

During Emperor Jiajing's reign (1521-1566) in the Ming Dynasty, there were four close friends, Mao Peng, Tian Lun, Gu Du and Liu Ti, who attended the Imperial Examinations and were selected as *Jinshi* together. Soon, they were sent to take up their positions away from the capital. Before their departure, they swore together that none of them should break the law or desert his duty, which is the scene in this painting.

There happened to be a criminal case that Tian Lun's elder sister, in order to seize all the family properties, poisoned her brother-in-law, and sold her sister-in-law Yang Suzhen to a businessman, while Liu Ti, the chief executive, did not care it at all. When Mao Peng as an official supervisor visited, Yang Suzhen told her sad story to him. Mao Peng wrote a petition for her, and advised her to launch her case in Xinyang City where Gu Du served as the chief official. Yang went all the way to Xinyang, and stayed in an inn. Learning Yang's miserable experience, the old owner of the inn took her to the government for justice. Unfortunately, Gu Du had already been bought off by Tian Lun and accepted bribes, he prisoned Yang Suzhen, and lashed the old man. The old man returned to his inn, and happened to find that the civil servants sent by Tian Lun to bribe Gu Du checked in. He somehow got the letter that Tian had written to Gu from the servants, went to Mao Peng's office, and exposed the case. Mao Peng upheld justice. He sentenced Tian Lun's elder sister to death, punished the corrupted Tian, Liu, and Gu – three faith-breakers, and released Yang Suzhen.

贾元春省亲回到宫中后，忽想起大观园中景致。她知道临幸之后，贾政必定将园林锁闭，不让人进去骚扰。于是她下了一道谕，命宝玉和她的诸位姐妹搬入园内居住、读书。宝玉住进了怡红院。

这一日恰逢阳春三月，春光明媚，微风轻拂，落英缤纷。宝玉闲暇无事，便来到花园，坐在桃花下面读起《西厢记》来，不想被来此葬花的黛玉撞见。宝玉只好将书交给黛玉。黛玉拿过书，坐下就看，只觉字字珠玑，句句精妙，越看越舍不得放手。宝玉见她看得出神，不禁感慨自己就是那“多愁多病身”的张生，黛玉就是那“倾国倾城貌”的莺莺；把自己和黛玉比作是一对恋人。黛玉一听，羞得满脸通红，恼怒万分，说宝玉拿淫词艳曲欺负她，转身欲走。宝玉赶忙上前，又说好话，又赔不是，并不断地贬损自己，最终逗乐了黛玉，两人又玩闹起来。

宝黛阅《西厢》

Baoyu and Daiyu Sharing the *Romance of the West Chamber*

After Yuanchun's return to the palace from her visit to the Grand View Garden, she was sure that her father, out of a zealous reverence for the emperor and herself, would have kept it all locked and allowed no one else to enter. That would be a pity. So she ordered Jia Baoyu and all her younger sisters to move to the garden, which was not to be closed. Baoyu chose the Happy Red Court as his residence, while Lin Daiyu, his cousin, chose the Bamboo Lodge.

One day about the middle of the third lunar month, Baoyu came to a garden to kill time. Sitting down on a rock under a blossoming peach tree, he began to read the *Romance of the West Chamber* (one of the most famous Chinese dramatic works, which tells a story of a pair of lovers, Zhang Sheng and Cui Yingying, consummating their love without parental approval, and was forbidden to read at Baoyu's age). He had just reached the line, red peach blossom were falling when a little gust of wind blew over, and a shower of petals suddenly rained down from the tree above, covering his clothes, his book and all the ground around him. Baoyu was so intoxicated that he didn't find Daiyu's arrival. Failed to conceal, Baoyu had to pass her the book. Daiyu put down her things and began to read. The more she read, the more she liked it. Baoyu saw she loved the book, and began to compare himself to Zhang Sheng while Daiyu to Cui Yingying. He implied that Daiyu and he were a couple falling in love. Daiyu was ashamed and annoyed, and cried. She reproached Baoyu for bullying her with such inappropriate words. Baoyu hurried to apologize and even disparaged himself, which eventually made Daiyu smile through her tears.

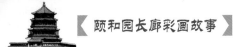

陶渊明是东晋著名辞赋家、散文家和田园诗人。这幅画描绘的是他的散文名篇《桃花源记》中的场景。

一天，武陵一个渔夫划船沿溪边捕鱼，遇到一片桃花林，继续前行，又看见一个山洞，洞口隐约有光亮，便从洞口走了进去。走出洞口后，土地平坦开阔，房屋整齐有致；田地肥沃，小路交错相通；人们耕田劳作，悠闲愉快。村里人看见渔夫，大吃一惊，问他从哪里来，并争着邀请渔夫去家里做客。他们自己说前代祖先为了躲避秦朝时候的战乱，带妻子儿女和同乡人来到这个与人世隔绝的地方，已不知道外面是什么朝代。渔夫停留了几天，告辞离去。村里人告诉他说，不可以把这里的情况对外人说。可是他出去后就报告了太守；再来时无论怎么寻找，也找不到桃花源了。

桃花源记

The Source of the Peach Blossom

This painting depicts a scene in *The Source of the Peach Blossom*, a famous prose of Tao Yuanming, who was one of the most influential poets in Chinese history.

One day, a fisherman in Wuling (present-day Changde, Hunan Province) rowed his boat along a stream, fishing. He suddenly found himself in the midst of woods full of peach blossoms along both banks. The fisherman was so curious that he rowed on. At the edge of the woods was the source of the stream. He found a hill with a small glimmering opening so he went ashore and stepped in. After several moments' walk, he suddenly caught sight of a wide-open field: the land was flat and spacious; everything such as the houses, fertile fields, and beautiful ponds was arranged in symetrical order on the land; paths crisscrossed the fields in all directions; in the fields people were busy with farm work; all people, men and women, the old and the young, appeared happy. They were surprised to see the fisherman, asking where he came from, and they enthusiastically invited him to their homes to entertain him. They told him that their ancestors, bringing their families and the village people, had come to this isolated haven to escape the turmoil of the Qin Dynasty (221-206 BC) and ever since then they had been cut off from the outside world. They knew neither the Han Dynasty (202 BC-220AD) nor the Wei (386-534) and Jin (265-420) dynasties. The fisherman told them all the things that they wanted to know. Before the fisherman took his leave, the villagers entreated him not to talk to others about their existence. When the fisherman came back home, he, however, reported his adventure to the prefect, who immediately sent people to look for this ideal world, but in vain.

神通广大的孙悟空，被骗到天上，封了个“弼马温”。他得意了十来天，才知道自己做的是最末一等官。一气之下，闯出了南天门，回花果山当“齐天大圣”去了。玉帝闻之，恼怒不已，命托塔李天王和哪吒三太子擒拿孙悟空。没想到第一个回合，李天王手下的先锋就被孙悟空打败了。哪吒急忙飞身来到水帘洞外，变成三头六臂，手持剑、刀、绳索，脚踏火轮，朝孙悟空迎面打来。孙悟空也变成三头六臂，把金箍棒一晃，变作三条，和哪吒对打起来。刀光剑影，枪来棍去，地动山摇。孙悟空眼疾手快，趁混乱使了个分身法，纵身跳到哪吒脑后，朝他左臂一棒打去。哪吒挨了一棒，只好负痛败下阵来。 李天王见连败两阵，只好收兵，奏报玉帝。玉皇大帝也没了主意，只得封孙悟空做了“齐天大圣”，并派他看管桃园。下文接《大闹蟠桃会》。

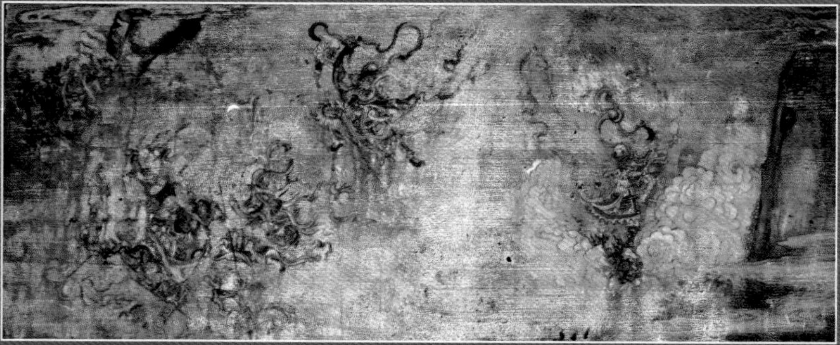

孙大圣斗哪吒三太子

Monkey King Fighting Nezha

The magnificent Monkey King was tricked into going to heaven and was bestowed a lowly title of Protector of the Horse. He was happy for less than a dozen days when he eventually learned of his inferior rank. Ashamed and angry, he went out of the South Gate of Heaven, and returned to his home the Mountain of Flowers and Fruits to continue his life as the Great Sage Equaling Heaven (which was self-granted). The Jade Emperor was furious on hearing this and decreed the Heavenly King Li and his third son, Prince Nezha, to catch the Monkey King. The pioneering general of the Heavenly army, however, was easily defeated by the Monkey King during the first round of the battle.

Nezha hurried to reinforce his partners. He transformed himself with three heads and six arms, which made him look most ferocious. He held six kinds of weapons, trod on the Wheels of Wind and Fire, and rushed straight at the Monkey King, who also turned himself into the same shape; he was brandishing his magic cudgel, and immediately there appeared three magic cudgels in his hands. The duel was quite fierce. The Monkey King was more sharp-sighted and quick-handed. He plucked one of his hairs from his head in the midst of the fray, and changed it into his own double to mislead Nezha, while his real self leapt round till he was behind Nezha and hit him on his left arm. Receiving such a painful blow, Nezha was unable to hold on, so he was forced to make a retreat from the battle field. This had all been observed by Heavenly King Li, who ordered a general to report to the Jade Emperor. The Jade Emperor had no idea of how to deal with the Monkey King, and finally had to grant him Great Sage Equaling Heaven and dispatched him to take charge of the Imperial Peach Orchard. The following story is *The Monkey King Ruining over the Peach Feast.*

颐和园佛香阁 TOWER OF BUDDHIST INCENSE

STORIES BEHIND THE LONG CORRIDOR PAINTINGS IN THE SUMMER PALACE

《颐和园长廊彩画故事》

孙悟空拜师学法，练就一身本领，就缺少一件称心的兵器。于是他来到水晶宫，向东海龙王借宝。悟空试了多件兵器，都不满意。龙王便领悟空去试定海神珍铁。看见珍铁金光万道，可变大变小、变粗变细，悟空满心欢喜，走近一看，原来这棒两头都是金箍，中间是一段乌铁，上面刻有“如意金箍棒一万三千五百斤”字样。悟空喃喃道：“这个宝贝太粗太长，如果细些短些才用得顺手。”话音刚落，只见金箍棒果然就短了几尺、细了一围。悟空大喜，遂把它变成了一根小细针，放在耳朵里，随后又向龙王要了一身披挂：一双藕丝步云履，一副锁子黄金甲，一顶凤翅紫金冠。孙悟空穿戴整齐，举着金箍棒，赶回花果山去了。画面上，是悟空正在龙宫借宝的情景。

龙宫借宝

Monkey King Forcing the Treasure out of the Dragon King

Having finished learning from his master, the Monkey King acquired a variety of skills and found everything was in place except that he lacked a favorite weapon. So he went to the Crystal Palace of the Eastern Sea to borrow a precious weapon from the Dragon King. This is the scene shown in the painting. He tried several weapons, but none of them won his heart. The Dragon King then led the Monkey King to try the magnificent, precious, sea-conquering iron piece hidden deep inside the treasure of the sea. On their arrival, the piece suddenly radiated millions of bunches of golden light. The Monkey King went over, found it was a piece of iron pillar. Seizing it with both hands, he said, “It’s too thick and too long! If it were a bit thinner and shorter it would do.” To his surprise, the pillar immediately became thinner by several feet and shorter by a round. The Monkey King said again, “Better to be much smaller!” The piece really became smaller in portion.

Delighted, he found it was a piece of black iron circled on both ends with gold. Carved on the piece were the characters: As-You-Will Gold-Banded Cudgel: 6,750 kilograms. The Monkey King played it for a while, and found it quite fit. He held the cudgel, and shouted, “Smaller, smaller, and smaller!” The cudgel turned into a needle, and he put it inside his ear. The Dragon King was greatly shocked by the scene. The Monkey King then asked for a set of outfit to go with the cudgel. The Dragon King of the Eastern Sea had to summon all his three brothers, and they presented a pair of lotus-root cloud-walking boots, a suit of golden chain corselet, and a phoenix-winged purple gold helmet. The Monkey King put on these carefully, held his magic cudgel, and left for Mountain of Flowers and Fruits. The four dragon kings were most indignant, and discussed to send a memorial to Heaven.

赤壁之战之前，孙权和刘备联合，准备共同抗御曹操。但是，周瑜心胸狭窄，忌贤妒能，一心想除掉刘备和诸葛亮。一次，他假借商议破敌之计，瞒着诸葛亮，请刘备到江东会面，欲害之。刘备接到邀请，信以为真，执意前去，关羽随行。

周瑜见刘备只带20余人，心中窃喜，忙命刀斧手埋伏在营帐周围，到时以掷杯为号，一齐动手；随后迎刘备至军帐内，设宴相待。席间敬酒时，周瑜猛然看见关羽站在刘备身后，威风凛凛，不怒而威。他惊出一身冷汗，连忙恭维道："将军过五关、斩六将，勇猛非凡，天下闻名。"不敢轻举妄动。过了一会儿，刘备不见诸葛亮，心知有诈，便起身向周瑜告辞。刘、关二人来到江边，见诸葛亮正在船中等候。诸葛亮将刘备、关羽送上船，并告诉他们，如若不是关羽在此，今天刘备凶多吉少。

刘备江东赴会

Liu Bei Going to the Banquet in the East of the Yangtze River

Prior to the Battle at Chibi, Sun Quan and Liu Bei were allies and they united to resist Cao Cao. Zhou Yu, however, was narrow-minded and jealous at the prominence of Liu Bei and Zhuge Liang, and always sought opportunities to get rid of them. Once, under the guise of discussing the strategy of breaking the enemy, he invited Liu Bei to come to dominion, without telling Zhuge Liang, with the intention of killing Liu. Liu Bei thought it a sincere invitation, accepted it, and determined to go; Guan Yu accompanied.

Zhou Yu, seeing Liu Bei only brought 20 men with him, was thrilled. He arranged 50 assassins to hide around the camp, and told them that, as soon as he threw his cup on the ground, they should immediately take action. He welcomed Liu Bei, led him into the camp, and held the banquet. After a while Zhou Yu proposed a toast, but noticed a grand ferocious general standing with Liu Bei. Knowing he was Guan Yu, Zhou Yu was scared and said, "General Guan killed six generals when passing through five passes. You are well known for your extraordinary intrepidity and fighting skills." The feast went on for a while, and Liu Bei asked why Zhuge Liang (at that time he was visiting Sun Quan) did not come. Zhou Yu mumbled without a clear answer. Guan Yu then gave Liu Bei a hint. Liu Bei understood, rose from his seat, and bade farewell to Zhou Yu. When they arrived at the bank, they found Zhuge Liang waiting in a boat. Zhuge Liang told Liu Bei, "If Guan Yu had not been there, you would have been killed." Liu Bei, after a moment's reflection, saw that it was true. Then Zhuge Liang saw Liu and Guan off, and continued to stay there alone, confronting Zhou Yu and other unfriendly counterparts.

唐朝年间，秀才裴航进京赶考，不料名落孙山，便乘船回家，同行的有一位樊夫人，美貌过人。他不禁写诗向她表示倾慕。可是樊夫人早已为人妻，但她还是回了一首诗，裴航不解其意。

数日后裴航路过一个叫蓝桥的地方，遇到一个叫云英的姑娘，生得姿容绝世。裴航越看越喜，要娶云英为妻。云英的母亲让他找到玉杵臼，捣药100天，方可娶云英。裴航听了，到处打听并倾其所有，好不容易才买到了玉杵臼。回到蓝桥，裴航日夜捣药。裴航对爱情坚贞不渝的精神感动了月亮上的玉兔。它每天夜晚趁裴航睡觉的时候，下凡帮他捣药。最后云英的母亲终于答应把云英嫁给他。迎亲那天，樊夫人也来了，原来她是云英的姐姐，两姊妹都是仙女。樊夫人上次遇见裴航，见他诗作得好，人也长得英俊，有意把妹妹嫁给他。裴航和云英相亲相爱，白头偕老。蓝桥捣药的故事也流传至今。

蓝桥捣药

Grinding Medicine at a Blue Bridge

During the Tang Dynasty, there was a scholar named Pei Hang. He took part in the Imperial Examinations in the capital but failed. Disappointed, he had to go back home by boat. He encountered a beautiful young lady, Mrs. Fan, on the boat. Pei Hang could not help admiring her, and wrote a poem to express his feelings. The lady was already someone else's wife; in response to his fancy, however, she also wrote a poem which Pei Hang did not quite understand the underlying meaning.

Several days later, he passed a place called Blue Bridge, and encountered an attractive girl Yunying. Unable to hold his love, Pei Hang implored her mother to marry the girl to him. The old dame responded, "I am old and sick, and if you really want to marry my daughter, you must get a jade stick bowl, and then grind herbal medicine for me for 100 days." Pei Hang then searched everywhere for the bowl. He eventually bought the bowl, using up all his property. Back at the Blue Bridge, he ground herbal medicine all day and night. His firm commitment to love touched the Jade Bunny on the moon, and every night after he fell asleep, the Bunny came to help with the work. The old dame finally permitted him to marry Yunying. On the wedding day, Yunying's elder sister, Mrs Fan, showed up. Actually the two were both fairies. When Mrs. Fan first encountered Pei Hang, she thought Pei Hang a brilliant and handsome man, so she liked him, and planned to introduce him to his younger sister anyway. The young couple lived happily ever after, and their love story is still told by people today.

王羲之是东晋时期的大书法家。笔势飘若浮云，矫若惊龙。羲之清高风雅，尤爱养鹅。会稽有一老妇，养有一鹅，声音清亮。羲之为官至此，托人带重金去买，老妇不卖。他又乘车前往观赏，老妇以为他爱吃鹅肉，连忙杀鹅以款待他。羲之为此长叹数日，深为惋惜。一次，羲之探知山阴有一道士，养有好鹅，亲往观看，并求道士卖给几只。道士要羲之书写一篇《道德经》，便以群鹅相赠。羲之满口应允。书罢，羲之将鹅装入笼内，满载而归。从此“羲之爱鹅”传为佳话。

羲之爱鹅

Wang Xizhi Loving Geese

Reputed as the Sage of Calligraphy, Wang Xizhi (303-361) was one of the most famous calligraphers in ancient China, who developed calligraphy into a transcendent art form. His works were sometimes as elegant as floating clouds while sometimes as vigorous as flying dragons". Such a man, high-hearted and well-mannered, had affection for geese. One day, Xizhi learned that an old lady kept a white goose, which had a silvery voice, singing like a flowing river or sometimes a deep musical instrument. So he asked someone to buy this goose for a high price, which was refused by the woman. Then Xizhi himself went to see the goose. After the old lady heard this, she thought that Xizhi wanted to eat the goose meat. Hence she killed the goose and cooked it to entertain him. Unexpectedly Xizhi felt deeply sorry for this and couldn't help sighing for days.

Realizing Xizhi loved geese so deeply, his attendants often went on secret expeditions in search of geese. When they heard that a Taoist raised some good geese, they right away told Xizhi; the latter was overjoyed at the news and set off immediately. The geese were indeed excellent, with elegant posture. Then Xizhi entreated the monk to sell him some. At beginning the Taoist refused, but bargained, "I have known you for long and if you write one scripture from the *Tao Te Ching* for me, I'll give all geese to you." Xizhi accepted. Having finished, Xizhi requested his attendants to cage the geese and return home. Thereupon, "Xizhi loving geese" became a much-told story.

他们是商纣王手下的两员大将，一个眼观千里，一个耳听八方。这两个人原是棋盘山上的桃精和柳鬼，会很多妖术，后来被商纣王差往前线，与周国的姜子牙作战。姜子牙每次设下的计谋都被两妖识破。大将杨戬见这两妖非同一般，便来到金霞洞，请教师父。杨戬回到军中，令军中舞动红旗，擂鼓鸣锣，以迷惑千里眼和顺风耳。

两妖听得周营中擂鼓鸣锣不止，便走出帐来。千里眼举目一望，只见红旗招展，眼花缭乱；顺风耳侧耳一听，只闻得锣鼓喧天，震耳欲聋。姜子牙遂派人到棋盘山，把桃树柳树统统挖尽，放火焚烧，断了妖根。晚上，两妖领兵来劫周营。不料姜子牙神机妙算，早有准备，众兵将把千里眼、顺风耳团团围住。这两怪妖根已断，神通难施，姜子牙趁机将他们铲除。

千里眼和顺风耳

Thousand-Mile Eye and Wind-Following Ear

They were two generals under King Zhou of the Shang Dynasty (1600-1046 BC). Originally, they were a peach tree elf and a willow tree ghost who lived in a mountain called Qipan, and they were masters of witchcraft. Just as his name implied, the Thousand-Mile Eye's sight could cover one thousand miles, and the Wind-Following Ear could hear any sound produced in any corner of the world. King Zhou sent them to fight against Jiang Ziya of the Zhou State.

During the battles, they sabotaged every trap set by Jiang Ziya. Knowing the extra-ordinariness of the two, General Yang Jian of the Zhou State went to consult his master in the Jin Xia Cave. Once back with the army, Yang Jian ordered his soldiers to wave red flags, knock drums, and hit gongs so as to confuse their enemies' extraordinary sight and hearing.

The two heard the noise from the Zhou army's camps, and came out to see what happened, but they were totally dazzled and deafened by the chaotic scene. Jiang Ziya took advantage of the situation, sent 3,000 men to Qipan Mountain, uprooted and burned all the peach and willow trees; thus, the roots of their enemies were completely ruined. That night, the two devils launched a secret attack against Zhou army's camp, which to their dismay, was foreseen by the smart Jiang Ziya. The well-prepared soldiers of the Zhou army ambushed the Thousand-Mile Eye and the Wind-Following Ear, and since their roots had been destroyed, they were incapable of conducting their witchcraft. After killing them, Jiang Ziya won victory after victory.

陶弘景，字通明，丹徒秣陵（今江苏江宁）人，是南北朝时期著名的道教思想家、医学家、炼丹家、文学家。他自幼聪明异常，十五岁著书立作，好道术、喜山水、善琴棋、工书法、通医学。齐高帝曾召他陪伴太子读书。后来，陶弘景远离尘世，隐居句曲山（今茅山）。

梁武帝早年便与陶弘景相识，他继位后，想让陶弘景出山为官、辅佐朝政。陶弘景于是画了一张画，两头牛，一个自在地吃草，一个戴着金笼头，被拿着鞭子的人牵着鼻子。梁武帝一见，便知其意，不再勉强。但是每逢凶吉、祭祀、征讨等大事，朝廷都派人向他去请教。所以，陶弘景被称为“山中宰相”。

山中宰相

The Reclusive Prime Minister

Tao Hongjing (456-536), courtesy name Tongming, was a native of present-day Jiangning, Jiangsu. He was a thinker, alchemist, pharmacologist and writer in the Southern and Northern Dynasties (420-589), took interest in Taoism, had a love for nature, and was expert in both medicine and creating prose. Besides he was talented at musical instruments, chess and painting. He once tutored the crown prince and princes at Emperor Gao of Qi's (427-482) invitation. Later, he lived in seclusion on today's Maoshan Mountain in Jiangsu.

Tao Hongjing was also knowledgeable about five element theory, geography, astronomy and meteorology. After Emperor Wu of Liang (464-549) succeeded to the throne, he often dispatched someone to ask advice from Tao Hongjing about the time to schedule major events such as sacrifices and punitive expedition. Therefore, he was called the reclusive prime minister.

During his retirement on Maoshan Mountain, Tao Jinghong compiled the *Bencao Jing Jizhu* (*Collected Commentaries to the Canonical Pharmacopoeia*), a commentary on the *Shennong Bencao* (*Canonical Pharmacopoeia of Shennong*). The original text contained notes on 365 drugs, while Tao added 365 more. He initially divided the drugs into seven broad categories – mineral, plant, insect, mammal, fruit, vegetable and grain, which has been used as a standard for more than 1,000 years.

画中身穿红斗篷的是薛宝钗的堂妹薛宝琴。一次，薛宝琴同邢夫人的侄女邢岫烟，李纨的堂妹李纹、李绮到贾府游玩。贾府上下都很高兴，把她们请进大观园住下。贾母特别看重薛宝琴，让她做了王夫人的干女儿，还送了她一件凫裘（用野鸡毛织成的斗篷）。

时值隆冬大雪过后，大家聚在一起赏雪作诗。李纨让宝玉去折枝红梅，一会儿，宝玉拿着一枝红梅回来。邢岫烟、李纹、宝琴三人分别以“红”、“梅”、“花”为韵，即兴赋诗。

众人都说宝琴作得最佳。正说着，贾母来了，大家说笑了一阵。贾母便起身回去，刚出门，只见白雪中，宝琴披着凫裘，旁边的丫环手里抱着一瓶红梅。原来，她看那梅花开得好，余兴未尽，也去采了一枝。贾母见宝琴人品好、才华高，有心把她许给宝玉；但是得知宝琴已经订亲，只得作罢。

薛宝琴雪中折梅

Xue Baoqin Plucking Plum Blossoms in Snow

The girl in red in this painting is Xue Baoqin, Xue Baochai's cousin. Once, she came to visit the Jia Family, along with Lady Xing's (Jia Baoyu's aunt) niece Xing Xiuyan, and Li Wan's (Jia Baoyu's sister-in-law) two cousins Li Wen and Li Qi. The Jia Family was delighted, and arranged them to stay in the Grand View Garden. Grandmother Jia was very fond of Xue Baoqin; she asked Lady Wang (Jia Baoyu's mother) to take the girl as her god-daughter, and also bestowed her a fuqiu (a kind of precious cloak made with wild chick feathers) as gift.

It was in winter. One day, after a heavy snow, people were gathering to appreciate the snow-covered scenery and to compose new poems. Li Wan then asked Jia Baoyu to pluck some plum blossoms. After a while, Baoyu came back with a bunch of red plum blossoms. Xing Xiuyan, Li Wen, and Baoqin improvised a poem rhymed on Red, Plum, Blossom, respectively.

Folks said Baoqin's poem was the best. Just then, Grandmother Jia came, they chatted and laughed for a while, and then Grandmother Jia rose to take her leave. Just outside the door, she saw Baoqin wearing the fuqiu with a maid holding a vase of red plum blossoms walking in the white show, and the girl looked so beautiful. Baoqin found the plum blossoms too beautiful to resist, and decided to pluck one more bunch. The Grandmother wanted to marry Baoyu to Baoqin, but when she knew the girl had already engaged and would get married soon, she had to swallow her regret.

画中的四位老者均是秦末汉初的著名学者。他们不愿意当官，长期隐居在商山（今陕西省丹凤县境内），出山时都80有余，眉皓发白，故被称为“商山四皓”。刘邦久闻四皓的大名，曾请他们出山为官，但被拒绝。刘邦建立汉朝登基后，立长子刘盈为太子，封次子如意为赵王。后来，刘邦见刘盈懦弱、平庸，而次子如意却聪明伶俐、才学出众，便有意废刘盈而改立如意为太子。刘盈的母亲吕后知道后，非常着急，按张良的主意，请来了商山四皓。有一天，刘邦与太子一起饮宴，他见太子背后有四位老人，问后知是商山四皓。四皓上前谢罪道，他们听说太子是个仁义之士，又有孝心、礼贤下士，就一齐来作太子的宾客。刘邦知道大家很同情太子，又见太子有四位贤人辅佐，消除了改立太子的念头。后来，刘盈顺利继位，为惠帝。

商山四皓

Four Venerable Elders from Shangshan Mountain

The title refers to the four elders in the picture. They were erudite and informed, full of stratagem. In order to dodge the war in late Qin Dynasty (221-206 BC), they hid themselves in Shangshan Mountain (in today's Danfeng County, Shaanxi Province), devoted themselves to learning. Liu Bang (Emperor Gaozu of Han, reigned 202-195 BC), admired them and invited them to assist him, but was refused.

After his enthronement, Liu Bang made his eldest son Liu Ying the crown prince and conferred his second son Ruyi as the Prince of Zhao. Later he discovered that Liu Ying was cowardly and mediocre, yet Ruyi was smart and intelligent. Thus Liu Bang intended to depose Liu Ying and support Ruyi as the successor to the throne. Upon hearing this, Liu Ying's mother Empress Lü was worried and asked Zhang Liang (?-189 BC) for help. According to Zhang Liang's advice, Empress Lü went to ask the four venerable elders to support Liu Ying to govern the state.

One day, Liu Bang had a dinner with Liu Ying. When he saw the four elders behind Liu Ying, he felt surprised and soon knew that they were the four venerable elders, who then bowed to the emperor and said, "We hear that the crown prince is a filial son with talents and lofty ambition and he respects the officials regardless of their rankings. Hence, we are willing to assist him." Liu Bang realized that everybody now showed sympathy for the crown prince. If he insisted on deposing him, Ruyi would be trapped into a very isolated situation. Therefore, the crown prince Liu Ying became the second Emperor of the Western Han Dynasty, historically known as Emperor Hui of Han (reigned 195-188 BC).

穆桂英对杨宗保心生爱慕，手下得知姑娘心意，便向宗保去提亲。然宗保死活不依，穆桂英只好亲自出马，羞怯地说道："你若答应了我的亲事，我便砍了降龙木，率全家和你一起去投军。你何苦偏寻死路？""我以身报国，虽死犹荣。""你不死在抗辽战场上，却死在这小山寨，有何荣耀？宋军没有降龙木，如何去破敌人的天门阵？倘若敌人攻破三关，入主中原，生灵涂炭，你哪点报了国？那时你杨家将的世代英名将毁于一旦，你又有何脸面去见祖宗？"宗保此时静下心来，觉得这番肺腑之言入情入理，不禁由敬生爱。再看穆桂英体健貌美，武艺出众，有这样一位妻子，也觉称心，于是便答应了这门亲事。宗保回到营中，杨延昭听说他与草寇私定终身，大发雷霆，要将他推出斩首。穆桂英此时带领人马赶到，帮助宋军大破天门阵，杨延昭这才饶恕宗保、接纳了这位儿媳。

穆桂英招亲

Mu Guiying's Engagement

Mu Guiying, however, fell in love with Zongbao; when she learned that her followers had him in the prison, she was violently angry because it broke her heart. Her followers realized her sentiment, and proposed that Zongbao become their master. But Zongbao did not accept, so Mu Guiying had to take action by herself, and she offered, "If you promise to marry me, I'll cut down the Dragon-Conquering Wood, and follow you in your fight against Liao with all my forces. Why would you be so stubborn and pick the path of death now?" "I am willing to sacrifice myself for my country, and my death will be glorified," answered Zongbao. "You will die in a minor mountain castle rather than in the battlefield against Liao invaders; what kind of glory is that? The Song army doesn't get the Wood, and how can they destroy the enemy's formation? If the enemy ends up as the main power of central China, people will be in extreme misery, so how is it that you imagine you are truly serving your country? At that time, the reputation of your famous Yang Family will be completely ruined, and won't you have any pride to face your prominent ancestors?"Zongbao calmed down, took her speech as heartfelt and reasonable, and his feelings toward her began to change from awe to love. Besides, he thought that marrying such a capable, attractive, and prominent woman would be delightful. So they were engaged.

After Zongbao returned to the Song bastion, Yang Yanzhao ordered him to be executed, because he had broken the army regulaion to make marital commitment while fighting the enemy. Meanwhile, Guiying, leading her soldiers, came to surrender to the Song forces, and vanquished the Sky Gate Formation. Seeing this, Yanzhao forgave Zongbao.

春秋战国时期，俞伯牙擅弹古琴，技艺高超。一次，他乘船外出，兴致骤起，弹起古琴，曲未终，弦断。这时，岸上走来一个樵夫，说琴声悦耳，听得出神，没想打扰伯牙弹琴。伯牙请他上船，两人相叙。樵夫叫钟子期，家有老父，靠打柴度日，子期虽贫寒，但博学诗书，与伯牙说古道今，谈琴论乐，十分投机。伯牙每弹一曲，子期都能讲出曲子的内容、风格和伯牙弹奏时的心情。两人相约一年后再相会。第二年，伯牙如约而至，子期却没有出现。伯牙上岸寻访子期，碰见子期的老父，得知从两人分别后，子期愈加刻苦读书，因劳累过度离开了人世。伯牙来到坟前，取出古琴，边弹边哭。没有了知音，弹奏完毕，伯牙扯断琴弦、把心爱的琴摔得粉碎。

伯牙摔琴谢知音

Boya Breaking a Fiddle

Yu Boya was an accomplished *qin* (a kind of seven-string Chinese musical instrument) player during the Spring and Autumn Period or the Warring States Period, but was lonely without any close friends. One day, he went out on a boat, and played *qin*. Suddenly one of the strings broke. At this moment, a woodsman came near, saying, "My name is Zhong Ziqi. I became lost in beautiful sounds; I never expected to disturb you." Boya felt amazed and invited him to talk on the boat. The two talked about everything from the ancient to the current, from the *qin* to all kinds of music. Each time Boya played, Ziqi could name the piece as well as the style and Boya's feelings while playing. When Boya's will was towards high mountains in his playing, Ziqi would say, "How towering like Taishan Mountain!" When Boya's will was towards flowing water in his playing, Ziqi would say, "How majestic the rivers and oceans!" Before parting they promised to meet there again next year.

In the following year, Boya returned and waited for a few days but Ziqi hadn't arrived. Hence Boya went ashore to look for him. On the way, he encountered Ziqi's father, who told, "After your departure, Ziqi read more industriously. Unfortunately he died from exhaustion several months ago. He asked us to bury him on the bank where you met so that his soul would come for your appointments." Indeed Boya saw a new grove not far away. In front of the grove, Boya played and wept. Finished, Boya sighed, "Without Ziqi, who can be my friend and soul-mate?" Boya sighed to the sky, broke the *qin* into pieces at the grave and lamented.

王徽之，字子猷，是大书法家王羲之第五个儿子。他一生玩世不恭，放荡不羁。一个雪后的夜晚，王徽之想道：如果在这样一个夜晚能和好友把酒弹琴，将是一件非常美好的事情。他便立刻命人备船前往。舟行河中，波光粼粼，他一路欣赏，拂晓时分到了好友家。然而他却命仆人掉转船头回家。仆人不解，他说道："我乘兴而来，沿途美景不断，如入仙境。如今兴致已尽，又何必要见朋友呢？"王徽之不恋官场，不贪富贵，对竹子却爱得如痴如狂。有次他专程前往观赏一种名贵竹子。见那竹子果然长得青翠欲滴，出类超俗，子猷竟发起呆来，连主人的招呼也没听见；直到暮色渐浓，才不舍离去。走了一程，又觉余兴未尽，于是调马回头。见院门已关，他又透着门缝细细观赏。子猷喜好游历四方，每至一地，便立刻命人栽竹，一天都离不开竹子。

子猷爱竹

Wang Ziqiu Loving the Bamboo

Wang Huizhi (343-386), styled himself Ziqiu, was the fifth son of Wang Xizhi. He was a real unconventional and uninhibited cynic throughout his life. One winter's night after a heavy snowfall, a bright, full moon rose and the white snow glistened. Wang Huizhi was enjoying the beauty of nature, while suddenly he thought, "What a great pleasure it would be to play the *qin*, drink the wine and enjoy the scenery together with a friend!" Then he asked his servant to prepare a boat for him to visit one of his friends. The boat moved forword sprightfully. When he saw the sparkling ripples on the river, he felt as if he entered a fairyland. He arrived at his friend's home at day break, however, he asked the servant to sail the boat back. The latter asked him why. He said, "I come here due to a whim, which has been satisfied. There is no more need to see him."

Wang Huizhi never clung to power or wealth, but loved the bamboo very much. Once he made a special trip, taking all day and night, to appreciate a kind of rare bamboo. The beautifully green bamboo actually grew otherworldly as he had hoped. He appreciated the bamboo deeply in his heart and even didn't hear his host's call, and didn't leave until the darkness fell. Though having ridden for a short distance, he turned his horse and headed back. Seeing the door had already been closed, he peered through a crack in the door to appreciate the bamboo. Wang Huizhi liked to travel. He lived in an abandoned house every time he traveled. And he asked all the people he knew to plant bamboo as soon as they settled down. When asked by friends why he took such pains to do so, Ziqiu, pointing to the green bamboo, laughed, "How can I spend a day without it?"

红孩儿是牛魔王和铁扇公主的儿子。他听说吃了唐僧肉可以长生不老，就等着唐僧经过。这一天，他望见唐僧远远而来，便用苦肉计，将自己绑在树上，就等唐僧上钩。唐僧果然发了慈悲，救下了红孩儿并让悟空背他。悟空早就认出了这个妖怪，暗自盘算准备找个机会摔死他。哪知红孩儿也早有准备。悟空正待下手之际，霎那间，乱石奔走，尘土飞扬。风停时，唐僧已不见踪影。

悟空知道是红孩儿捣的鬼，召出土地、山神，问明妖怪来历，一路寻到红孩儿的住处。悟空和红孩儿展开了一场恶战。红孩儿斗不过悟空，便吹起一阵毒烟毒火。悟空只得跳出火阵。他请来龙王降雨，却灭不了三昧真火；化成牛魔王的样子，又被红孩儿识破；无奈之下，只得到南海请来观世音菩萨，降服了红孩儿。为此，孙悟空与牛魔王、铁扇公主又结下冤仇，过火焰山时颇费了一番周折。

红孩儿计擒唐僧

The Red Boy Catching Priest Tang Trickily

The Red Boy, son of the Bull Demon King and the Princess Iron Fan, heard that if he ate a piece of fresh of Tang Seng he would live as long as heaven and earth, and decided to wait for a chance. One day, seeing Tang Seng coming, he came up with a self-suffering trick to lure Tang Seng close. Seeing a child hung in a tree, Tang Seng "saved" him, and asked the Monkey King to carry him. The Monkey King had already recognized the child was a devil, and planned to kill him by throwing him on a rock. The Red Boy, however, was well-prepared. All of sudden, he created distraction with a strong whirl of wind that blew all the stones around and dust everywhere, and when the wind stopped, he and Tang Seng disappeared.

The Monkey King then summoned the local land gods, asking about the evil spirits on the mountain, and then set out to search for his master. He went to the Red Boy's residence and had a good fight with him. The Red Boy could not quench win by force, so he conjured up poisonous smoke and fire. The Monkey King had to escape from the fire field. He invited the dragons kings to help him, but the water could not the True Samadhi Fire; he tranformed into the Bull Demon King, the boy's father, but was looked through. Knowing he was unable to win, he went to the South Sea, and asked for Kwan-yin's help, who then subdued the Red Boy. Thus, the Monkey King earned the hatred of the Bull Demon King and the Princess Iron Fan. Afterwards, when they passed the Mountain of Fire, they had to overcome many difficulties created by the couple.

弥勒是佛教里的一个神通广大的胖和尚。相传，他有个神袋，专门用来收妖装魔。弥勒用此袋收了六个童子。这些童子本领高强，一有机会就到人间，为非作歹，祸害百姓。所以，弥勒佛总是小心翼翼地看管他们，每次出门都把他们装在袋里带着。但弥勒总有疏忽的时候，一日，六童子之一的黄眉童儿趁弥勒外出赴会，偷了神袋，来到人间为非作歹，擒住了唐僧。孙悟空搬来的各路诸神，皆被神袋收了去。幸得弥勒前来指点悟空，悟空抡起金箍棒，与黄眉童子战了几个回合，佯败而去，跑进一块瓜地，变作一个西瓜。黄眉童子追了半日，早已干渴，一见瓜地，便唤种瓜人摘瓜，几口便吃了下去。悟空在其肚子里拳打脚踢，痛得妖怪满地打滚。这时，种瓜老人走进跟前，现出真身，那妖一见是弥勒佛，跪在地上，连连告饶。弥勒提起那怪，取下神袋，将其装进去，驾云回极乐世界去了。

六子闹弥勒

Six Children Bothering Mile

Maitreya, a powerful figure in Chinese Buddhist legend, had a magic bag which was exclusively used to subdue devils. Maitreya trapped six children inside the bag. These six children were all monsters of destructive capabilities, and would seek any chance to do harm to the world; therefore, Maitreya had to carefully supervise them. Every time he went out, he would take them with him in the bag. However, there was a time when Maitreya was careless. One day, when Maitreya was absent, the Yellow Brow Child stole the magic bag, and went to harm the people in the world, and caught Tang Seng. In order to save his master, the Monkey King invited various gods and heavenly soldiers to help him, but they all ended up trapped in the magic bag.

Fortunately, Maitreya came to give him an idea. Next time when the Monkey King confronted the Yellow Brow Child on the battle field, he pretended to be unable to hold on and lured the monster into a melon patch, where the Monkey King turned himself into a big ripe melon. The monster chased the Monkey King for quite a while so felt thirsty. He saw the watermelon field, and asked the farmer to get a watermelon for him. The farmer plucked the one changed by the Monkey King, and the monster ate it in a few bites. Then the Monkey King was in the monster's stomach, hitting, kicking and grabbing inside. The monster was in great agony, rolling all over the ground. At that moment, the farmer came over, and revealed his original identity – he was Maitreya. Seeing his master, the Child knelt down and begged for forgiveness. Maitreya put him into the magic bag, and went back to the West Paradise with his belongings.

东汉末年，董卓专权，残忍暴虐，司徒王允一直想除掉董卓。一天，他信步来到后园，为无计可施而垂泪，忽然听到叹息声。走过去一看，原来是府中歌伎貂蝉。貂蝉自幼被王允收养，学习歌舞，美而聪慧，王允待若亲女；貂蝉感激王允养育之恩，常思报效。她看见王允最近愁眉不展，知道必有国家大事，又不敢多问，才躲在此处哀叹。王允见状，计上心来。他请貂蝉正坐，向她流泪跪拜说："如今奸臣董卓当道，欲阴谋篡位。董卓有一义子吕布，助纣为虐，骁勇无比。满朝文武，皆束手无策。如今只有你能拯救天下苍生。"他随即将他的连环计向貂蝉全盘托出：由于董、吕父子二人均是好色之徒，他打算先将貂蝉许嫁吕布，然后献给董卓。让貂蝉伺机离间二人，致使吕布杀掉董卓，为国家除患。貂蝉当即表示甘愿献身，助王允实施"连环计"。

王司徒巧使连环计

Strategy of Combining Tactics

During the end of Eastern Han Dynasty, the Prime Minister Dong Zhuo's subsequent tyrannical and cruel behavior aroused the wrath of many courtiers of the Han, but they could do nothing. Among the upright courtiers, Wang Yun, the Minister over the Masses, was desperate to get rid of Dong Zhuo, but failed to develop an adequate plan, because Lü Bu, Dong's foster son, was a valiant general and was seen beside his father almost all the time.

Late at night, Wang Yun walked in the garden alone, shedding tears of worry. Just then he heard a girl grieving in the garden. Tracing the sound, he found Diao Chan, a song girl who was brought up in his household but whom he had been treating like his own daughter. When asked, the girl knelt down, "You have been treating me so well since I arrived. I know that in recent days you have been vexed by worries, but I didn't dare to ask. I wish I could help you in some way to repay your kindness to me."

An idea then struck Wang Yun, and then he told Diao Chan his scheme. Because of the fact that Dong Zhuo and Lü Bu were both lechers Wang Yun wanted to cast a bone between them using a strategy of combined tactics: Wang Yun first married Diao Chan to Lü Bu but then dedicated her to Dong Zhuo as a concubine. He let Diao Chan plant the seed of dissension between them and which ultimately led to Lü Bu's slaying his adoptive father.

张良的祖父、父亲都是战国时期韩国的相国，后来秦灭韩，张良便决心报仇。一次张良刺杀秦始皇，但未成功，于是开始流亡。一天，张良在桥上漫步，遇见一位老人。老人见张良走来，故意把鞋扔下桥，让张良给捡回来，张良取回鞋后，老人又让张良给他穿上。张良心里想：既然已经把鞋捡回来了，索性好人做到底吧。于是他俯下身子，跪在老人面前，帮老人把鞋穿好。老人大笑走了。张良感觉奇怪，便跟在老人身后；老人约他五天后的黎明在此会面。前两次会面，张良都来晚了。老人很生气，教训他：跟老人约会不应该迟到。第三次张良半夜三更就跑到桥上等老人。老人看到张良后很高兴，交给他一本《太公兵法》，并告诉他：熟读此书后即可当帝王之师。张良此后日夜诵读，终于成为一个足智多谋、文武兼备的人，帮助刘邦赢得了天下、建立了汉朝。

张良进履

Zhang Liang Picking up Shoes for an Elder

Zhang Liang's grandfather and father were both prime ministers of the State of Han during the Warring States Period (475-221 BC). When the Sate of Qin destroyed the Han Zhang Liang determined to extract revenge on Emperor Qin Shi Huang (reigned 246-210 BC). Yet he failed to assassinate Qin Shi Huang and was forced into a fugitive life.

It's said that one morning Zhang Liang took a stroll on a bridge and met an elder. When Zhang walked near, the elder dropped his shoes down an embankment intentionally and asked Zhang to fetch the shoes. Zhang turned angry, however, seeing him so old, Zhang felt pity on him and got the shoes. He then tolerated him and picked up the shows. When he was back, the elder asked Zhang to put them on for him. Zhang then knelt down and respectfully did so. Uttering no thanks, the elder swaggered away.

Feeling surprised at the elder's behavior, Zhang followed him behind. The elder smiled, "You are doomed to do something and I'm willing to instruct you! Come to meet me here at dawn five days later." Yet Zhang was late, twice, and the elder berated him. For the third time, Zhang rushed to the bridge at midnight, waiting there. At this time, the elder was satisfied. He then gave Zhang a book on military strategy and tactics written by Jiang Ziya. Thereafter, Zhang was buried in that book day and night and grasped its pith. Soon heroes raised one after another to overturn the Qin Dynasty. Zhang Liang, relying on his wisdom and strategy, became Liu Bang's important counselor and helped him win the country.

刘备听徐庶推荐，说诸葛亮很有学识，又有才能，就和关羽、张飞带着礼物到隆中（今湖北襄阳县）卧龙岗去请诸葛亮出山辅佐他。恰巧诸葛亮这天出去了，刘备只得失望而归。过了数日，听说诸葛亮已回，刘备又和关羽、张飞冒着大风雪第二次去请。不料诸葛亮又外出闲游去了，刘备只得留下一封信，表达自己对诸葛亮的敬佩，并请他出来帮助自己挽救国家危难。转眼新春已至，刘备斋戒三天，第三次访诸葛亮。离茅庐半里之外，刘备便下马步行。到时，诸葛亮正在睡觉。刘备不敢惊动他，一直站到诸葛亮自己醒来，才彼此坐下谈话。刘备不辞劳苦，三次访贤，终于感动诸葛亮，请得他出山相助。

三顾茅庐

Liu Bei Visiting the Grass-Roof Farmhouse Three Times

On Xu Shu's recommendation Liu Bei set out to visit Zhuge Liang at Sleeping Dragon Ridge, Longzhong (today's Xiangyang County, Hubei Province), along with Guan Yu and Zhang Fei, in order to entice him to serve as his assistant. But on the day they arrived, Zhuge Liang was not at home, and they had to turn back. Several days later, after hearing Zhuge Liang had come back, Liu Bei, Guan Yu and Zhang Fei, under heavy snow and harsh wind, went to visit Zhuge Liang again; unfortunately, Zhuge Liang had gone for another excursion before they arrived, and Liu Bei had to leave a letter for him. In the letter, Liu Bei expressed his admiration for Zhuge Liang and sincerely asked him to help save the country.

A drawing of Liu Bei Visiting the Grass-Roof Farmhouse Three Times

Soon the spring came. Liu Bei cast lots to find the propitious day for another journey in search of Zhuge Liang. Before setting out on the selected day, he fasted for three days. Half a mile to the farmhouse, Liu Bei got off the horse, and began to walk. When he arrived, Zhuge Liang was sleeping. Liu Bei was unwilling to interrupt him, and waited until Zhuge Liang woke up. Then they had a good talk. Zhuge Liang was moved by Liu's sincerity and perseverance, and presented his famous Longzhong Plan, which formed the basis for the grand plan of Liu Bei and later the Three Kingdoms state of Shu.

“举案齐眉”是一个形容夫妻相敬相爱的典故。梁鸿是东汉时期著名的隐士，志趣清高，聪颖过人，博学多识。很多人家向他提婚，但都被他婉言拒绝。同县一个又丑又胖的女子孟光，衣着朴素，到了30岁还不肯出嫁，却说只有梁鸿那样的人，她才肯嫁。梁鸿听说后，便娶她为妻。

孟光嫁给梁鸿后，满心欢喜，精心打扮，想让梁鸿高兴。然而，梁鸿竟一直不理她。孟光觉得很委屈，梁鸿说：“我的妻子应该能与我一同隐居深山、过清苦的生活；而不是像你这样衣着华丽、施粉涂脂。”孟光听了，不再把精力放在容貌、衣着上，辛勤地操持家务。后来，俩人到霸陵山隐居。每天，男耕女织，闲时，吟诗弹琴自乐，生活非常幸福。梁鸿爱妻子，孟光敬丈夫。每次吃饭，孟光总是把盛饭的托盘高高举在眉前，请丈夫用饭，以此表示敬意。这就是这个典故的由来。

举案齐眉

Raising the Tray up to the Eyebrows

“Raising the Tray up to the Eyebrows” is a famous idiom in China and describes a couple having respect and love for each other. Liang Hong, a famous recluse in the early Eastern Han Dynasty (25-220), lost parents during his childhood. And his circumstances became more and more poor. However, he never accepted charity from others. In addition to his wisdom and profound knowledge, he was well-known and many women proposed to him. There lived a lady named Meng Guang, fat and ugly. She was already 30 years old, and often dressed simply and was unwilling to marry anyone except Liang Hong. Hearing this, Liang Hong married her.

Feeling joyful, Meng Guang began to dress gorgeously and wear make-up in order to please him. However, Liang Hong didn’t care to look at her. Meng Guang then asked for the reason. While Liang Hong told, “My wife should live a simple life together with me. Dressing gaudily and daubing face with thick make-up are not my idea of wifely virtues.” Thereafter, Meng Guang, never attaching importance to dressing, handled the housework industriously and attended to Liang Hong elaborately. Later, they sequestered themselves from the world and led a happy life: Liang Hong tilled the land and Meng Guang weaved cloth, taking pleasure in reading poems and playing musical instruments in their leisure. When having meals, Meng Guang often lifted the bowl up to her eyebrows to express her respect to Liang Hong. This’s the origin of the idiom.

唐贞观年间（627～649年），僧人玄奘从长安出发，一直西行，历经千辛万苦，来到佛教发源地天竺（今印度）取回了真经，前后用了17年的时间。从此，佛教得以在中国弘扬、传播。

由于当时交通极其困难，玄奘取经这个故事本身就带有了传奇色彩。到了明代，小说家吴承恩在民间口传的基础上，创作了《西游记》，又加进了不少神话色彩，更增强了故事的可读性和趣味性。小说中的唐僧、孙悟空、猪八戒、沙僧等人物形象在中国家喻户晓，老幼皆知。画中是师徒四人在西行过程中的一个情景。

唐僧取经

Xuanzang's Pilgrimage

During the years of Zhenguan (627-649, the reign of Emperor Taizong of the Tang Dynasty), a Buddhist monk, Xuanzang, went west all the way from Chang'an (capital of Tang, present-day Xi'an, Shaanxi Province) to the cradle of Buddhism, Sindhu (present-day India) in order to obtain Buddhist religious texts called sutras. He overcame huge difficulties, and the whole journey took 17 years. The pilgrimage and his study on Buddhism played a significant role in the spread and popularization of Buddhism in China.

A drawing of Xuanzang's Pilgrimage

Because of under-developed transportation in ancient times, Xuanzang's journey to the west was adventurous and became legendary; Wu Cheng'en (1500-1582), a famous novelist in the Ming Dynasty, collected materials among the folktales and wrote the *Pilgrimage to the West*, one of the Four Great Classical Novels of Chinese literature. Wu Cheng'en added many mythic elements to the novel, which endowed it with readability and popularity. Characters in the novel including Xuanzang (or Tang Seng) and his three protectors – Sun Wukong (Monkey King), Zhu Bajie, and Sha Wujing (Sha Priest) – are known to every household in China. The scene in the painting is that of Xuanzang and his disciples on their way to the West.

文彦博（1006～1097年）是北宋著名的宰相，学识广博，文武具备。他既是著名的政治家，又是杰出的军事家，宋夏战争期间，他采用积极防御、提高军队战斗力的方法，维护了宋政府在边疆的利益。文彦博共事仁宗、英宗、神宗、哲宗四朝，任将相50余年，安民治国、名闻四方。其任官时间之久，在中国历史上是绝无仅有的。文彦博一生虽位尊权重，但从不恃权骄横。

这幅画画的是文彦博小时候的一个故事：一天，文彦博和小伙伴在林旁空场上玩球，有个小朋友无意之中把球踢进树洞里。大家纷纷卷起衣袖，挤上去用手掏。因为洞太深，谁也够不着。有人试着用木棍去夹，也无济于事。众人一时没了主意。这时，文彦博端来一盆水，倒进树洞，球便随水浮出洞口。从此，文彦博灌水得球的故事，就一直流传下来。

灌水得球

Retrieving the Ball by Pouring Water

Wen Yanbo (1006-1097), a famous prime minister in the Northern Song Dynasty (960-1127), was knowledgeable and prominent both in the literary field and in the military field. He held an important position in political and literary history of China; additionally, during the war between the Nothern Song and Western Xia, he implemented a military strategy of active defense, which successfully enhanced the combat effectiveness and safeguarded the interests of the Song government in the border areas. He was on his position for 50 years, and served a total of four emperors. He was well-known for his contributions to social and national stability and prosperity. His long term of serving as an official is unprecedented in China's history. Although he took high positions and had mighty power, he had never been proud and lofty. He used to hang out with friends, drinking and composing poems. When he was at the dinner table with friends, they never ranked themselves as officials but according to their ages (as is Chinese tradition).

This painting is based on a story which happened in Wen Yanbo's childhood. One day, Wen Yanbo and other children were playing a ball by woods. A boy unintentionally kicked the ball into a hole in a tree. Then all the boys tucked up their sleeves, and tried to retrieve the ball using their bare hands. However, they failed. Someone tried to get the ball with a stick, but failed too. While the boys were at a loss, Wen Yanbo carried a basin of water and poured it into the hole. The ball emerged floating on top of the water. The enlightening story has been widely told ever since.

一次，曹操的大将张郃被张飞、魏延杀败，连失三寨，损兵折将，退到瓦口关，凭借天险闭关坚守。张飞、魏延领兵追到瓦口关，一连攻打几天，都没有攻破。

一天，张飞和魏延到瓦口关两边观察道路，忽然看见几个百姓背包在山间偏僻小路上攀藤附葛而走。张飞心中一亮，急忙吩咐手下军士唤那几个百姓前来。张飞从他们口中得知山中有一条小路可以直通瓦口关背后。张飞、魏延大喜。

第二天，魏延领一支军马来到关下攻打，张飞却带领轻骑绕至关后。张郃披挂上马，正要下山迎敌，忽闻关后火起，忙领兵前去察看，却见张飞迎面而来。张郃见魏延、张飞前后夹攻，无心再战，寻径而逃。

猛张飞智取瓦口关

Zhang Fei Seizing the Wakou Pass

Once, Zhang He, one of Cao Cao's generals, was defeated by Zhang Fei and Wei Yan of the Shu State. Losing three encampments and many of his men, Zhang He retreated to the Wakou Pass (in today's Sichuan) in order to hold on by hiding in the dangerous surroundings. Zhang Fei and Wei Yan leading their troops went after him, but for several days, their chase had failed. Zhang Fei saw formal attacks could not be effective, and he ordered a retreat.

One day, Zhang Fei and Wei Yan were patrolling and observing the roads by the pass, and saw some people carrying bags while treading their way along a remote mountainous path. Zhang Fei got an idea, and he hurried to order his soldiers to bring those people to him. After inquiring, he learned there was a path which directly led to the back of the Wakou Pass. Zhang Fei and Wei Yan were very happy about that, and for this piece of information Zhang Fei rewarded these people by taking them into his camp and giving them a good meal.

The next day, Zhang Fei sent off Wei Yan to make a frontal attack on the pass, while he himself with 500 light-horsemen attacked it from the rear by way the local people told him. Upon hearing Wei Yan's attack, Zhang He girded on his armor and was about to meet enemy head on, but he was told fires had started behind the pass. Zhang He leading his troop rushed to the spot on fire, and found that Zhang Fei was waiting for him. Zhang He saw his army was attacked from both the front and rear, and realized that he was fighting a losing battle. So he had to escape with some 10 followers.

晴雯虽天生争强好胜，但心灵手巧无人能比。一天晚上，宝玉一进门就唉声叹气。原来，贾母送给他一件珍贵的孔雀裘，可他不留神给烧了一块。工匠们因不认得这材料，都不敢接活儿。第二天宝玉还得穿着它去见老太太，因而心中十分焦急。晴雯着了风寒，本来躺在一边休息，听说后挣扎着翻身起来。她拿过大衣，仔细打量后，说需用孔雀金线织补。可是宝玉房中只有她一人会补。她怕宝玉着急，只得咬着牙，狠命撑着，缝补起来。一直忙碌到后半夜她才完成。看着补过的孔雀裘简直和原来一模一样，晴雯咳嗽一声，身子不由自主地倒下来。宝玉赶忙叫人服侍她睡下。后来在宝玉的精心照料下，晴雯的病才慢慢地好起来。

晴雯病补孔雀裘

Qingwen Stitching the Peacock Feather Robe at Ill

Although Qingwen was a brash and competitive maid, she was famous for her weaving skill. One night, Jia Baoyu returned to his chamber, and began to whine and sigh. The Grandmother Jia just gave him a precious peacock feather robe, however, he carelessly burned a hole in the back. No craftsmen dared assume the task of repairing it, since they had never seen anything like this before. Baoyu was worried because he would have to wear it to meet his grandmother the next day.

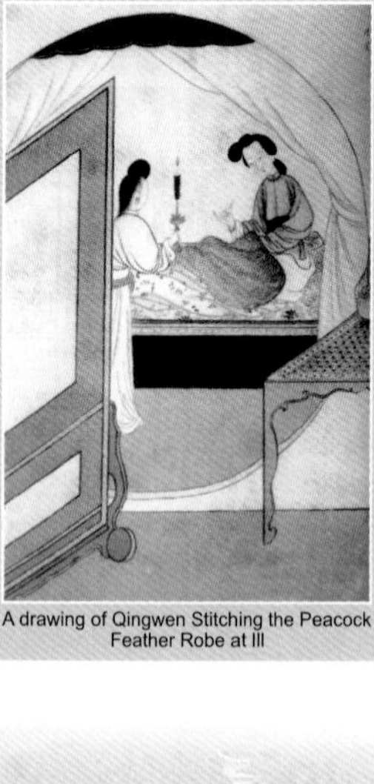

A drawing of Qingwen Stitching the Peacock Feather Robe at Ill

Qingwen had a bad cold, and was lying on her bed resting. On hearing this, she got up, had a careful look at the robe, and then wanted to repair it with golden peacock threads. Despite feeling dizzy and lacking strength, she set out to do the job, because she was the only one there who could do the darning. She carried on until well after the midnight when the work was done. Her job was nice, and the robe was as good as before. But her health deteriorated; she coughed, and then passed out. Baoyu hurried to place her in bed. Later, under the care of Baoyu, she gradually recovered.

唐朝时候，有个道士罗公远，道术十分高明。唐玄宗得知后，把他招进宫里，陪伴着自己玩乐解闷。这年中秋节，皓月当空。玄宗望着月亮，心里格外高兴，恨不得能飘上月宫，与嫦娥共品桂花酒。站在一旁的罗公远看出了玄宗的心思，随即抽出身后的宝剑，向空中挥去，只见一条绚丽的彩桥从月宫伸下来，玄宗乘着彩云，随着罗公远向月宫飞去。嫦娥听说人间的皇帝来了，便带着仙女出来迎接，吴刚也用馥郁芳香的桂花酒款待唐玄宗。仙女们随着乐曲翩翩起舞。美妙的曲子、优美的舞蹈、甘甜的美酒，玄宗很快便喝得酩酊大醉。

唐玄宗素来精通音律，将一切默默记在心中。日后他回忆月宫仙娥的音乐歌声，亲自谱曲编舞，创作了著名的“霓裳羽衣曲”。

唐玄宗夜游月宫

Emperor Xuanzong of Tang Visiting the Moon Palace in a Dream

There was a Taoist named Luo Gongyuan in the Tang Dynasty, and his mastery of Taoist ceremony was prominent. On learning that, Emperor Xuanzong summoned him to the royal palace so he could accompany him in his leisure time.

During Mid-Autumn Festival, the moon was full and bright. The emperor was pretty delightful, and could not help imagining that he flew to the Moon Palace. His mind was penetrated by Luo Gongyuan, who then waved his sword toward the sky. Unbelievably, a colorful cloud bridge stretched out from the moon to them.

Riding on colorful clouds, the Emperor flew after Luo right to the Moon Palace. Learning the emperor of the mortal world was coming, Chang’e, a legendary fairy living in the Moon Palace, led maids to welcome him. Wu Gang, a legendary man who was in charge of cutting the laurel in the Moon Palace, entertained the emperor with delicious sweet-scented osmanthus wine. Maids in the Moon Palace began to dance to music. The Emperor drank in the melodies, the beautiful dancing as well as the delicious wine.

A Portrait of Li Longji (Emperor Xuanzong of Tang)

Emperor Xuanzong was a master of music, and he secretly recited the melody. Later, according to his memory, he composed the famous *Song of Rainbow Skirts and Feather Robes.*

这幅画中的女子是《红楼梦》里贾宝玉的妹妹探春。她和宝玉同父异母，是贾政的侍妾赵姨娘所生。看到贾府日渐衰落，探春心中不安，想方设法兴利除弊，以图重振没落的贾府。但贾家的颓势已无法挽救。最后，探春由父亲贾政作主，远嫁他方，重振家业的愿望就此成了泡影。

探春在大观园的时候住在秋爽斋，与众姐妹及宝玉结了个“海棠诗社”，每个人又都起了个别号。宝玉因住怡红院，号“怡红公子”；黛玉住在潇湘馆，就叫做“潇湘妃子”；宝钗住在蘅芜院，称为“蘅芜君”，湘云老家原来有个 “枕霞阁”，就号“枕霞旧友”，探春住的秋爽斋，附近有许多芭蕉，因此她便自号为“蕉下客”。

蕉下客

The Stranger Under the Plantain

The girl in this painting is Jia Tanchun, Jia Baoyu's younger half-sister. Her mother, Concubine Zhao, was the second wife to Jia Zheng. Tanchun witnessed the Jia Family's decline and felt anxious. She tried every means to save the Jia Family from disintegration when she temporarily took over the family's financial affairs. However, the Jia Family was destined to decline. Eventually, under her father's arrangements, Tanchun was married off a faraway land. Her marriage was ultimately unhappy and her dream of restoring her family eventually amounted to nothing.

A drawing of Jia Tanchun

Tanchun used to live in the Studio of Autumn Fressness in the Grand View Garden, and established a poetry society, called the Begonia Poetry Society, with her sisters and Baoyu. Each member chose a pen-name. Baoyu, because he lived in the Happy Red Court, was called the Prince of Happy Red; Lin Daiyu living in the Bamboo Lodge was called the Queen of Bamboos; Xue Baochai living in the Alpinia Park was called the Lady of Alpinia; while Shi Xiangyun was called the Old Friend of Pillowing Red Clouds, because there was a Pavilion of Pillowing Red Clouds in her hometown. Jia Tanchun styled herself the Stranger Under the Plantain as there were lot of plantain trees around her chamber.

这天，贾宝玉、薛宝琴、邢岫烟、平儿四个人一同过生日，大家凑在一起，在大观园里摆上酒席，宝玉建议行酒令，大家一致赞成。活泼、爽快的史湘云见众人相聚，十分高兴，故意嬉闹。大家怪她捣乱，不由分说先罚了她一杯。酒令行到香菱时，香菱一时想不起来，湘云在一旁挤眉弄眼，悄悄地教给她，又被众人罚了一杯。轮到湘云行令，她想借酒令拿丫环们取笑，可丫环们都起来罚湘云喝酒。就这样，众人热热闹闹地玩了半天。等到散席时，竟发现湘云不在了。众人莫名其妙，来到院中假山后面，只见湘云躺在石凳上睡得正甜。山石上，芍药花争相怒放，微风吹过，湘云的头上、脸上、身上都落满了花瓣。扇子掉在地上，也被落花掩盖。湘云面带微红，娇柔妩媚，醉梦中还嘟哝着酒令。大家看着湘云，不由笑起来，赶紧上前把她推醒，说说笑笑地拥着湘云回屋去了。

史湘云醉卧芍药裀

Shi Xiangyun Getting Drunk at the Feast of the Peony

A drawing of Shi Xiangyu

One day, Jia Baoyu, Xue Baoqin, Xing Xiuyan and Ping'er were having a birthday party. They held a feast in the Grand View Garden; Jia Baoyu suggested playing a drinking game. All of the participants agreed, but the lovely and open-minded Shi Xiangyun became naughty; she insisted on a finger-guessing game. Everyone condemned and punished her by making her drink a cup of wine. When the drink game went on to Xiangling's turn, she got stuck. Shi Xiangyun helped her cheat, and was forced to drink another cup of wine. For her turn, she tried to make fun of the maids, and all of the maids stood up and urged her to drink a cup of wine as a penalty. Everyone had a good time. After dinner, they discovered that Xiangyun was missing. They had no idea where she had gone, and went to look for her. At last, they found her lying on a stone bench behind a rockery in the courtyard. She was sound asleep. The blossoming peony on the rockery shed petals all over her due to the breeze, and heaped-up peony petals wrapped in a white silk handkerchief made an improvised pillow for her head. Her fan, dropped to the ground, was almost entirely covered with flower leaves. Her face was peach pink, which added to her beauty. She was still mumbling the words of the drinking game. Seeing this they all laughed; they woke Xiangyun and walked her to the chamber.

马超，世代将门之后，武艺高强，父亲死后，投奔了汉中的张鲁。恰逢刘备攻打益州，张鲁就派马超出兵迎战。张飞闻马超攻关，非要去战马超。随后，刘备亲率大军，命张飞为先锋，引军至关上。次日天明，马超兵到。只见马超纵骑持枪而出，狮盔兽带，银甲白袍，气质非凡。张飞见马超，便要下关，刘备止之，待马超阵上人马皆倦，遂选五百骑，跟着张飞冲下关来。张飞、马超两马齐出，二枪并举，约战百余合，不分胜负。刘备怕张飞有失，急命收军。张飞回到阵中，歇息片刻，又出阵与马超厮杀。两人精神倍加，又斗百余合。刘备再次收军，二将各回本阵。

张飞夜战马超

Zhang Fei Fighting Ma Chao at Night

Ma Chao, a descendant of an honored militarily family, received good fighting training as well as military education. After his father died, he came under Zhang Lu's command in Hanzhong (in present-day Shaanxi). It was the time when Liu Bei's troop was attacking Yizhou Prefecture. Zhang Lu sent Ma Chao to counterattack. Learning Ma Chao was going to emerge on the battle field, Zhang Fei was determined to face him. So Liu Bei dispatched Zhang Fei as his lead general, and led the troop into the pass. The next morning, Ma Chao and his troop arrived. Ma Chao rode out, spear in hand, wearing a lion helmet, a beast plate, a sliver corselet and a white robe. His dress and bearing were so extraordinary, so were his abilities superior. Zhang Fei wanted to fight him immediately, but was stopped by Liu Bei. Until Ma Chao's men and horses were tired from being on the battle field, Liu Bei selected 500 warriors to accompany Zhang Fei to fight Ma Chao. It was a good fight. They fought like tigers for long periods on two occasions with no signs of either one gaining an upper hand. Fearing that Zhang Fei would get hurt, Liu Bei ordered him to stop for a rest. Zhang Fei went back to his side, rested his steed for a while, and rushed to fight again. After another lengthy period, the two competitive rivals seemed to wax fiercer than ever, and had no intention of stopping.

天色已晚，刘备劝张飞回关上，来日再战。张飞不肯罢休，恰马超换了马，也来到阵前，大叫夜战。张飞性起，骑上刘备的坐骑，冲向马超。两军齐声呐喊，点起千百个火把，照耀得如同白昼。到二十余合，马超见不能赢，拨马便走。张飞追去，马超暗中取出铜锤，突然回身打去。张飞早有提防，闪身躲过，掉转马头往回撤，马超又赶来。张飞拈弓搭箭，回射马超，马超亦躲过。二将遂各回本阵，双方收兵歇息。第二天，军师诸葛亮来到关上，见两军相持不下，施计离间马超和张鲁，陷马超于困境。马超看出张鲁并非仁义之君，便投奔了刘备。

张飞夜战马超

It was then getting late. Liu Bei tried to persuade Zhang Fei to return to the pass and continue his fight the next day. Zhang Fei, however, was getting quite excited because of the fight; he simply would not let it go. At that moment, Ma Chao had changed his horse, came back to the battle field, and demanded a night fight. The excited Zhang Fei rode Liu Bei's steed and rushed out to accept the challenge. The two continued their long fight. Soldiers of both sides all shouted for their generals, and lit thousands of torches, lightening the battle field as brightly as daytime. At the 20th bout, Ma Chao found he was still unable to win, turned his horse back, and pretended to terminate the fight. Zhang Fei went after him, while Ma Chao suddenly turned back and threw a bronze hammer toward Zhang Fei. Zhang Fei, however, was cautiously prepared; he dodged the sudden attack, stopped chasing, and turned back. But Ma Chao in turn began to chase after him. Zhang Fei took out his bow, and shot an arrow at Ma Chao. But Ma Chao also successfully dodged it, and the arrow flew by. Then each returned to his own side, and the day's fight eventually ended. The next day, Zhuge Liang arrived at the pass. Liu Bei consulted Zhuge Liang and they agreed that such a valiant and highly skilled general like Ma Chao would be a waste if any harm fell on him or Zhang Fei. Then Zhuge Liang said he had a little ruse left that would bring Ma Chao over to their side. He bribed one of Zhang Lu's advisors and cast in a bone between Zhang Lu and Ma Chao, which trapped the latter. Ma Chao finally realized Zhang was not a virtuous lord, and eventually defected to Liu Bei.

周瑜几次欲讨还荆州落空，便假意将孙权的妹妹嫁给刘备，骗刘备过江，欲将之困于东吴，以荆州相换。不料弄假成真，刘备与孙夫人结成良缘。后来，赵云按诸葛亮的吩咐，假称曹操起兵杀奔荆州，催刘备速回。刘备信以为真，携孙夫人离去。周瑜、孙权听到消息后，派兵追赶。

刘备泣告孙夫人道，当初孙权与周瑜同谋将夫人嫁给刘备，是为了先夺荆州，再杀刘备；此刻孙权部将在后追赶，周瑜部将于前堵截，只有孙夫人才能解救。孙夫人大怒，一面大骂周瑜，一面喝令推车前进。周瑜部将碍于她是孙权之妹，不敢阻挡。行不到数里，孙夫人闻知追兵又到，便让刘备先走，她与赵云在后掩护，再次责退追兵。等到追兵带着孙权亲赐的“尚方宝剑”赶到时，刘备、孙夫人早已远去。

刘备智激孙夫人

Liu Bei Wisely Stimulating Lady Sun

Several times, Zhou Yu had tried to seize Jingzhou, but all of the attempts failed. Then he married Sun Quan’s younger sister to Liu Bei, trying to trick Liu Bei into coming to the Eastern Wu. Then he could hold and ransom him, exchanging Liu for Jingzhou. Unfortunately, Liu Bei and Lady Sun really fell in love with each other, and established a good marriage. Later, Zhao Yun falsely claimed that Cao Cao’s army was about to attack Jingzhou, and urged Liu Bei to go back. Liu Bei thought it true, and left along with Lady Sun. Zhou Yu and Sun Quan learned the news, and sent troops to chase them.

Liu Bei wept to Lady Sun, “Originally, our marriage was a trick arranged by your brother Sun Quan and Zhou Yu, so they could hold me and might recover Jingzhou. When they achieved their goal, they would kill me. Careless of consequences I crossed the river and came to marry you, for I admire you, a brave and intelligent heroine. And now they try to kill me and my followers on the way back on the excuse that Jingzhou is in danger. With Zhou Yu’s troops blocking the way ahead and Sun Quan’s generals chasing behind, it was only you, my wife, who could extricate us from this danger.” Lady Sun was furious; she reproached Zhou Yu’s subordinates, pushed their way ahead while severely abusing Zhou Yu. Zhou Yu’s subordinates had to let them go. Learning Sun Quan and Zhou Yu’s troops were combined and again chased after them, Lady Sun asked Liu Bei to go first, and then she stayed behind with Zhao Yun to cover for her husband. The arriving troops were reproached severely by Lady Sun again and had to turn back. When Sun Quan sent another troop to catch them, Liu Bei and Lady Sun had already made it far away.

金国元帅四太子金兀术屡次带兵进犯中原，这一年冬天，他调集60多万人马，迫近朱仙镇。岳飞领兵60万，在朱仙镇扎营，一连几仗，大败金兵。金兀术又急又气，正在进退两难之时，军师献计摆“金龙绞尾阵”，待阵势已毕，金兀术派人到宋营下战书。第二天，两军正杀得难解难分之际，阵外狄雷、樊成、关铃三个小将听说岳家军在此酣战，特赶来投奔。三个人锤打、枪挑、刀砍，把“金龙阵”冲得七零八落，阵脚散乱，金兀术拨马绕阵而逃。这时候，岳家军中共有四位使锤：岳云银锤摆动，严成方金锤使开，何元庆铁锤飞舞，狄雷铜锤并举，一起一落，只杀得金兵尸如山积，血若川流。这就叫“八大锤大闹朱仙镇”。只一阵，金兵弃寨而逃，败走20余里，路上又中了刘锜元帅的埋伏，最后只剩下五六千。当夜金兀术收拾残兵败将，悄悄逃回金国。朱仙镇一战使岳家军声威大震。

八大锤大闹朱仙镇

The Battle at Zhuxian

The Marshal Jin Wuzhu of the Jin Dynasty (1115-1234) had led his troops to invade central China several times. This time in winter, he summoned an army of over 600,000 men and marched on Zhuxian (a town near present-day Kaifeng, Henan). On hearing the news, Yue Fei gathered an army of 600,000 men, which made camp at Zhuxian and confronted the Jin army. The Song army won several battles, which defeated their enemy's spirit.

Jin Wuzhu was agitated because he was trapped in dilemma. His military counselor came up with an idea of using the Gold Dragon Twisting Tail formation, and after the formation was set up, Jin Wuzhu sent a challenging letter to the Song army. Yue Fei deployed his men right away, and the next day, when the battle reached a stand-off, Di Lei, Fan Cheng and Guan Ling, who intended to join Yue Fei's army, rushed to reinforce the Song troops, and now there were eight hammers in the battle: Yue Yun's two silver hammers, Yan Chengfang's two gold hammers, He Yuanqing's two iron hammers, and Di Lei's two bronze hammers. Knowing the dramatically changing circumstances, Jin Wuzhu rode around his formation, found a way out, and escaped. The eight hammers' power lifted up the Song army's spirit, and the four generals, leading their men, killed many Jin soldiers. This was the famous battle at Zhuxian. The Jin army deserted their camp, and fled more than 20 miles. On the way, they were ambushed by Marshal Liu Qi's troop, and were left with a paltry 5,000 to 6,000 men. That night, Jin Wuzhu picked up his defeated men and left for his own country. The battle established the glorious reputation of Yue Fei's army.

颐和园南湖岛 SOUTH LAKE ISLAND

STORIES BEHIND THE LONG CORRIDOR PAINTINGS IN THE SUMMER PALACE

《颐和园长廊彩画故事》

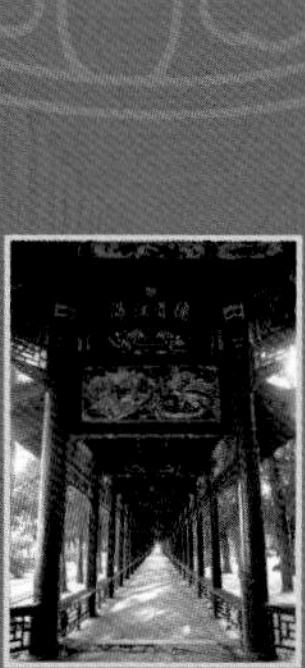

麻姑是中国道教中的神话人物，东晋道教学者、著名炼丹家葛洪曾在《神仙传》中对麻姑有出神入化的描写。相传，农历三月初三是住在昆仑山上的神仙西王母的寿辰。每当寿辰之日，她都要设蟠桃会，宴请众仙。八方神仙，四海龙王，天上仙女都赶来为她祝寿。百合、牡丹、芍药、海棠四位花仙采集了各色鲜艳芬芳的花卉，邀请仙女麻姑和她们同往。麻姑用灵芝草酿成仙酒，带到蟠桃会，献给了西王母。因此，过去民间为妇女祝寿时，常常绘“麻姑献寿”的图画相赠。

据传，麻姑原是建昌（江西省南城县）人，她勤劳美丽，后得道升天。汉桓帝时，曾投胎转世于一个普通人家。她掷米成珠，分给贫苦百姓。麻姑曾对人说，她亲眼看见东海三次变为桑田，“沧海桑田”的成语就出自于此。唐朝代宗年间，颜真卿曾为麻姑山撰文立碑，不幸被雷火击毁。

麻姑献寿

Magu Presenting a Birthday Gift to the Queen Mother of the West

Magu is a legendary Taoist immortal associated with elixir of life, and symbolic protector of females in Chinese mythology. Ge Hong, a Taoist philosopher and alchemist of the Eastern Jin Dynasty introduced her stories in his work, *Biographies of Divine Immortals*. The third day of the third lunar month was supposed to be the birthday of the Queen Mother of the West who lived on the Kunlun Mountains in the far west. And every year on this day, she would invite immortals to attend her Peaches of Immortality. The four flower fairies – lily, peony, fragrant peony, and caval vine – collected brightly-colored and aromatic flowers and invited the fairy Magu to go with them. Magu then brewed a kind of immortal wine with special fungus, brought it to the fest, and presented it to the Queen Mother. Traditionally in ancient times when celebrating a woman's birthday, people often presented a picture painted with “Magu Presenting Her Birthday Gift”.

It's said that Magu was born in Jianchang (present-day Nancheng County, Jiangxi Province). Diligent and charming, she cultivated herself according to a religious doctrine and became an immortal. During the reign of Emperor Huan (132-167) of Han, she was reborn into a common family. In this reincarnation, she threw rice grains into the air and changed them into pearls, and distributed among the poor, providing relief to them. She once told people she had witnessed the blue ocean turning to mulberry fields for three times, from which derived the Chinese of Canghai Sangtian (blue ocean, mulberry fields), meaning gerat changes over the course of time. Yan Zhenqing (709-785), a great calligrapher during the Tang Dynasty, once erected a stele for her in Linchuan, Jiangxi Province, which was later destroyed by lightning.

相传很早以前，有一个牧牛郎，父母早亡，与一头老黄牛相依为命。一天，老牛开口说话，说织女要到银河洗澡，如果牛郎能趁机拿到织女的衣裳，就可以娶她为妻。牛郎按照老牛所说，躲在河边的芦苇中，待织女和众姐妹跃入清流之后，牛郎拿走了织女的衣服。众仙女见状，四下逃散。牛郎请求织女嫁给他，织女早已爱上老实本分的牛郎，便答应了他的请求。婚后一家人生活得很幸福。

但是这事很快便让王母娘娘知道，她派天兵天将下凡强行把织女带回天上。牛郎悲痛万分，拉着一双儿女，日夜追赶织女。原来清浅的小河变成了波涛汹涌的天河，牛郎和织女被隔在两岸，只能相对哭泣流泪。牛郎带着两个孩子日夜舀水，他们的忠贞爱情感动了喜鹊。千万只喜鹊飞来，搭成鹊桥，让牛郎织女走上鹊桥相会。王母娘娘无奈，只好允许两人在每年七月七日于鹊桥相会。

牛郎织女

The Cowherd and Girl Weaver

There lived a cowherd. After his parents died, he was drove out of the house by his brother and sister-in-law, only with an ox accompanied. One day, the ox said to him, "The Girl Weaver from heaven was about to bath in the Milky Way and if you can steal her clothes, you can marry her." The cowherd then quietly concealed himself among the reeds on the bank. The Girl Weaver and her sisters came. While they were bathing, the cowherd jumped out of the reeds and took the Girl Weaver's clothes away. When the fairy girls saw this stranger, they felt panic-stricken and ran away. Only did the Girl Weaver stay in the river shyly because she had no clothes to put on. Then the cowherd begged the Girl Weaver to be his wife. Only if she accepted the request, he would return her clothes. Seeing the frank cowherd, the Girl Weaver fell in love with him and agreed. After the marriage, they led a happy life and gave birth to a boy and a girl.

Unfortunately, the Queen Mother of the West soon found out and ordered heavenly soldiers and generals to bring the Girl Weaver back. The cowherd was deeply grieved, chasing after his wife day and night. However, the Milky Way was changed from a shallow river into deep surging torrent. The couple could do nothing but weep tears from opposite sides of the river. The cowherd and his children never stopped scooping, which moved the magpies. Thousands of magpies flied up into heaven and formed a bridge across the Milky Way for them. The Queen Mother of the West had no choice but permit that they meet once a year on the seventh day of the seventh lunar month.

元宵节这天，王子服表兄吴生约他郊游，后吴生因家中有事，留下子服一人游玩。忽然，一女子手拈梅花，冉冉而来，子服目不转睛地盯着这女子，少女发现后扔下梅花，笑着走了。子服拾花回家，藏在枕下，因思念少女，不吃不喝，身体瘦弱，难以支撑。吴生得知后，前来探望，子服告以实情。吴生骗他说，女子是子服的表妹，名叫婴宁，住在西南山中三十里处，并说等子服病好，一起去找婴宁。子服听后十分高兴，病很快就好了。

一日，子服等不及吴生，按吴生所指来到那个地方，果然见到了婴宁。子服住了几天，便带婴宁回家成亲。婚后，日子过得美满幸福。一天，婴宁对子服说自己原是狐女，子服知道后，并不介意，夫妻仍像以前一样恩爱。

婴宁

Yingning

One day, Wu Sheng invited Wang Zifu, his cousin, out for an excursion; but, suddenly, Wu had an emergency to handle and return home, living Wang alone. At that moment, a beautiful girl caught Wang's eye. He stared at her quite regardless of appearances; the girl noticed him, either. She walked away smiling, only throwing a twig of plum blossom on the ground. Wang then picked it up. He returned home confused, "What's her intention?" He hid the flower under his pillow and lay on the bed, neither talking nor eating. As soon as Wu Sheng heard this, he came to see Wang, who told the truth. Then Wu said he would inquiry for Wang; in a few days, he came to tell Wang that the girl was one of his own cousins, named Yingning, living not far away. Moreover, Wu promised to try to arrange a marriage for them. Wang, from this moment, was rapidly restored to health.

In fact, Wu Sheng told a lie; he only wanted to comfort Wang. The girl didn't exist. In the following days without Wu Sheng's return, Wang could wait no more and looked for the girl himself. Unbelievably, Wang found Yingning and expressed his affection to her. Afterwards Wang brought Yingning home. When asked about her parentage, Yingning just smiled, giving no answer. Seeing she was industrious and dexterous, Wang's mother approved their marriage. One night, Yingning told her husband, "I didn't tell you before, because we had known each other such a short time. Since you and your mother have been so kind to me, I'm going to tell you the truth. I'm, acutally, the daughter of your uncle and a fox. After my father's death, my mother and I was driven away. And when my mother went away she put me in the charge of a ghost; with whom I remained for a period of over 10 years." Hearing this, however, Wang didn't care about. The couple still led a happy life as before and the next year they gave birth to a child.

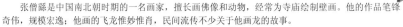

张僧繇是中国南北朝时期的一名画家，擅长画佛像和动物，经常为寺庙绘制壁画。他的作品笔锋奇伟，规模宏逸；他画的飞龙惟妙惟肖，民间流传不少关于他画龙的故事。

一年，张僧繇在安乐寺的墙壁上画了四条龙，个个栩栩如生，呼之欲出，他却不肯把眼睛画上。众人问他原因，他说如果画上眼睛，龙就会飞走。人们不信，说他吹牛，议论纷纷。张僧繇无奈，只得来到壁前，当着众人的面，提笔给一条龙画上了眼睛。刚落笔，只见那条龙昂头躬身，破壁飞去，惊得在场人面面相觑。后来，用“画龙点睛”比喻作文或说话时在关键地方加上精辟的语句，使内容更加生动传神。

画龙点睛

Adding a Finishing Touch to the Picture of a Dragon

During the Southern and Northern Dynasties (420-589), there was a famous painter called Zhang Sengyou, a native of Suzhou, Jiangsu Province. He was also a general and a procurator of Wuxing County. Zhang Sengyou excelled in painting human figures and animals and always painted frescos for Buddhist temples. Anyone that had seen his work evaluated that his work was imposing and exquisite, full of peculiarity, especially the vivid Chinese dragons he painted.

Many legends about his dragons spread, and the following one is the best-known. Once he painted four dragons in Anle Temple in Jinling (today's Nanjing, Jiangsu). They were so full of life that they made as if to come off the wall. However, none of them had eyes. The onlookers felt this odd and asked why he hadn't painted the eyes. He answered, “Eyes are crucial for dragons. With the eyes painted on, the dragons will break away from the wall and fly off.” Nobody believed this. As the days passed, some argued that he just talked big and some criticized that he had told a lie, thus he grew a little infamous. Therefore, Zhang Sengyou had no choice but to come in front of the fresco, take up his brush and add eyes to one of the dragons. All of a sudden heavy rain came on the heels of the lightening and thunder. No sooner had he finished than the dragon flew into the sky amid a thunderstorm, which delivered a great shock to onlookers. When the weather cleared, there were just three dragons on the wall.

Since then, the idiom “Adding a Finishing Touch to the Picture of a Dragon” is used to describe how, when painting, writing or speaking, the addition of just one or two key brushstrokes, sentences, words or phrases could enhance the content.

贾宝玉和林黛玉互相钟情，是封建的伦理道德所不允许的。贾府的长辈也都不喜欢林黛玉。贾母、王夫人、王熙凤遂瞒着宝玉、黛玉两个人，商议把符合她们心愿的薛宝钗嫁给宝玉，但对宝玉却说娶的是黛玉。婚礼一过，宝玉不答应也不行了。于是，贾府上下忙着给宝玉、宝钗准备婚事。

这一天，黛玉出来散心，走到山石后边，只见一个丫头坐在那儿哭。原来是老太太屋里的一个傻丫头，因为宝玉娶宝钗的事，说了一句“以后对宝钗是叫宝姑娘，还是叫宝二奶奶呢？”被掌嘴，并赶出房门。

黛玉素来和宝玉最知心，两个人情投意，听此一番话，顿觉五雷轰顶，心中又急又气，昏昏沉沉便往回走。刚一进屋，黛玉哇的一声，喷出一口鲜血，就昏死过去。

痴丫头无意泄机关

Innocent Maid Revealing Secret Unintentionally

Jia Baoyu and Lin Daiyu fell in love with each other, which was against the reigning feudal ethic and morality. The seniors of the Jia Family did not like Lin Daiyu either. Grandmother Jia, Mrs. Wang (Baoyu's mother) and Wang Xifeng (the de facto head of the Jia Family) meant to marry Baoyu to their favorite – Xue Baochai, and they arranged the wedding, but told Baoyu, who had set his heart on Daiyu, it was Daiyu whom he was going to marry. They reckoned after the wedding, even if Baoyu resisted it, it would be in vain. Thus, the whole family was busy in preparing the wedding. Daiyu was totally unaware of this matter.

One day, Daiyu went out for a walk. When she walked behind a rock, she found a maid sitting there crying. The maid, who was called numskull, was from Grandmother Jia's chamber. Since Baoyu was going to marry Baochai, she asked, “How should we address Baochai after the wedding ceremony? Miss Baochai or Mrs. Bao?” and then she was slapped and driven out of the Grandmother's chamber.

Daiyu always took Baoyu as her intimate friend, and they were deeply in love. Hearing the maid's unfortunate words Daiyu felt thunderstruck. She turned back to her Bamboo Lodge in a state of walking unconsciousness. But her body felt as though it weighed a thousand tons, her legs were as limp, and her feet were as wobbly as if she were walking on cotton-wool. It seemed a long way. when she approached her residence, a stream of blood came gushing from her mouth, and then Daiyu passed out.

东汉桓帝时，长安霸陵有个很固执的人，叫韩康。他本出身于名门望族，勤奋向学，精通诗书礼乐。东汉末年，朝政腐败，政治黑暗，民不聊生。韩康无意于仕途，便隐姓埋名。他经常到深山采药，然后拿到集市上出卖，以此为生。他卖的药，总是一个价钱，三十年从没变过。有一次，一个不认识韩康的女人来买药，韩康开口还是老价钱。这个女人便开始讨价还价，韩康就是不答应。这幅画就是韩康卖药的情景。女人气得说道："难道你是'口不二价'的韩康吗？"韩康一听，羞得满脸通红，背地里叹道："我本为了避名，才以卖药为生。现在连女人都知道我了，我还卖什么药啊！"于是，他便逃进深山隐居，再不出来卖药。后来，汉桓帝听说了韩康的事情，觉得这个人很有意思，就请他出来做官。韩康不得已只好应承下来，可半道上又跑了回去，一直到死再未出山。

韩康卖药

Han Kang Selling Medicinal Herbs

During the reign of Emperor Huan of Han (146-167), there lived a scholar named Han Kang, who was from the top drawer. He was diligent about his study and became a master of academy and music. However, in the end years of the Eastern Han Dynasty, consort clans and eunuchs struggled for power in subsequent reigns, and the politics became more and more corrupt. People sank into poverty and destitution. On seeing this, he retired from the official career. He earned a living by trekking to mountains to pick medicinal herbs and then sell them on the market. But he was a stubborn man, who refused to bargain and kept his prices the same for 30 years. Hence he was well-known, and was called "One-Price Han Kang".

Once a woman, who didn't knew Han Kang, came to his stand, selected some herbs and began to bargain, which is depicted in this painting. Of course, Han Kang refused her as usual. The woman said angrily, "you are so peculiar. You are Han Kang, aren't you?" Upon hearing this, Han Kang felt ashamed and said to himself, "I was going to live incognito, however, now even a woman has known me for my bad stubbornness. How can I continue to sell herbs here?" he then scuttled away and lived in seclusion in the mountains. Later, Emperor Huan of Han heard of this and thought Han Kang a special man. He then dispatched someone to invite Han Kang to the court. Han Kang had to accept. However on the way to the court, he escaped to the mountain because he didn't dare to face people. And he never came out of the mountain again after that.

武松武艺高强，胆识过人，整日游走江湖，结交天下豪杰。这一天，武松来到景阳冈，肚中饥渴，远远望见一酒家，酒旗上写有“三碗不过冈”五个字。武松来到店内坐下，便叫店主人斟酒。他连喝三碗，又招呼添酒。然而，店主人却道：“凡客人来我店中喝酒的，三碗便醉了，过不得前面的山冈。”武松笑道：“我喝了三碗，怎么不醉？”酒家道：“我这酒，初入口时，醇浓好喝，少刻时便倒。”武松正在兴头上，听此言很是不快，嚷道：“快拿酒来，又不是不给你钱！”店主无奈，只好由他。武松前后共喝18碗，结了酒钱，拿起哨棒、包袱起身便走。店主人见状，前来阻挡说，前面景阳冈上有只老虎，经常晚上出来伤人，已经伤了二三十条性命。可是不论店主人如何劝说，武松执意前行。下文接《武松打虎》。

“三碗不过冈”

Three Bowls of Wine and You Can’t Cross the Ridge

Wu Song, excellent at martial arts, was bolder and more sensible than most ordinary people. He traveled throughout the country, and made friends with his contemporaries. One day on his way home, he came to a place called Jingyang Ridge. He was hungry and thirsty from walking; further up the road he saw a tavern, outside which hung a flag with characters “Three Bowls of Wine and You Can’t Cross the Ridge”. Wu Song entered the tavern, took a seat, put down his bundle and cudgel, and called up the owner to pour wine for him.

After drinking up three bowls, he found the owner was no longer serving him. He rapped on the table and called the owner: “Host! Where’s wine?” The owner came out and said, “Guests in my tavern usually got drunk after draining three bowls, unable to surpass the mountain ahead.” Wu Song laughed it off and said, “I have had three bowls, and why am I not drunk?” The owner said, “This wine seems mellow and delicious; you don’t feel anything at first, but you will be down after a moment.” Wu Song was feeling quite well so he was a bit annoyed at the owner’s response, he said, “Fetch your wine quickly! I’m not drinking for free, am I?” Seeing that the wine had little effect on Wu Song, the owner had to let it pass. At last, Wu Song had drained a total of 18 bowls of that special wine, paid the bill, and picked up his cudgel and bundle, taking his leave. The owner hurried to stop him, and said there was a fierce tiger on Jingyang Ridge ahead, which often preyed upon people at night and had already killed almost 30 strong men. However, no matter how hard the owner tried to persuade Wu Song to stay, Wu Song was determined to go. With his bundle and cudgel in hand, Wu strode off towards Jingyang Ridge. The following story is *Wu Song Beating the Tiger*.

陶渊明（376～427年），又名陶潜，浔阳柴桑（今江西九江）人，是东晋时期著名的文学家。他的曾祖陶侃是晋朝名将，祖父和外祖父也均为晋朝名人。但到陶渊明时，家势已经衰弱，生活相当艰辛。他29岁步入仕途，做过几次小官；39岁出任县令时，因不愿“为五斗米折腰”，辞官归隐。此后，他以酒遣怀，以菊为伴，再没有出仕。

陶渊明以爱菊出名，有许多咏菊的诗篇。如“采菊东篱下，悠然见南山”（出自《饮酒》第五首），“秋菊有佳色”（出自《饮酒》第七首），“松菊犹存”（出自《归去来兮辞》）等，皆为名句。陶渊明一生坎坷流离，仕途曲折颠簸，他曾做过《五柳先生传序》概括自己清苦的一生以及处世哲学，如“闲静少言，不慕荣利……尝著文章自娱，颇示己志。忘怀得失，以此自终。”

陶渊明爱菊

Tao Yuanming Loving the Chrysanthemum

Tao Yuanming, also known as Tao Qian or Mr. Wuliu, born in presend-day Jiujiang, Jiangxi, was a noted literator, proser and one of the most influential poets from the Eastern Jin Dynasty. He came from a notable family which had descended into poverty. His great-grandfather was Tao Kan, a famous general and governor during the Eastern Jin, and his grandfather was also a celebrity during the time. He was selected to be a government official at 29, and had taken several low-ranking positions, but his disgust at the corruption and infighting of the court was steadily on the increase. At the age of 39, when he was appointed a county chief, he was reluctant to “bowing for five bushels of grain (it’s a figurative expression of the humble salary that low-rank officials got at that time),” and resigned and lived in seclusion. After that he drank to pass his time, took the chrysanthemum as his friend, and never returned to the political arena.

Tao’s love for the chrysanthemum was well-known, and he left behind many poems that praised this flower, such wonderful sentences as “Plucking the chrysanthemum by the east fence, I sees the south mountain at leisure” (quoted from his fifth poem *Drinking*), “The chrysanthemum in autumn has special beauty” (from his seventh poem *Drinking*), “The pine and the chrysanthemum still survive” (from *Lyrical Ballad of Returning to Nature*). Tao led a restless and vagabond life, and his political life was even more troubled. He once wrote about his poverty and loneliness as well as his life philosophy in *Preface of the Biography of Mr. Wuliu*, such as “To be leisurely, calm, and speak less; no admiration for fame and wealthy…write for one’s own entertainment; disregard gains and losses...”

高衙内霸占林娘子未遂，又被林冲惊吓，一病不起。太尉高俅听说后大怒，设下一条狠计要除掉林冲、为他的义子出气。高太尉假借要看宝刀，把林冲诱入军机重地，反诬他“手持利刃，蓄意杀人”，将其发配沧州；又重金收买押送的差役，让他们在途中了结林冲性命。

两个差役押解着林冲直奔沧州。走了几天，来到一个叫野猪林的地方，差役准备在这里下手。差役假意让林冲休息，又声称不放心，掏出绳子把林冲绑在树上；绑好后，举起木棍便向林冲劈头打去。这时，从树后跳出一个胖和尚，抡起禅杖就打，吓得两个差役慌忙跪地求饶。林冲一看，原来是鲁智深。他和鲁智深乃是在大相国寺菜园结识。两人一见如故，惺惺相惜，当时就结拜为兄弟。鲁智深得知林冲被陷害后，一路暗中相随；到了野猪林看见差役加害，便挺身而出，搭救了林冲性命。

鲁智深大闹野猪林

Lu Zhishen Fighting in Wild Boar Forest

Gao Yanei became sick due to the great shock, and was forced into bed all day long. On hearing this, Gao Qiu, Lin Chong's senior Minister, broke out in a rage, and vowed revenge on Lin Chong. Later, Gao Qiu and his followers made up an excuse that Gao Qiu wanted to have a look at Lin Chong's precious sword, which tricked Lin Chong into coming to the forbidden office of the military ministry. Then Lin was framed with attempting to assassinate Gao and sentenced to exile to Cangzhou, Hebei Povince. Even so, Gao Qiu did not want to let Lin off as he had offended Gao Yanei. Gao Qiu bribed the guards and secretly instructed them to kill Lin Chong on the way.

Days later, they came to the Wild Boar Forest, where pine trees and cypresses reached toward the sky and withering plants twisted with each other covering the ground – it seemed the right place for murder. The two guards told Lin to stop by a tree for a rest. They tied him fast to the tree, saying that it was for safety concerns. Only after they finished did they reveal their real purpose and readied their cudgels to kill him. When the cudgel was just about to fall upon Lin Chong's head, it was knocked away. A fat monk jumped out from behind the tree and brandished his staff, ready to fight. The guards were scared and knelt down, begging for forgiveness. Lin Chong opened his eyes, and the first person he saw was none other than Lu Zhishen, his sworn brother. When the two first met in the vegetable gardern of the Great Monastery of Assisting the State, they were impressed by each other, and became sworn brothers. Knowing that Lin Chong was framed and exiled, Lu Zhishen had been secretly protecting him all along the way.

鲁智深路见不平，行侠仗义，三拳打死恶霸镇关西后，被迫在五台山出家为僧。后来因为酒后闹事，违犯戒律，被打发去了东京大相国寺看守菜园。当地一些无赖整天偷菜，发现看管菜园的人换了，他们也不在意，反而想给鲁智深一个下马威。然而，鲁智深三拳两脚就把为首的两个无赖踹进了粪池，其他的人吓得跪地求饶。

第二天，他们拿着酒菜向鲁智深赔礼。正吃得起兴，门外大树上的乌鸦叫个不停，吵得人心烦。无赖们便要搬梯子上树去捣毁乌鸦窝，鲁智深和他们一起来到树下，弯下腰去，把大树连根拔起，无赖们都惊呆了，赶忙拜鲁智深为师，让他传授武艺。

鲁智深倒拔垂杨柳

Lu Zhishen Uprooting a Willow Tree

This story, taken from the *Outlaws of the Marsh*, is about Lu Zhishen, one of 108 heroes on the Mount Liang. Before coming to Mount Liang, he served as a constable in Weizhou, Shaanxi Province. However, when he saw a local tyrant nicknamed "Lord of West Town" was forcibly taking a girl from common family, he, in a fit of anger, killed the tyrant with just three punches. To avoid arrest by the government, he fled to Wutai Mountain and became a monk. Since he did not follow the Buddhist code, ate meat, drank wine and made trouble when he was got drunk, he was sent to the Great Monastery of Assisting the State in the then capital city, Kaifeng, where he was put in charge of a vegetable garden.

Near the garden there lived a band of local hooligans, who frequently came to steal the vegetables. None of the previous watchmen dare to stop them. As soon as they heard that a new monk had been employed there, they schemed to show their power over him. But it turned out this was in vain. Lu Zhishen had a great deal of physical strength so ruffians barely seemed like real opponents. Unfortunately they suffered a nasty beating at his hands and the two leaders were kicked into a manure pit. The rest were so frightened that they knelt down and begged for mercy.

The next day they came again with wine and food to apologize. While they were enjoying the food, some crows up in a tree outside the door cackled nonstop, which upset the men inside. The hooligans said they'd take care of it and using a ladder attempted to destroy the nest. Lu Zhishen followed them to the foot of the tree, looked it up and down; then he stripped off his cassock, bent down, grasped the trunk and uprooted the tree. The gang was astonished and implored Lu Zhishen to teach them martial arts.

黄忠是蜀汉军中的“五虎上将”之一，是历史上有名的老将军。有一次，曹军大将张郃引兵攻打葭萌关，守军抵挡不住，向刘备告急。刘备接到告急文书，请军师诸葛亮及众将商议。诸葛亮认为须是张飞亲往，方可敌退张郃。然张飞此时正兵屯瓦口，镇守阆中，亦是紧要之地。这时老将黄忠请战，诸葛亮激黄忠说：“将军虽勇，但已年迈，恐非张郃对手。”黄忠不服，大步走下堂，拿起大刀，抡动如飞；又取壁上硬弓，一连拉断两张。刘备、诸葛亮大喜，令黄忠点将。黄忠力荐另一位老将严颜。赵云不免担心：若葭萌关一失，益州危在旦夕；两位老将，未必堪当此任。但诸葛亮却对二人信心十足。果然，黄忠二人到了葭萌关，先用计大败张郃，又智夺曹操屯粮积草之地天荡山，最后攻下汉中定军山，大获全胜。众将心服口服。

黄忠请战

Huang Zhong's Plea for a Fight

Huang Zhong, one of the Five Tiger Generals of the Shu army (the other four were Guan Yu, Zhang Fei, Zhao Yun and Ma Chao), achieved greatness in his old age. Once, Zhang He, a general of the Cao Cao, was leading his army in an attack of the Jiameng Pass (in present-day Sichuan Province). The defense troop could not hold on and request reinforcements from Liu Bei. On receiving the letter, Liu Bei consulted Zhuge Liang and his followers. Zhuge Liang said no one could win over Zhang He except Zhang Fei, but Zhang Fei was far away in Wakou Pass, leading his troop defending Langzhong, which was also of strategic importance, so a general had to be chosen to meet the enemy head-on.

At that moment, the eldest general, Huang Zhong, pleaded for permission. Zhuge Liang suggested that Huang was too old to rival Zhang He. Huang Zhong did not buy Zhuge Liang's suggestion. He went to the center of the camp, got a broadsword, and brandished it quickly; then he picked two hard bows on the wall and pulled till they snapped. Liu Bei and Zhuge Liang were quite delighted, and asked him to choose an assistant. Huang chose General Yan Yan. Zhao Yun said it was not trustworthy to send two old generals to reinforce the Jiameng Pass, since the pass was the gate to Yizhou Prefecture, and once it fell to enemy occupation, Yizhou would be in danger. But Zhuge Liang had a lot of faith in the two old generals. As a matter of fact, Huang Zhong and Yan Yan leading their troop defeated Zhang He's army, then wisely seized Tiandang Mountain where Cao Cao stored grain and fodder, and occupied the Dingjun Mountain in Hanzhong. Their full victory won admiration from all the generals and soldiers.

西凉大将马腾欲害曹操，被斩。马腾的儿子马超武艺高强，勇猛过人，闻讯后誓杀曹操，以报父仇；随即率兵攻下长安、占领潼关。曹操手下有一员虎将许褚，力大无比，听说曹军儿员大将接连败于马超，心中不服，定要与他拼个高下。这一天，两军对阵，马超挺枪纵马，许褚拍马舞刀，斗了100多回合，不分胜负。马匹困乏，双方回营更换战马再战，又战100余回合，仍不分胜负。许褚杀得兴起，索性卸了盔甲，赤体提刀，与马超决战。两人越战越勇，又战30余回。突然间，许褚举刀砍去，马超侧身闪过，乘机一枪直刺许褚心窝。许褚扔掉手中大刀，一把握住来枪，夹在腋下。二人较力，拗断枪杆，各执半截断枪在马上乱打。双方阵营怕有闪失，均派兵解救。慌乱中许褚臂中两箭，慌忙退入寨中。马超回到营中，连赞许褚英勇。

许褚裸衣斗马超

Xu Zhu Stripping for a Fighting with Ma Chao

Ma Teng, a general of the Western Liang Regime, collaborated to kill Cao Cao, but was failed and beheaded. Ma Chao, Ma Teng's son, was a prominent and ferocious general who promised to take his revenge on Cao Cao. He led an army and seized Chang'an and Tongguan Pass. Cao's army was defeated during several battles, and Cao Cao was almost killed in battle. He took off his red robe and cut off his beard which marked his identity, and managed to escape.

Xu Zhu, a ferocious warrior served as a bodyguard to Cao Cao, was grandly-proportioned and particularly great in strength. When he heard several generals of his army were defeated by Ma Chao, he felt unworthy, and challenged Ma Chao to a duel. Ma Chao took up the challenge, and the pair rode forth to engage in a battle on horseback. They fought over 100 bouts, but neither had the advantage. By then, both of their steeds were spent, so each retired to their own lines to change a fresh mount. After another 100-round fighting, neither Xu's sword nor Ma's spear could get an upper hand. Suddenly, Xu Chu galloped back to his own side, stripped off his heavy armor and rode back to battle-field bare-chested. More that 30 bouts elapsed, and Xu Chu, summoning up all his force, plunged towards Ma Chao with sword held high to strike. Ma evaded the strile but rode in with his spear at Xu's heart. At the critical moment, Xu threw down his sword and clamped the spear firmly under his left arm. Then a struggle for the spear ensued. With his enormous strength, Xu Chu snapped the spear-shaft into two, each holding one half. Fearing for their warriors, both sides sent aides into the field. In the chaos, Xu Chu received two arrow wounds and had to retreat. Back at his camp, Ma Chao repeatedly spoke highly of Xu Zhu to his followers.

荣国府二老爷贾政的大女儿元春被封为贵妃，皇帝恩准她元宵节回贾府省亲。为迎接元春，贾府专门修了一座大观园。元宵节之日，贾府男女老少一大早就跪在大门外迎候贵妃。元春乘坐绣凤金銮大轿，前呼后拥来到大观园。园内雕梁画栋，金碧辉煌：既有竹林掩映的江南风景，也有桑榆成阴的乡间田舍。元春在大观园里转了一遭，便与贾母、王夫人相见，几人呜咽抽泣，互诉思念之苦。随后，元春依次见过了迎春、探春、惜春及黛玉、宝钗等姐妹。见到弟弟宝玉，元春又哽咽起来。恰时盛宴齐备，元春命众兄弟姐妹分别按大观园各处景色各展才华题诗一首，以示庆贺。接着，元春去看戏，向众人发了赏赐物品。最后和大家含泪惜别，上轿回宫。

元春省亲

The Homecoming of an Imperial Concubine

This story, taken from the *A Dream of Red Mansions* by Qing Dynasty novelist Cao Xueqin, which is one of the Four Great Classical Novels and is often acknowledged to be the zenith of Chinese classical fiction. The novel contains nearly 30 major character and hundreds of minors ones. With the love tragedy among Jia Baoyu, Lin Daiyu and Xue Baochai as the main thread, and the change from prosperity to decline of the four great clans of Jia, Shi, Wang, and Xue as the background of the story, the novelist made a painstaking description of the daily life and a life-like portrayal of numerous figures, truly but vividly delineated the inevitable doom of the four clans and the decline of feudal society in general.

Jia Yuanchun, the eldest sister of Jia Baoyu, was conferred as the highest-ranking imperial concubine, and the emperor allowed her to visit her family on the coming Lantern Festival. The Jia Family built a Grand View Garden for her visit. On the early morning, all the members of the Jia Family knelt down by their house gate to welcome Yuanchun. Accompanied by many followers, Yuanchun paraded to the garden. The pillars and balks of the garden were colorfully painted, and the decoration themes were magnificently varied. Yuanchun took a tour of the garden, and then met with her grandmother and mother. They could do nothing but sob, while Yuanchun complained bitterly, “What is the use of all this luxury and splendor if I have to be seperated from my family?” Then she met her brother and sisters, and couldn’t weeping again. Just at that moment, the reception feast was ready. All good things must come to an end. After the feast, she bade farewell to her family in tears and returned to the forbidden royal palace.

北宋年间，西夏国侵犯中原，大将杨宗保率兵镇守边关，抗击敌人，不幸身亡。这时西夏兵破边关，大举进犯中原。朝廷百官贪生怕死，无一人敢领兵迎战。宗保的祖母佘太君忍住悲痛，率领全家出征抗敌。杨家兵将攻无不克，战无不胜，杀得西夏兵逃回老营。宋军追至山下，见一深谷，正欲进兵，一将军急忙阻拦。原来这是一条绝谷，杨宗保正是误入此谷丧生。全军只得扎下营来，进退两难。回到帐中，穆桂英经过询问，确信绝谷内定有栈道可以飞越天险，直捣敌营。于是她骑上宗保生前的坐骑闯入峡谷，靠着识途的老马和采药老人的帮助，找到了栈道，直插敌营，一举歼灭了敌军，保卫了的边疆。

画中的情景是穆桂英正在采药老人的指点下，寻找栈道。

穆桂英绝谷寻栈道

Mu Guiying Finding a Path Through the Valley of the Dead

During the years of the Northern Song Dynasty, the Western Xia State often invaded the central China. General Yang Zongbao fighted the Western Xia army and defended the border, unfortunately sacrificed his life. The Western Xia army was about to break through the border defenses and mount a massive invasion of the central China. Officials of the court, however, were all frightened, and no one dared confront the Western Xia army.

Yang Zongbao's grandmother, She Taijun, overcoming the extreme sadness at the loss of Zongbao, took the mission in this national crisis, enlisted her family, and led the army to resist the enemy. The army led by the Yang Family was courageous and capable. They achieved victory after victory, and drove the Western Xia army back to their base. When chasing after the enemy, they arrived at the mouth of a deep valley. Soldiers were about to pass it before one of the generals stopped them. He explained that it was a dead valley, and General Zongbao lost his life for mistakenly entering into it. The army was in dilemma, and had to make camp.

Mu Guiying, Zongbao's wife, after some consultation, believed that there was probably a path to crush the enemy's base. Leading a squad, she entered the valley, riding her husband's horse. Under the guidance of an old horse and an old herb-collector, she found the path, crushed the enemy's base, and annihilated the Western Xia army. She eventually defended the border of her country, and at the same time fulfilled her husband's ambition. The scene in the painting shows Mu Guiying searching for the path under the guidance of the old herb-collector.

安大业从小聪明机智，俊美出群。父母视他如掌上明珠，希望他将来能成就大业。长大后，村中人争着给他说媒。一天晚上，大业母亲梦见仙女对她说大业将娶一位公主为妻，于是婉言谢绝了所有提亲的人。但几年过去了，也不见有公主到来。

一天，大业正在房内读书，只见几个婢女拥着一个窈窕少女进屋。经问，得知少女是圣后府上的云萝公主，大业惊喜万分。二人坐下对弈，精通棋道的大业连败。下完棋，公主要走，大业不舍，公主拿出一千两黄金，要大业盖新房，等新房盖好后再来与大业相会。公主如约赶到后，大业向公主求婚。公主说，如果结为夫妻，他们只能在一起生活六年；但两人要是作棋友、酒友，可生活三十年。大业还是想先成婚。二人遂成亲，先后有了两个儿子。六年期满，公主果然一去不返。

云萝公主

Princess Yunluo

An Daye was a man of extraordinary quality and appearance, being quiet his parents' pet. Many match-makers offered marriage proposal. One night An Daye's mother dreamed that a fairy told her that her son Daye should marry a princess at some future day. Therefore, she graciously refused all proposals. Yet several years had passed, no princess appeared.

One day when An Daye was reading alone in his room, a beautiful princess endowed with a fairy-like loveliness walked in with several maids. It turned out to be Princess Yunluo. Daye was pleasantly surprised and was much struck by her beauty. He just stood there in silence, as did the princess. It was an awkward moment. Suddenly, a clever maid saw a chess-board on the table and suggested that they play. Daye hurriedly took out the pieces and started the board game with the princess. Daye hadn't met any real opponents before he encountered the princess, but now ended up defeated. The princess got up to leave. She gave Daye a large sum of money to build a new house and a promise to return when it was finished. Then she disappeared in the clouds.

When the house was completed, the princess came to meet Daye as she had promised. At night, Daye proposed to the princess, who said, "If we become a couple, we'll live together for just six years, but we can get along with each other for 30 years if we simply remain friends, filling up the time with chess, wine, conversation and good cheer. What's your thought?" "We might as well get married." Then, that night, they got married and later had two sons. Yet the princess left six years later, as she said she would, without saying anything, leaving Daye to yearn day and night.

诸葛亮率领蜀军在祁山（三国时魏蜀必争之地）和魏军对峙，山路崎岖，粮草渐少，魏将孙礼设下一计：他带兵装扮成运粮队伍，却在粮车上装满干柴茅草、硫磺硝烟，引诱蜀军前来抢粮；待蜀兵抢车之际，放火烧车，外以伏兵，内以夹攻，企图一举大破蜀军。诸葛亮正为军中缺粮踌躇，忽哨探来报，祁山西边有魏军数千辆粮车运粮，运粮官是孙礼。诸葛亮笑着说："孙礼料我缺粮，车上装载的必是茅草引火之物。"随即决定将计就计。

这天夜里，诸葛亮派马岱引兵三千，摸到孙礼运粮车队之前。正值西南风起，蜀兵到上风处放起火来，一时车仗尽着，魏军大乱。又有两路蜀军杀来，将孙礼团团围住。魏军人马乱窜，死伤无数。孙礼领着残兵败将狼狈逃走。

诸葛亮计破孙礼

Zhuge Liang Defeating Sun Li

Zhuge Liang was leading the Shu army in a confrontation against the Wei army at Qishan Mountain (a crucial spot for both the Wei and the Shu in a military sense). The mountainous area was very arduous for trafficking fodder and grain, and the Shu army's storage was quickly depleting. Sun Li, a general of Wei, set a stratagem: he led a troop disguised as the grain carriers, and tried to induce the Shu army to seize the "grain" carriages, which were indeed full of dry grass, wood, and other combustibles; if the Shu army rushed up, they would ignite the carriages, and with the ambushing force nearby, they might crush the Shu army in one decisive strike.

Zhuge Liang was considering about the shortage of grain and fodder, when a scout came to report that there were many carriages with grain to the west of Qishan Mountain; the general in charge was Sun Li. Zhuge Liang responded, laughing, "Sun Li knows my army is short of grain. The stuff inside the carriages must be grass or other fire-friendly items." Then he decided to set a trap to break the trap.

That night, Zhuge Liang sent Ma Dai leading 3,000 men to secretly rush at Sun Li's carriages. When the southwest wind began to blow, the Shu soldiers, in the safe areas along the way, began to set fires, with the wind blowing they ignited the Wei army's carriages. Soon all the carts were in a blaze that lit up the sky. The Wei army was immediately thrown into chaos. Soldiers and horses of the Wei army scattered everywhere, and the dead were too many to count. Sun Li, leading the remnants of his defeated army, made a dash through the smoke and fire of the battle and escaped.

这一年中秋节，荣、宁二府随贾母到大观园赏月。众人散去，黛玉和史湘云却毫无睡意，便来到山坡下的池塘边。但见夜空一轮皓月，池中一盘月影，清风吹过，碧波微皱，令人心旷神怡，二人诗兴大发。黛玉先起："三五中秋夕"，湘云接道："清游拟上元"，两人便这样你一句我一句地联起诗来。正在兴头上，黛玉停下来指着水面上的一个黑影，疑是有鬼；湘云胆子大，捡起一块石头扔了过去，池面上飞起一只白鹤。

湘云见景生情，马上念了一句："寒塘渡鹤影"。黛玉连声叫好，沉思片刻，对道："冷月葬花魂"。湘云拍手称赞，转而说道："好是好，只是太颓废了，你现在有病，不应作这种过于凄凉的诗句。"正说着，栊翠庵的尼姑妙玉走了过来，邀她们进庵喝茶，于是三人一起来到了栊翠庵。

寒塘渡鹤影

The Crane's Shadow Sliding Through the Cold Pond

On the night of a Mid-Autumn Festival, all family member accompanied Grandmother Jia to watch the moonlit scenery in the Grand View Garden. This big family reunion made Lin Daiyu feel so disconsolate that she had slipped out to the corridor to shed tears; while Shi Xiangyun came to comfort her. After everyone else left, Daiyu and Xiangyun did not feel sleepy at all; they came to a pond by a hill. The big bright moon was in the sky, and the pond mirrored the moon. When the breeze blew, the smooth water surface of the pond rippled, which looked fantastic. The two began to compose poetic sentences about the wonderful view. Just at the moment when they were getting excited about the composition, Daiyu stopped and pointed at a shadow in water. She suspected it was a ghost. Xiangyun picked up a stone and threw at it – a white crane flew out of the pond.

Xiangyun immediately thought of a sentence to describe the scene, "The shadow of a crane sliding through the chilly pond," which won Daiyu's repeated praises. After thinking for a while, Daiyu continued, "The soul of the flower buried under the cool moonlight." Xiangyun applauded, but then said, "Your sentence is certainly good, but it is too depressing. You are ill now, so you should not compose these kinds of sentences and sadden yourself." At that moment, Miaoyu, who was a young, beautiful and very learned nun from the Buddhist nunnery of the Jia Family, came over. She had been listening to their reciting. However, on hearing the last two lines, she thought they seemed the height of refinement and sounded too mournful, so she came out to prevented them from going on. She then invited the two to her residence to drink tea.

诸葛亮亲率30万精兵伐魏，直奔陈仓道口而来。陈仓地势险要，城虽不大，但深沟高垒，易守难攻。诸葛亮领兵一连攻打20多天，未能破城，只好退兵。一日忽有哨探回报说，陈仓守将郝昭病重。诸葛亮遂命魏延、姜维领兵五千直奔陈仓城下，如见火起，合力攻城，却同时命关兴、张苞暗出汉中。三日后，魏延、姜维领兵来到陈仓城下，见城上并无旗号，更无守军，二人惊疑不定，不敢攻城。忽听城头一声炮响，四面旗帜齐竖，诸葛亮站在城头，魏延、姜维慌忙下马，拜伏于地。原来，诸葛亮命魏延、姜维二人领兵取城实乃稳众人之心；他本人暗藏于军中，随关兴部队披星戴月，赶到陈仓，使敌不能调兵。大军到后，暗探在城内放火，发喊相助，令魏兵惊疑不定。兵无主将，必自乱，因而攻城易如反掌。正如兵书上所言“出其不意，攻其不备”。

诸葛亮奇兵袭陈仓

Zhuge Liang Seizing Chencang with a Special Force

Zhuge Liang gathered an army of 300,000 men to attack the Wei State; he marched toward the Chencang Crossroad. The crossroad was very dangerous, and the general, Hao Zhao, who was in the charge of its defense, had ordered a barrier of deep ditches and high walls built to resist the attack. Therefore, for more than 20 days, Zhuge Liang was unable to seize it, but had to retreat. One day, a scout reported that Hao Zhao was very ill. Zhuge Liang thought an opportunity was coming. He dispatched Wei Yan and Jiang Wei with an army of 5,000 men to attack the barrier, and if they saw a blaze, then attacked. But then, he summoned Guan Xing and Zhang Bao and gave them secret instructions.

Three days later, Wei Yan and Jiang Wei reached Chencang. They spotted no flags or soldiers on the barrier. Being suspicious, they did not dare to launch their attack abruptly. Suddenly, the wall was thick with flags, and there appeared Zhuge Liang. Wei Yan and Jiang Wei hurried to kneel down to show their great admiration for Zhuge Liang. In fact, dispatching Wei Yan and Jiang Wei to attack the barrier was misdirection in order to calm the people of this people; Zhuge Liang hid himself among his soldiers, went all the way to Chencang over night along with Guan Xing and Zhang Bao so that the enemy would have no time for deployment. He had sent spies into the city. When the Shu's army came, they set fires and began to shout, which made the Wei soldiers frightened and hesitant. Since Hao Zhao was sick, there was no leader commanding the Wei army at that moment, and the city was soon in chaos. Under such circumstances, it was easy to seize Chencang. This was, thereafter, used as an example of "attacking the unprepared" in military academies.

高衙内仗着义父高俅的势力，欺压百姓，调戏妇女，无恶不作。一天他在岳庙遇见八十万禁军教头林冲貌美的妻子，便上前纠缠。幸亏林冲及时赶到，高衙内才悻悻离去。可是，自从见了林娘子，高衙内邪念不断，整日焦躁不安。仆人富安给他出了个暗害林冲、强占林娘子的主意。

第二天，林冲的好友陆谦（已经被高衙内收买）请他到酒楼喝酒。林冲出来不久，富安跑到林冲家对林娘子说，林教头在陆谦家里喝酒，昏倒了。林娘子急忙赶到陆谦家，却见高衙内等在那里。林娘子知道上当，正要回去，不料门被紧紧关上。高衙内百般调戏，林娘子拼死反抗。丫环赶忙来找林冲。林冲听说，跑到陆谦家里，高喊开门。听到丈夫的声音，林娘子使劲推开高衙内，急忙去开门。林冲闯进屋来，高衙内早吓得魂飞魄散，拼命夺路而逃。林冲还要追赶，娘子百般劝阻，方才罢手。

高衙内戏林娘子

Gao Yanei Harassing Mrs. Lin

Under the powerful influence of his adoptive father, Gao Qiu, a high-ranking official at the time, Gao Yanei often randomly bullied folks and harassed attractive females. One day, he came across the wife of Lin Chong, who was the trainer of the 800,000 Imperial Guards. Lin's beautiful wife caught the eye of Gao Yaonei, and suffered sexual harassment from the latter. Fortunately, Lin Chong came in time and rescued his wife. Gao Yanei and his followers had to leave resentfully. After meeting Mrs. Lin, however, Gao Yanei became obsessed with her attractiveness, and grew anxious all the time. Fu An, one of his followers, thought up a dark schemes.

The next day, Lu Qian, who was a close friend of Lin Chong but had already been bribed by Gao Yanei, invited Lin to have a drink at a restaurant. Lin Chong, without any doubt, left home. Soon after, Fu An went to tell Mrs. Lin that Lin Chong was drunk at Lu's home and that he had passed out. Shocked, Mrs. Lin went hastily to Lu Qian's home, but found Gao Yanei was waiting for her there. She realized the trap. Gao Yanei tried to rape her by every means, but she fought like a tigress. Her maid hurried to get Lin Chong. At the news, Lin Chong was furious. He rushed to Lu Qian's house, and shouted fiercely calling the door open. Knowing her husband had arrived, Mrs. Lin felt a little more empowered. She pushed Gao Yanei away and opened the door. Seeing Lin Chong entering the house, Gao Yanei was scared to death, but he managed to escape. Lin Chong wanted to go after him, but was stopped by Mrs. Lin.

赤壁之战后，曹操领残兵败将逃命，一路上连遭伏兵劫杀，最后只剩三百余骑往华容道撤去。此时正值隆冬严寒之时，人皆饥倒、马尽困乏。行不远，大将关羽提刀跨马，截住去路。谋士程昱说，关羽欺强而不凌弱，恩怨分明。因曹操待关羽有恩，于是程昱建议曹操亲自求情，可脱得此难。曹操从其言，纵马向前，请求关羽念昔日之情，放曹军一条生路。关羽是个义重如山的人，想起曹操许多恩义与后来过五关、斩六将之事，不觉动心。又见曹军惶惶，皆欲垂泪，于是勒马，命众军四散摆开。曹操见关羽回马，便和众将一齐冲过去。关羽回身时，曹操已与众将过去了。关羽大喝一声，曹军皆下马，哭拜于地。关羽越加不忍。正犹豫间，曹将张辽纵马而至。关羽和张辽是故友，今日见了，又动故旧之情，长叹一声，放他们离去。

华容道关羽义释曹操

Releasing Cao Cao at Huarong Trail

During the Battle at Chibi, Zhou Yu's fire ships, carried by the southeastern wind, sped towards Cao Cao's fleet and set it aflame. In a short time, a large number of Cao's soldiers were burned or drowned to death. Cao was defeated utterly. He gathered the remnant army and escaped towards Huarong Trail, a narrow shortcut in the woods. However, under instruction from Zhuge Liang, Guan Yu and his soldiers had already stationed there.

It was the time of greatest wind cold, Cao's men were starving, and the horses exhausted. Seeing Guan Yu, they dropped into desperation. Upon being cut off, Cao Cao rode forward and appealed to Guan Yu to remember his kindness in former day. Guan Yu was indeed a very mountain of goodness and could not forget the great kindness he had received at Cao Cao's hands, and the magnanimity Cao had shown over after he smashed through five passes and killed Cao's six generals. Seeing the plight of the defeated men, Guan Yu pulled at the bridle of his steed, ordered his men to stand aside. When Guan Yu turned to look back, they had all passed. Suddenly, Guan Yu uttered a great shout, Cao's soldiers jumped off their horses immediately and knelt on the ground crying for mercy. Under such a circumstance, Guan Yu was even reluctant to take action. Then, Zhang Liao, one of Cao Cao's generals, arrived. Zhang Liao was also an old friend of Guan Yu. Meeting his defeated friend in such a situation, Guan Yu let out a long sigh, and eventually allowed the enemy to pass through without challenge.

Upon returning, Guan Yu pleaded guilty and asked for death, but Zhuge Liang fully understood the compassion and mercy of Guan Yu and forgave him at last.

画上的两个女子是三国时期江东有名的美女——大乔和小乔。世人称她们为“江东二乔”。大乔嫁给了孙权的兄长孙策，小乔则做了都督周瑜的夫人。诸葛亮想联合孙权，共抗曹操，见孙权对拒曹一事犹豫不决，便想出一个办法。一天，他去看望周瑜，对他说，曹操造了一个铜雀台，金碧辉煌，极其壮丽。他知道大乔和小乔是绝色美女，因此想把二乔置于铜雀台，以享晚年。周瑜心中一惊，诸葛亮又不紧不忙地说，曹操的儿子曹植作过一首《铜雀台赋》，里面有：“揽二乔于东南兮，乐朝夕之与共。”诸葛亮于是建议把二乔送给曹操，免得曹操过江攻打东吴。周瑜勃然大怒，咬牙切齿，誓与曹操势不两立。这样，双方决定联合对付曹操，便有了后来著名的赤壁之战。其实，诸葛亮假装不知道周瑜和二乔的关系，借用《铜雀台赋》来激怒周瑜，使他下决心坚决抗曹。

江东二乔

The Two Ladies of the Qiao Family in Jiangdong

The two ladies, the Elder Qiao and the Younger Qiao, in this painting were the most attractive ladies in Jiangdong (southeast of the lower reaches of the Yangtze River) during the Period of the Three Kingdoms. The Elder Qiao married Sun Quan's elder brother Sun Ce and the younger one married Zhou Yu, one of the most capable military strategists of Sun Quan. Zhuge Liang intended to collaborate with Sun Quan to resist Cao Cao, but Sun was hesitant. In order to form a federation with Sun, Zhuge Liang came up with an idea.

One day, he paid a visit to Zhou Yu, and told him that Cao Cao had learned the Two Qiaos were all tremendously attractive and intended to seize them, so he built an extravagantly decorated and grandly shaped Bronze Sparrow Mansion in hope of spending his rest life with them. Zhou Yu was shocked. Then Zhuge Liang recited a quote from *Ballad for the Bronze Sparrow Mansion* by Cao Cao's son, Cao Zhi (192-232), "To seize the two Qiaos from the southeast, and entertain them all day long." Zhuge Liang proposed Zhou Yu to donate the two ladies to Cao Cao to avoid Cao Cao's attack on Jiangdong.

Zhou Yu became furious, and he swore he would fight fiercely against Cao. Thus, the two sides decided to collaborate with each other, and afterwards, the Battle of Chibi took place. Actually, Zhuge Liang pretended that he did not know about the relationship between Zhou Yu and the Two Qiaos, and deliberately aroused Zhou Yu's hatred by reciting the ballad, so that Zhou would be determined to confront Cao Cao.

一天夜晚，李白和堂兄弟们聚会在桃花园，明月悬空，春风徐徐，送来桃李的芬芳。李白和兄弟们饮酒赋诗。李白乘兴写了一篇100多字的散文名篇《春夜宴诸从弟桃花园序》。主要表达光阴似箭，日月如梭，人生如梦，当尽情欢乐；也暗示出作者放荡不羁，高傲蔑俗的性格。 这幅画是取“秉烛夜游”的语意而绘制。

秉烛夜游

The Candle-Lit Party

One night, Li Bai and his cousins had a party in the Peach Flower Garden. It was in spring. The big bright moon hung in the sky, and the mild breeze brought the sweet scent of the peach flowers and the plum blossoms. People at the party drank wine and composed poems. In his delight, Li Bai wrote his famous essay, *Ode to the Feast of Entertaining My Cousins on a Spring Night in the Peach Flower Garden*. The essay of more than 100 words expresses the author's attitude toward life – life is too short and dreamlike; people should commit to Carp Diem and live their lives to the fullest. The fantastic description of the candle-lit party also reflects Li Bai's personality – unconventional and uninhibited, proud, reluctant to conform, and defiant of the vulgar. The probable meaning of the essay is as follows:

The heaven and earth are an inn for all things, while time a passenger passes through the ages. The floating and changeful life is like a dream, and how much time does it allowed for our enjoyment? So the ancients liked to light their candles to make merry in the nights. That's a good idea. For me now, the spring scenery is so charming, while the nature colorful. It's such a pleasing thing that my bros and I happily rally here, a garden filled of the odour of peach blossoms, to chat over wine. All my bros are gifted scholars, however, I'm too talentless to compose an appropriate poem to express the pomp. The elegant sight scene is not yet all covered, but our topics are already turned into elegant taste. So let's make our feast amongst blossoms, swilling our wines and enjoying the moon while intoxicated. However, without good poems, how could we express our graceful feelings? So let's emulate the ancients, thoes who cannot make a poem would be punished to drink three cups of wine. The painting is based on the sensations created in the party according to Li's description.

典韦是曹操手下的一员猛将，几次救过曹操性命，倍受器重。张绣败降曹操后，每日宴请曹操，曹操见张绣的婶婶邹氏姿容艳丽，便霸为己有。张绣气愤，欲起兵反曹，可又顾虑典韦的勇猛。

一日张绣请典韦饮酒，趁典韦酒醉之时，盗走他的战戟。半夜，张绣派人放火，又领兵冲进曹营。典韦听到喊杀之声起身，寻不见战戟，拿了士兵的腰刀，冲出营。典韦身无片甲，在敌人枪、箭的攻击下，伤痕累累，却毫无惧色，奋力死守寨门，曹操才得以脱身逃命。后来，典韦后背中枪，倒在血泊之中。

战宛城典韦救主

Dian Wei Saving His Master in the Battle at Wancheng

A portrait of Cao Cao

Dian Wei was a ferocious general subordinate to Cao Cao. Famous for his enormous strength, Dian Wei excelled in wielding dual halberds, each of which was said to weigh 40 *jin* (20 kg). Since he had saved Cao's life several times, he was well respected and well treated.

Having been defeated, Zhang Xiu, governor of Wancheng City (present-day Nanyang, Henan Province), surrendered to Cao, and every day he held feasts to flatter Cao. On seeing Zhang Xiu's aunt, Cao Cao was attracted to her beauty, and intended to forcibly occupy her. Zhang Xiu was humiliated and angry; he intended to rebel against Cao, but was afraid of Dian Wei's ferocity. One day, Zhang Xiu invited Dian Wei to have a drink, and after Dian Wei got drunk, Zhang stole Dian's special weapon, dual halberds.

At midnight, Zhang Xiu sent his men to set a fire, and he himself led an army and rushed Cao's encampment. Dian Wei was awakened by the noise. Unable to find his halberds, he took an ordinary sword from a soldier, and rushed out of his camp. He did his utmost to hold the gate of the encampment and without the protection of armor or corselet, the fearless general was severely wounded and won enough time for Cao Cao to escape through the back gate. Soon after, Dian Wei was impaled with a spear through his back, and he fell down in pool of blood. This fatal injury claimed his life. Only after assuring that he was dead did the enemies dare to come forward.

杨延昭见穆桂英有勇有谋，命她掌挂三军大印。桂英率领宋军大破辽军，斩了敌军主将，骇得辽兵闻风丧胆。然而，当宋军回朝后，宋真宗竟听信谗言，解除了杨家的兵权。

转眼20多年过去，西夏国崛起，图谋中原。此时，穆桂英已不在军中，且杨家兵将老的老，死的死。西夏有恃无恐，大军直逼都城。朝廷上下无人敢带兵抗敌，皇帝只得张榜招贤。此时，奸臣王强为了一己私利，保举儿子王伦应招比武，妄图抢得帅印。穆桂英的儿子杨文广和女儿杨金花背着母亲，参加比武，杨文广怒斩王伦，夺下帅印交与穆桂英。穆桂英深感朝廷薄恩寡义，已心灰意冷，不愿再为朝廷效力。老太君佘赛花深明大义，极力劝说桂英以国家为重。在民族危难之际，年过半百的穆桂英重新披甲上阵，统领宋军拼死抗敌，大破西夏军。

穆桂英挂帅

Mu Guiying Taking the Title of Marshal

Mu Guiying's talent and skills soon made their due impression on the Yang Family and foes, and was recommended into the army to fight against the Liao. She leading the Song army defeated the Liao army, and killed their commanding general, demonstrating her peerless valor. However, when the Song army returned in triumph, the emperor Zhenzong was poorly advised by some corrupt officials, and removed the military commanding power of the Yang Family and decreed they must return to their hometown and farm for a living.

20 years passed, Mu Guiying was no longer in charge of military affairs and the once capable generals in the Yang Family had grown old or passed away. With nothing to be afraid of, the army of Western Xia (1038-1227), a regime founded by the ancient nomadic tribes of Tangut, invaded central China and marched on Song's Capital. Officials in the court did not dare to lead the army out against this enemy, and the emperor had to put out notices to recruit new generals and leaders. A corrupt minister, Wang Qiang, urged his son, Wang Lun, to attend the martial arts competition for the recruitment, so that his family might get all this military power. Yang Wenguang and Yang Jinhua, son and daughter of Mu Guiying, attended the competition, concealing their mother. In the competition, Yang Wenguang knocked down Wang Lun, and thus received the seal of marshal; then he turned it over to his mother. Initially, Mu was reluctant to accept the assignment because she was dissatisfied with the unfair treatment rendered by the imperial court to the generals of the Yang family after they defeated the Liao's invasion. But she was persuaded by She Taijun, her grandmother-in-law. In such a national crisis, 50-year-old Mu Guiying put on her corselet to command the Song army and later decisively defeated the enemy.

赤壁大战之前，周瑜苦思破曹之计，老将黄盖自告奋勇，愿诈降曹操、以作内应。第二天，周瑜召集各位将军于帐下说，曹操兵将充足，人马齐备，令将士领取三个月的粮草，准备长期对抗。然话音未落，黄盖劝道，不如弃甲倒戈，及早投降。周瑜大怒，说黄盖扰乱军心，喝令将其斩首。众将官一齐跪地请求，周瑜免黄盖死罪，但要杖打一百军棍。两边军士把黄盖拖翻在地，拿起军棍打了五十下。众将又苦苦哀求，周瑜这才罢休。众将官急忙上前扶起黄盖，只见他被打得皮开肉绽，鲜血迸流。看的人无不下泪。只有坐在一旁的诸葛亮不动声色，他早就看出周瑜和黄盖演的是“苦肉计”。黄盖写了一封降书，托人带过江去，送给曹操。早有眼线将黄盖被责一事禀奏曹操，因此曹信以为真。不料赤壁一战，正是黄盖引着火船冲入曹军水寨，对大败曹操起了重要作用。

苦肉计黄盖受刑

Huang Gai's Self-Torturing to Win the Enemy's Trust

Prior to the Battle at Chibi, Zhou Yu was racking his brains in search of a way to defeat Cao Cao. An old general, Huang Gai, recommended himself to offer a false surrender. The next day, Zhou Yu gathered all his generals to have a meeting. He said Cao Cao had plenty of troops and supplies, so it was impossible to break him in one strike, and his fellow generals should prepare supplies and get ready for a long fight. Huang Gai immediately said that they might as well surrender. Zhou Yu was furious, ordered the lictors to remove Huang and execute him. General Gan Ning begged for forgiveness for him, but was driven forth with blows. All generals knelt down to beg for Zhou's mercy. Zhou then cancelled death penalty, but turned to the lictors and bade them deal the culprit 100 blows as punishment. The fellow generals intended to continue to beg him, and Zhou Yu pushed over the table and scared them away. Huang Gai was thrown to the ground, and 50 blows were given. All his colleagues, again, prayed for remission. Zhou told Huang, "If you dare disrespect to me again, you should be punished for both faults", and then let him go.

The generals hurried to help Huang Gai who was now severely wounded. Everyone was in tears, and only Zhuge Liang sat calmly aside. He knew it was the self-torturing trick played by Zhou Yu and Huang Gai. Huang Gai was carried to his camp. That night, he wrote a letter of collaboration to Cao Cao. Cao believed him. During the Battle at Chibi, however, Huang Gai led a fleet of fire boats rushing into the marine forces of Cao's army, which contributed significantly to the defeat of Cao Cao.

孙悟空听说吃仙桃可以益寿、成仙，就放开肚子吃起来。这天，王母娘娘开蟠桃盛会宴请众仙，派仙女去桃园摘桃。仙女来到桃园门口，被把门的土地神拦住，说若要摘桃，必须先通报大圣。土地神找不到大圣，仙女们也等不及，便进园摘桃。然而蟠桃树上的桃子，青的多，红的少，众仙女正在议论，不想却把睡在树上的悟空惊醒。悟空得知王母娘娘没有邀请他参加蟠桃盛会，不禁大怒。他一个筋斗，闯入瑶池，吹一口仙气，准备宴会的人便东倒西歪地睡去。悟空便狂吃痛饮。酒足饭饱后，他又拔下毫毛，变作一个口袋，把好吃的东西装满，想带回花果山给小猴子们品尝。走到太上老君炼丹的地方，他见四下无人，又把老君炼的金丹吃了个精光，才混出南天门，回花果山。

大闹蟠桃会

The Monkey King Ruining over the Peach Feast

The story goes on to relate that the Monkey King was quite satisfied that his name, the Great Sage Equaling Heaven, was on the register of office without caring about the grading of his job, the rank, or the salary. On learning that anyone who ate these peaches would become an Immortal and become as eternal as Heaven and Earth, the Monkey King ate his fill of them. Being satisfied, he made himself only two inches long, and fell asleep on a branch. It happened to be the day when the Queen Mother of the West was holding a peach feast to entertain immortals and deities. The fairies were sent to pluck peaches, but stopped by the keeper of the yard, the land god, who said that it should report to the Great Sage first. However, the land god could not find the Great Sage. The fairies could not wait, and they went into the orchard to pick peaches. But they found there were not enough ripen peaches on the trees, and began to complain, which awakened the Great Sage.

When he knew that the Queen Mother did not invite him to her feast, the Great Sage flipped to the Jade Pool in a fury, and blew a hypnotic whirl at the people preparing the feast. After they fell asleep, he not only ate the delicacies but also took away as many as he could by putting them into a bag – he wanted the little monkeys in the Mountain of Flowers and Fruits to have a taste of the delicacies of Heaven. When he passed by the studio where the Supreme Lord Lao Zi used to create elixir, he saw it was unguarded. So he sneaked into the studio, and ate up all the golden pills of refined elixir stored in a gourd. Then he tricked the guards at the Heavenly Gate, left Heaven, and went back to his hometown, the Mountain of Flowers and Fruits.

这诗句出自南北朝时期著名诗人谢灵运的《登池上楼》。谢灵运（385～433年）是东晋名相谢玄（343~388年）的孙子，南朝宋武帝（363～422年）时曾出任永嘉太守，但并不得意，不久隐居会稽。谢灵运经常放浪于山水之间，创作了大量的山水诗，成就很高，是我国山水诗作的开创者之一。

登池上楼》就是他的山水诗中著名的一首。这首诗是诗人出任永嘉太守时，在海滨病倒卧床期间所作。诗大意是：这一天，诗人病有好转，便命人卷帘开窗，观赏大自然的景色。这时正值春天，窗外流水潺潺、青山高峻、春风融融、春光明媚；池塘边碧草初萌、柳枝渐绿。诗人以清新明快的笔调，表现了自己久病初愈后，看到秀丽的自然景色时无比欢快的心情，抒发了对大自然的无限热爱。这幅画就是根据这首诗写意而成。画中展现的正是谢灵运命人卷帘开窗、远眺时的情景。

:衾枕昧节候，褰开暂窥临:

The Quilt and Pillow Oppose the Weather; I Untie My Clothes and Look Out

Xie Lingyun (385-433), one of the most famous poets of the Southern and Northern Dynasties (420-589), was the grandson of the famous Prime Minister, Xie Xuan (343-388), in the Eastern Jin Dynasty. He used to serve as the Civil Governor of Yongjia (present-day Wenzhou, Zhejiang) during the reign of Emperor Wu of Song (reigned 420-422) in the Southern Dynasties, and being bored, he resigned and lived in seclusion in Kuaiji (present-day Shaoxing, Zhejiang). He loved traveling among mountains and rivers and wrote down many poems on nature. He was recognized as one of the founders of the poetry of nature's genre, focusing on the "mountain and water" instead of "field of garden" like Tao Yuanming. His poetry is allusive and complex.

The poem *Mounting a Tower over the Pond* is a well-known one in Chinese literary history. It was written when he was ill at a time when he was serving as the governor of Yongjia. The probable meaning of the poem is that one day, the poet's illness eased, and he had the window opened and enjoyed the natural scenery; it was in spring, he heard a babbling brook and was appreciating the steep green mountains in the bright sunlight; on the bank, the grass and the willows were exuberant. The fresh and vivid expression of the poem reflected his delight for recovery and for witnessing such a wonderful view as well as his love for nature. This painting is based on the sentiments reflected in the poem. In the painting, Xie Lingyun is ordering his servant to open the window so he can look out.

来到沧州后不久，林冲被派到城外去看管一个草料场。这一天，北风呼啸，大雪纷飞，林冲住的草屋被大雪压塌。他想起离草料场不远有一座荒废的山神庙，就从倒了的草屋里扒出条棉被，直奔山神庙而来。来到庙里，他掩上庙门，铺好被子，便坐下来喝酒驱寒。忽听得门外劈劈啪啪乱响。原来是草料场起了大火，火借风势越来越大。林冲正要出去救火，忽听门外有人说话。原来，高太尉知道林冲没死，又派心腹到沧州买通监狱的牢头，放火烧了草料场，想把林冲烧死。几个人放完火，来到山神庙前，说道："这么大的火，林冲是跑不出来了。就算不被烧死，烧了草料场也要定他的死罪。"林冲听出正是陷害他的仇人陆谦的声音，不由得怒火上心。他抄起花枪，冲出庙门，一口气杀了这几个仇人。这一来，林冲被逼得走投无路，只好去投奔梁山泊。

林冲风雪山神庙

Lin Chong Sheltering from Snowstorm in a Temple

Upon arriving in Cangzhou, Lin Chong was dispatched to guard a fodder storage field. One day, the north wind blew fiercely and heavy snow fell. The snow crushed the straw-made cabin where Lin Chong took shelter. Knowing there was a deserted temple nearby, Lin Chong pulled some cotton coverings out of the ruin and headed for the temple. Arriving at the temple, he closed the door, spread the cotton coverings on the ground, and sat supping his wine. Suddenly, he heard crunchy clacking noise outside. He leaped to his feet and peered through a vent in the wall and found it was the fodder yard on fire. The wind stoked the fire, and the fire became more and more fierce. When he was just about to open the door and dash to the fire, he heard someone talking outside.

They were sent by Gao Qiu. Gao Qiu had learned that Lin Chong did not die. He was unsatisfied with it and dispatched several close subordinates to buy off the jailers in Cangzhou. The jailers assigned Lin Chong to be in charge of a grain fodder storage field, and then they conspired to set fire there in an attempt to burn Lin Chong to death.

After this, the fire-raisers came to the front of the temple, and said, "Lin Chong could not survive such a huge fire, and even if he escaped, he will be sentenced to death for burning down a military fodder depot." By their voices, Lin Chong recognized them, one of whom was just his untrustworthy friend, Lu Qian. "Heaven took pity on me!" Lin Chong thought, and then he rushed out of the door and killed all of them. But he was left with no where to run but the Mount Liang.

苏小妹是宋代大文学家苏东坡的妹妹。相传她聪颖过人，能诗善文。但凡求亲者均被要求写一篇文章，由小妹亲自批阅、选择夫婿。

秀才秦观，字少游，投文中选，苏家便定下吉期。成亲那天，正是秦观中举之日，双喜临门，秦观不禁洋洋得意。这一夜月明如昼，秦观来到洞房，不料房门紧闭，只见庭中桌子上列笔、墨、纸、砚，又有三只纸袋装有三个题目。只有全部答对，才可以进洞房。秦观起手开封，取笔写就。前两题不费力就都猜中了。第三题却是对对子，“闭门推出窗前月”乍看容易，可是秦观左思右想，不得其

苏小妹三难新郎

Su Xiaomei Raising Three Quizzes to Her Groom

Su Shi was a renowned man of letters in the Song Dynasty. His father Su Xun and his brother Su Zhe were both famous literati, so was his younger sister, Su Xiaomei. It was said that she was extraordinarily smart and well-versed. She selected her husband among her admirers by asking them to write essays, and then she compared their work and picked the best. The essay written by a scholar, Qin Guan (literarily named Shaoyou), was selected, and the Su Family set the wedding day and began to prepare the wedding. The day of the wedding was the day when Qin Guan was promoted as *juren* (scholars who had passed the provincial academic examination) – a day of double happiness, and Qin Guan was quite proud of himself.

It was a full-moon night. Qin Guan came to the bridal chamber, but, to his surprise, the door was closed. There were brushes, ink, and papers on a table in the yard, along with three paper bags inside which were three quizzes. Only if he could answer all the three quizzes, he would get to enter the bedroom. He did the first two quizzes with ease, while the third one puzzled him. It required him to complete a couplet, and the first line given was “Closing the door, I pushed the moonlight out of the room” the line read easy, but it was hard to find the second line to fit it. Qin

对。苏东坡此时望见秦观在庭中徘徊踱步，有心相助，一时也想不出好对子来。

庭中有一只花缸，清水映着明月。秦观信步走来，倚着缸边出神。东坡看见，脑海中蓦然闪出一个佳句。但他怕直言相告会失了妹夫面子，便躲在阴影处，拣个小石子投向缸中。一缸清水刹时搅乱。秦观见状，不禁脱口而出："投石冲开水底天"。他急取笔墨，书写完毕，递给丫环，送给小妹过目。不一会儿，房门开了，苏小妹满面羞红地迎候他。

画中正是秦观倚缸沉吟，苏轼举石欲投，苏小妹待窗冥想的情景。

Guan thought for a long time, but still could not find a suitable one.

Su Shi watched Qin Guan wandering in the yard; he had the intention to help him, but also could not instantly produce a good line. There was a giant flowery vat in the yard, and the water inside the mug reflected the moon. Qin Guan wandered over and over, leaned by the mug while still concentrating on the quiz. Seeing such a scene, Su Shi suddenly came up with a good line; but being afraid of shaming his brother-in-law, he sneaked into a dark corner, picked a small stone, and threw it into the vat. The water in the vat as well as Qin Guan's aspiration was stirred up. He shouted out, "Throwing a stone, I crushed the sky under water." Then he hurried to write it down and asked a maid to hand it over to Su Xiaomei. After a while, the door of the newlyweds' bedroom opened, and Su Xiaomei shyly invited her husband in.

The scene in the painting is that of Qin Guan thinking by the vat, while Su Shi is about to throw the stone and Su Xiaomei is meditating by the window.

北宋年间，西夏国元帅殷奇率兵进犯中原，宋军溃败，文武百官无人敢领兵拒敌。穆桂英登台挂帅，带领杨家英雄儿女直奔边关。先锋杨排风自幼在杨家长大，原是个烧火丫头。她性情泼辣、勇敢，专爱耍弄刀枪，平日里常跟穆桂英习武，十八般武艺样样在行。这次西征，穆桂英见她武艺高强，便任命她为先锋将军。

嚣张狂妄的殷奇见穆桂英率军前来，便调兵遣将，设下埋伏，企图一举消灭杨家将。不料，被穆桂英慧眼识破。穆桂英将计就计，先派杨排风伏兵于密林，然后派人假败，诱出敌军主帅。殷奇见宋军败走，信以为真，拍马赶来。正行间，杨排风从林中跃出，威风凛凛，举枪就刺，殷奇不敌，落荒而逃，杨排风紧追不舍。殷奇逃回营中，急忙收兵，连夜后退。后来，杨家女将奋勇杀敌，大获全胜。

杨排风单骑取殷奇

Yang Paifeng Defeating Yin Qi Alone

During the middle period of the Northern Song Dynasty, the court was corrupt. Yin Qi, a marshal serving the Western Xia State, led his army to invade central China. No official in the court dared to lead the army to confront the enemy, except Mu Guiying. She took the position of the Marshal of the Song army, sorted out the troops, gathered supplies, and marched to the border. The pioneering general of the army was Yang Paifeng, who was originally a maid in the kitchen of the Yang Family. She loved practicing martial arts and excelled in all sorts of fighting. Thus, Mu appointed her as the pioneering general.

The presumptuous Yin Qi, learning Mu's army was coming, began to deploy his troops, and he intended to ambush the Song army in hope of annihilating them in one strike. However, Mu Guiying anticipated this strategy and set up a trap against the trap. She deployed Yang Paifeng and her troop to hide in a deep forest, and then sent an army to entice the enemy; the troop pretended to be defeated in order to seduce the enemy's marshal to chase them. Yin Qi saw the Song army retreating, thought the defeat was real, and rode to chase them down. When he was passing through the forest, the ferocious Yang Paifeng pounced, and thrust her spear directly to him. The fight went on for an extended period, and Yin Qi was losing his strength; he ran away. Yang Paifeng chased after him. Yin Qi managed to return to his camp. When he knew even a maidservant in the Yang family was a warrior skilled in martial arts, Yin Qi was greatly shocked, and ordered an overnight retreat. Later, the female generals of the Yang Family fought the enemy fiercely; they eventually achieved victory, and triumphantly returned to the capital.

吴国是春秋战国时期位于东南部的一个王国。公元前527年，王位落到公子僚的手里，本该继承王位的公子光一心要夺回王位。而后公子光结识了一个叫专诸的勇士，待他极为优厚。专诸十分感激，愿为公子光赴汤蹈火，虽死不辞。这时，公子光把自己所受的委屈和要刺杀吴王的心事都告诉了专诸，专诸马上表示愿意去刺杀吴王。这天，公子光在家中设宴招待吴王。吴王怕人行刺，穿上铠甲，带着护卫前来赴宴。当专诸端着那味香色美的红烧鱼走到吴王面前，吴王连声称赞，不料话音未落，专诸突然从鱼肚子里抽出一把短剑，向吴王胸膛刺去。剑刺透铠甲，穿出脊梁，吴王当场断气。堂下卫兵一拥而上，把专诸剁成了肉泥。这时，公子光带着人马杀散了卫兵，占领了王宫，登位做了国君。他就是中国历史上的阖闾。这个故事被人们取名为“鱼肠剑”。

鱼肠剑

The Fish-Intestines Sword

The Wu State was in southeast China during the Spring and Autumn Period. In 527 BC, Prince Liao seized power and came to throne. Prince Guang who should originally inherit the throne wanted to kill the new king and seized power back. Later, Prince Guang made acquaintance with a warrior named Zhuan Zhu. He treated him preferentially, and saw him as a member of his own family. Zhuan Zhu was so grateful that he was willing to do anything to serve, even die. The Prince then told him his suffering as well as his intention. Zhuan Zhu immediately promised to help him achieve his goal.

Knowing King Liao liked fish best, one day, Prince Guang held a feast entertaining the king. Fearing there might be an assassination, King Liao arrived with his corselet on and his guards surrounding him. When Zhuan Zhu carried a plate of delicious fish with brown sauce to King Liao, the latter was delighted, and praised it repeatedly. Suddenly, Zhuan Zhu took out a short sword from the belly of the fish, and thrust into the king's heart. The sword penetrated the King Liao's corselet and his body, and the king died on spot. The guards outside the dinning hall rushed in, and cleaved Zhuan Zhu into pieces; Prince Guang leading his men drove the guards away, occupied the royal palace, and seized the throne. He became King Helü of Wu. Listed as one of the Five Overlords of the Spring and Autumn Period, he reigned towards the end of the period.

In folklore, the sword Zhuan Zhu used to kill King Liao was named Yuchang, or "Fish Intestines", because it was small enough to be hidden in a fish.

麻姑是中国道教中的神话人物，东晋道教学者、著名炼丹家葛洪曾在《神仙传》中对麻姑有出神入化的描写。相传，农历三月初三是住在昆仑山上的神仙西王母的寿辰。每当寿辰之日，她都要设蟠桃会，宴请众仙。八方神仙，四海龙王，天上仙女都赶来为她祝寿。百合、牡丹、芍药、海棠四位花仙采集了各色鲜艳芬芳的花卉，邀请仙女麻姑和她们同往。麻姑用灵芝草酿成仙酒，带到蟠桃会，献给了西王母。因此，过去民间为妇女祝寿时，常常绘“麻姑献寿”的图画相赠。据传，麻姑原是建昌（江西省南城县）人，她勤劳美丽，后得道升天。汉桓帝时，曾投胎转世于一个普通人家。她掷米成珠，分给贫苦百姓。麻姑曾对人说，她亲眼看见东海三次变为桑田，“沧海桑田”的成语就出自于此。唐朝代宗年间，颜真卿曾为麻姑山撰文立碑，不幸被雷火击毁。

麻姑献寿

Magu Presenting a Birthday Gift to the Queen Mother of the West

Magu is a legendary Taoist immortal associated with elixir of life, and symbolic protector of females in Chinese mythology. Ge Hong, a Taoist philosopher and alchemist of the Eastern Jin Dynasty introduced her stories in his work, *Biographies of Divine Immortals*. The third day of the third lunar month was supposed to be the birthday of the Queen Mother of the West who lived on the Kunlun Mountains in the far west. And every year on this day, she would invite immortals to attend her Peaches of Immortality. The four flower fairies – lily, peony, fragrant peony, and caval vine – collected brightly-colored and aromatic flowers and invited the fairy Magu to go with them. Magu then brewed a kind of immortal wine with special fungus, brought it to the fest, and presented it to the Queen Mother. Traditionally in ancient times when celebrating a woman's birthday, people often presented a picture painted with "Magu Presenting Her Birthday Gift".

It's said that Magu was born in Jianchang (present-day Nancheng County, Jiangxi Province). Diligent and charming, she cultivated herself according to a religious doctrine and became an immortal. During the reign of Emperor Huan (132-167) of Han, she was reborn into a common family. In this reincarnation, she threw rice grains into the air and changed them into pearls, and distributed among the poor, providing relief to them. She once told people she had witnessed the blue ocean turning to mulberry fields for three times, from which derived the Chinese of Canghai Sangtian (blue ocean, mulberry fields), meaning gerat changes over the course of time. Yan Zhenqing (709-785), a great calligrapher during the Tang Dynasty, once erected a stele for her in Linchuan, Jiangxi Province, which was later destroyed by lightning.

“八仙”一般是指民间广泛流传的道教的八位神仙，即铁拐李、汉钟离、蓝采和、张果老、何仙姑、吕洞宾、韩湘子和曹国舅。这八位神仙好打抱不平，惩恶扬善。传说中，八仙有不同的法器：铁拐李有铁杖（或葫芦），汉钟离有鼓、张果老有纸叠驴、吕洞宾有长剑、何仙姑有荷花、韩湘子有箫管、曹国舅有玉版、蓝采和有大拍板。他们随身所携带的法器各有妙用。

八仙过海是传说故事之一。有一天，八位神仙结伴而行，到了东海，只见潮头汹涌，巨浪骇人。于是，他们各投一物于水中，以显“神通”，以便乘风逐浪渡海。后来，“八仙过海，各显神通”便成为一个典故，用来比喻依靠自己的特别才能而创造奇迹。

八仙过海

The Eight Immortals Crossing the Sea

The Eight Immortals are a group of legendary immortals in Chinese mythology living on the Penglai Mountain-Island, including: the Iron-Crutch Li, Zhongli of Han, Lan Caihe, Elder Zhang Guo, Fairy He (female), Lü Dongbin, Han Xiangzi, and Royal Uncle Cao. The Eight Immortals are considered to be signs of prosperity and longevity, so they are well-known to every household in China and are popular themes in ancient art.

The Eight Immortals loved to do justice for the people, and they punished evil and promoted good. It was said that each of them had his (or her) own unique equipment: the Iron-Crutch Li had his iron crutch; Zhongli of Han had a drum; Elder Zhang Guo utilized his paper-folded donkey to sustain his conduct; Lü Dongbin had a long sword; Fairy He had a lotus flower; Han Xiangzi had a flute; Royal Uncle Cao had a Jade board; and Lan Caihe had a giant flapper. Each of these had its own unique function.

The legendary story about their crossing the sea is very popular among people. One day, the Eight traveled together, and arrived at the Eastern Sea. The giant waves and the turbulent whirls in the sea looked quite scary. Instead of going across by their clouds, Lü Dongbin suggested that together, they should use their powers to get across. So they each threw their equipment into the sea, and performed their different skills, so that they could overcome the wind and the waves and cross the sea. Later, “The Eight Immortals cross the sea, each revealing its divine power” has become a classic proverb, which indicates the situation that everybody shows off their powers to achieve a common goal or create miracles.

魏、蜀两军交战于汉中，黄忠斩了曹操的爱将夏侯渊。曹操亲率二十万大军赶到，来为夏侯渊报仇。当夜黄忠领兵渡水，潜入敌营；正欲放火烧粮时，曹军大将张郃兵到，与黄忠混战起来。曹操听说蜀军前来劫粮，急令大将徐晃来助张郃，黄忠被曹军团团围住。

赵云在营中不见黄忠回来，忙领兵前来接应。渡过汉水，迎面遇上曹兵拦路，赵云冲上去，刺死曹将，杀散余兵。赵云见黄忠被曹军围着苦战，大喝一声，挺枪骤马，杀入重围，左冲右突，如入无人之境。曹操兵将望见“常山赵云”四字旗号，皆心惊胆战，无人敢阻。赵云且战且走，最终杀出重围，将黄忠救回本营。

据汉水赵云寡胜众

Zhao Yun Leading an Out-Numbered Winning

Xiahou Yuan, one of Cao Cao's favorite generals, stationed his troops on Dingjun Mountian and effectively resisted the advance of Huang Zhong. However, Huang used stratagem to behead Xiahou. Cao Cao nourished feelings of resentment against the slayer of his general and friend, and led his army of 200,000 men out against Dingjun Mountain to avenge Xiahou Yuan's death. At night, Huang Zhong leading his troops stole across the river and tried to burn the Cao's grain storage, but was found by Zhang He, Cao's general. Both sides had a fierce fight. Cao Cao learned that the Shu troops aimed to destroy his grain storage, and immediately sent another general, Xu Huang, to reinforce Zhang He. Thus, Huang Zhong and his troop were completely surrounded.

Huang Zhong did not return on time, so Zhao Yun girded on his armor and went out of camp to look for him. Crossing the river, Zhao Yun ran into Cao's vanguards but was blocked by Cao's soldiers. He killed the leading general, and disposed of the troops Wei; then he saw that Huang Zhong was surrounded but still fighting fiercely. Zhao Yun gave out a loud shout, held his spear firmly, and dashed at the encircling ring. The situation became very perilous for Zhao, as he and his soldiers were greatly outnumbered, but he was dauntless and daring. To and fro, back and forth, Zhao Yun marched on as though no one would think of standing in his way. Because of Zhao Yun's ferocity, Cao Cao's troops were frightened at the sight of his flag on which carried four Chinese characters, "Changshan Zhao Yun" (Changshan was Zhao Yun's hometown) and few of them dared to fight Zhao Yun. Finally, Zhao Yun rescued Huang Zhong and fought his way out toward his own camp. The day after the battle, Liu Bei arrived to inspect the battlefield. For his services Liu Bei gave Zhao Yun the title of General with the Might of a Tiger.

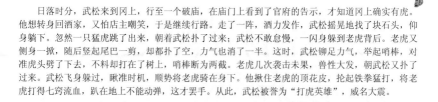

日落时分，武松来到冈上，行至一个破庙，在庙门上看到了官府的告示，才知道冈上确实有虎。他想转身回酒家，又怕店主嘲笑，于是继续行路。走了一阵，酒力发作，武松摇晃地找了块石头，仰身躺下。忽然一只猛虎跳了出来，朝着武松扑了过来；武松不敢怠慢，一闪身躲到老虎背后。老虎又侧身一掀，随后竖起尾巴一剪，却都扑了空，力气也消了一半。这时，武松铆足力气，举起哨棒，对准虎头劈了下去，不料却打在了树上，哨棒断为两截。老虎几次袭击未果，兽性大发，朝武松又扑了过来。武松飞身躲过，瞅准时机，顺势将老虎骑在身下。他揪住老虎的顶花皮，抡起铁拳猛打，将老虎打得七窍流血，趴在地上不能动弹，这才罢手。从此，武松被誉为“打虎英雄”，威名大震。

武松打虎

Wu Song Beating the Tiger

Wu Song didn't believe what the tavern owner told him and left for Jingyang Ridge. Soon after he saw a sign posted on a tree, which read, "Travelers are advised to go in groups over this mountain, especially at night, as the tiger here have taken several lives." Wu Song reasoned that it must have been written by the tavern owner who tried to scare customers into spending the night at his tavern. So he didn't pay attention to it and simply continued on his way. At sunset Wu Song reached an old temple and on the door there was another official announcement posted about hunting for tiger. Just then Wu Song realized and believed that there was indeed a tiger on the mountain. However he still wasn't willing to return to the tavern for fear that the owner would laugh at him. After a moment Wu Song felt too drunk to continue, so he found a stone, clambered onto its flat surface and prepared to have a sleep. Just then, a gust of wind whistled and a mammoth tiger jumped at him. At this sight Wu Song was awaken but managed to dodge behind the tiger, which leapt again but fanned the air. Wu Song evaded it successfully.

The tiger, flew into a rage; with a thunderous roar, it swept toward Wu Song with its tail. Wu Song jumped to avoid the attack. After several scary moments, the tiger effectively exhausted most of its strength. Seizing the opportunity, Wu Song lifted his cudgel and hit toward its head with all his strength; however, he had struck a branch of an old tree instead of the tiger, snapping the cudgel in two. The tiger then launched another attack. Wu Song threw away the last bits of his cudgel and jumped on to the back of the tiger. With his left hand, he grabbed the skin of the tiger's head and struck out at its eyes, mouth, nose and ears with his right hand. The tiger struggled frantically, but later lay prostrate on the ground and expired. Wu Song didn't stop swinging until the tiger died. Thus, Wu Song killed the giant tiger with bare hands, which made him widely known.

战国时期有一位书生东郭先生，他处处行善，却十分迂腐。一天，他赶着一头毛驴行路。突然，一只受伤的狼窜到他的面前，哀求救命。东郭先生让狼钻进口袋。一会儿，猎人追了上来，问东郭先生，看见一只狼没有；东郭先生谎称没有。猎人远去后，东郭先生把狼放了出来。狼刚一出来，就扑向东郭先生，想吃掉他。东郭先生大喊救命。这时，一位老农扛着锄头路过，东郭先生拉住他，请他评理。老农表示他不相信那么小的一个口袋能把狼装进去，让狼再钻一次；如果能钻进去，便让狼吃掉东郭先生。狼高兴地钻进了口袋。老农立即把口袋扎紧，抡起锄头，把狼打死。而后对东郭先生说，狼害人的本性是不会改变的，对狼仁慈太糊涂了。现在，“东郭先生”已经成为汉语中固定词语，专指那些不辨是非而滥施同情心的人。

东郭先生

Mr. Dong Guo

There was a scholar Mr. Dongguo in the Warring States Period. Over-influenced by the Confucism, he was merciful to anything. One day, he was on his way along with his donkey carrying a load of books. Suddenly, a wounded wolf rushed front and asked for help. Mr. Dongguo emptied his book-bag, let the wolf hide inside. A few moments later, a hunter came by and asked Mr. Dongguo if he had spotted a wolf. With the answer “no”, the hunter went off. In the bag, hearing the clop of the hunter’s horse fading away, the wolf asked Mr. Dongguo to let it out and give it something to eat.

Mr. Dongguo released the wolf; however, the wolf suddenly became ferocious and wanted to eat him. Just at the moment, an old farmer carrying a hoe passed by. Mr. Dongguo stopped him and said after he saved the wolf’s life it turned round and wanted to eat him, asking the farmer to do the justice for him. The wolf, however, firmly denied he had once saved its life. Then the farmer said he did not believe the bag was big enough to hold the wolf, so he asked the wolf to enter into the bag again to prove it; and if he could do that, he might eat Mr. Dongguo. Delighted, the wolf entered the bag. The old farmer immediately closed the bag, and beat the wolf to death with his hoe. Then he said to Mr. Dongguo, “The nature of wolfs will never change. It is unwise to be merciful to a wolf.” “Mr. Dongguo” has been a Chinese phrase symbolizing those universally merciful persons who cannot distinguish between the good and the evil.

扁鹊是战国时医学家，中国传统医学的鼻祖。他医道高明，经常周游列国，到各地行医，为民解除痛苦。有一次，扁鹊来见蔡桓公，说他病在皮肤，如果不及早治疗，恐怕病情会加重。蔡桓公听后不悦，声称没病。过了10天，扁鹊提着药篮去见桓公，对他说，病在血脉，若不抓紧医治，将会更加严重。桓公扭头不理，扁鹊只好退了出来。10天后，扁鹊又去见桓公，沉重地说，病在肠胃。桓公听后，大怒。扁鹊长叹而去。又过了10天，扁鹊又遇见了桓公，他二话不说，转身而出。桓公派人去问，扁鹊痛心地说，病在皮肤，可用药水热敷；病到血脉，可用针灸治疗；病入肠胃，可用汤药；现在病入骨髓，无药可医。几天之后，桓公浑身疼痛，果然病死。后来这个成语便用来比喻掩盖缺点，不愿改正。

讳疾忌医

Prevention in Order to Avoid the Doctor

Bian Que, a medical expert in the Warring States Period (475-221BC), is considered one of the originators of traditional Chinese medicine. His medical expertise was prominent, and he used to travel among the states and treat diseased people. Once, Bian Que paid a visit to Duke Huan of the Cai State, and said to the Duke that he had disease on his skin and if it was not treated in time, it would worsen. On hearing that, the king was quite unhappy, and he claimed that he was not sick.

After 10 days, Bian Que went to see the Duke again, and said the disease had invaded his veins and it would become much more serious if it could not be treated right now. The Duke turned his back on him, and Bian Que had to retreat. Another 10 days passed, and Bian Que called upon the Duke a third time. He told that the disease had entered his stomach and intestines. The Duke was furious and Bian Que had to leave, sighing. 10 days later, Bian Que happened to meet the Duke. When he saw the Duke, he immediately turned around and left.

The Duke sent one follower to ask him what was wrong, and the doctor sorrowfully said that if the disease was on the skin, it could be treated by pasting hot liquid medicine on the skin; that if the disease was in the veins, it could be treated with acupuncture; that if the disease was in the intestines, it could be treated by taking medicinal soup; but now the Duke's disease was in the marrow, and there was no treatment that could cure him. A few days later, the Duke felt pain all over his body, and died of the disease. This story leads to the idiom advising people that it is unwise to cover and try to avoid correcting their problems.

颐和园四大部洲 FOUR GREAT REGIONS

STORIES BEHIND THE LONG CORRIDOR PAINTINGS IN THE SUMMER PALACE

《颐和园长廊彩画故事》

汉宣帝初年，都城长安治安很乱，公子王孙为非作歹，小偷强盗横行霸道。正当汉宣帝为难之际，张敞自告奋勇去治理长安。张敞为人秉直公正，以忠诚著称。任职后，他首先处治小偷强盗。他置办酒席，宴请盗贼头目。待盗贼们醉如烂泥之后，张敞将他们一网打尽。之后，张敞开始惩办公子王孙，得罪了皇亲国戚。这些人找不到张敞的把柄，便向皇帝告发他“风流、轻浮，有失大臣体统”。原来，张敞相貌丑陋，妻子却很漂亮。张敞对她十分尊重爱护。有时早晨起来，见妻子端坐梳妆，便亲自为她描眉。这幅画画的就是此情景。后来，那些仇恨张敞的皇族便以此诬告张敞。当汉宣帝查问此事时，张敞理直气壮地答道，夫妻之间，相亲相敬，理所应当，何罪之有？汉宣帝见他说得在理，又知他治理长安确实很有成绩，深得百姓爱戴，就一笑了事。

张敞画眉

Zhang Chang Penciling the Eyebrows for His Wife

During the early years of Emperor Xuan of Han's reign (74-49 BC), the public security in Chang'an, the then capital city, was in disorder: local dignitaries did evil, and thieves and robbers ran amuck. The commoners suffered a lot. Even so, no one could control the evil forces until Zhang Chang recommended himself to govern Chang'an. After taking the post, Zhang Chang took the first aim at the thieves and robbers. He invited the gang leaders to a banquet. When they were drunk he rounded up the whole lot, and put them in prison. As to the near-royalty, Zhang Chang couldn't deal with them rashly, but only if he had good evidence. However, Zhang Chang caused offence to them, who then went and told Zhang Chang's "faults" to the emperor, complaining of his frivolous and disgraceful behavior as a high official.

Zhang Chang was not good-looking, yet his wife was beautiful. Zhang Chang respected her very much. He penciled her eyebrows for her, which became the accusation of the near-royalty. When asked about this by the emperor, Zhang Chang explained baldly, "There're more amorous matters than penciling the eyebrows between the married couple. Doesn't Your Majesty intend to investigate them one by one? In addition, it's beyond reproach for a couple to treat each other with respect." Realizing Zhang Chang was reasonable and was esteemed for his achievements in governing the capital, the emperor just smiled and let it go.

安家有两个兄弟，大成和二成，大成娶陈珊瑚为妻。珊瑚人品出众，温柔贤淑。大成母沈氏暴戾凶狠，对珊瑚非打即骂，珊瑚从无怨言。后来，沈氏竟逼大成休掉珊瑚。沈氏的姐姐于媪不满沈氏所为，把珊瑚接到自己家里，靠纺纱织布度日。珊瑚走后，沈氏想给大成另娶，可是沈氏恶名远扬，无人敢嫁。后来，沈氏给二成娶妻臧姑，臧姑比沈氏更加凶悍，重活累活都要沈氏包揽，致使沈氏操劳过度成疾。珊瑚知道后，用纺织换来的钱给婆婆做了很多好吃的，叫于媪的儿媳送去。沈氏病好之后，住在姐姐家，总夸姐姐的儿媳好。当沈氏得知东西是珊瑚用纺线赚的钱买来做给她吃的时候，倍觉羞愧，悔恨万分。后来，二成夫妇也痛改前非，一家五口过上了和睦、美满的生活。

珊瑚

Shanhu

There lived a filial daughter-in-law named Shanhu of extraordinary personality and virtue. In contrast was her mother-in-law, surnamed Shen, a woman of peevish disposition, who beat and scolded Shanhu unreasonably and randomly whenever she was unhappy. Even if Shanhu uttered no complaint, working from dawn to night. The old woman still made oblique accusations against Shanhu and finally drove her away. However, Dacheng, Shanhu's husband, was so meek that he dared not say a word. Lady Yu, Shen's elder sister, was angry at this and took Shanhu home. They lived together making a living spinning yarn, since Shanhu refused to go back her own home or marry some one else.

After Lady Shen drove Shanhu away, she wanted to make Dacheng remarry. But all villagers knew she was notorious for her ill temper; no one entertained her proposals. Several years later, Lady Shen's young son Ercheng got married. This daughter-in-law was even fiercer than Lady Shen, treating the old lady like her servant. Thus it came about that Lady Shen was in mortal fear of her daughter-in-law; and whenever her daughter-in-law was in a rage she would try and turn off her anger with a smile. Ercheng, being of a very weak disposition, dared not side with either. Lady Shen eventually fell sick due to the torment, only with Dacheng taking care of her beside her bed.

When Shanhu heard this, she bought and prepared some food for Shen, who quickly recovered from the illness. Shen didn't feel regret until she knew that it was Shanhu who had taken such good care of her. Meanwhile she burst into tears and was ashamed for what she had done to Shanhu; the latter still forgave her. Subsequently, they led a happy life together.

相传，远古时候天上有十个太阳。这十个太阳都是天帝的儿子，经常为非作歹。他们一同出现在天上，烤得大地冒烟，海水枯干，再加上猛兽的祸害，百姓简直无法生活。天帝派天神羿带妻子嫦娥下凡为百姓除害。羿杀死了九个太阳，只留下一个在天上；又杀死猛兽，百姓得以安定。然而当天帝知道羿杀死自己的孩子后，把羿和嫦娥贬为凡人，永远不准他们回天上。嫦娥不愿意作凡人，整天和羿吵闹；羿忍受不了，就去昆仑山上向西王母讨来不死神药。羿到家后，把王母的话转告给嫦娥：如果一个人吃了这药，就会升天成仙；如果两人一起吃，则长生不老。一次趁羿不在家，自私的嫦娥一个人偷吃了仙药，立刻飘到了空中。然而没有一位神仙欢迎嫦娥，嫦娥只得奔向清冷的月宫，和玉兔为伴。

嫦娥奔月

Chang'e Flying to the Moon

This is a well-known myth from ancient China. Long ago, there were 10 suns, all being the sons of the God of Heaven. Every morning, one of them was sent to give the world light, the other nine resting. One day, however, all of them appeared at the same time in the sky. The heat on earth baceme intense. Before long the seas dried up, and trees, as well as human beings, were burnt to death. Complaints of the common people could be heard everywhere. Houyi, a heavenly guardian, was sent to solve this problem for the people.

According to the God of Heaven's order, Houyi, with his wife Chang'e (an ancient beauty in the legend), descended to earth. Houyi was so angry at the disaster caused by the 10 suns that he shot down nine of them. The common people were then able to live a stable life. However, the God of Heaven got angry after hearing this. After all, Houyi shot and killed his nine sons. So he banished Houyi and his wife from the heaven and stripped them of their immortality. In the following days, Chang'e often quarreled with Houyi and complained, believing that if it had not been Houyi, she could be immortal like a fairy. Houyi then underwent all conceivable hardships, got to the Kunlun Mountain, a legendary holy mountain where immortals lived, and obtained an elixir from the West Queen Mother, a legendary figure of ancient times. Houyi returned home happily and told Chang'e what the West Queen Mother said, "We could be immortal if we both drink the elixir, but if only one of us takes it he will become a heavenly being and fly to the heaven." One night while Houyi was out, Chang'e secretly took all the elixir selfishly. And of course in heaven nobody liked such a selfish person so Chang'e had to fly to the isolated Palace of the Moon.

韩信是刘邦手下的一员大将，胸怀韬略，善于用兵。在楚汉相争的时候，他辅佐刘邦，打败项羽，夺得天下。

韩信小时候文武双全。后来，父母过世，韩信的生活十分穷困，再加上他不知道如何挣钱谋生，经常挨饿，生活凄苦。河边有一个老奶奶，靠给别人漂洗纱絮为生，人称“漂母”。她见韩信可怜，经常把自己带的饭分一半给他吃。韩信非常感激这位老人，对她说，将来一定好好报答老人的恩情。没想到，老奶奶一听这话，反倒生气，责备韩信没有出息；她只是见他可怜，给他饭吃，并不指望他的报答。韩信满脸通红，羞愧离开。然而，韩信一直不忘漂母的分食之恩，待他被封侯以后，派人到处寻找漂母，要以千金报答。

漂母分食待韩信

A Laundry Woman Sharing Food with Han Xin

Han Xin (?-196 BC), a great commander under Liu Bang, was full of military strategy and excelled in resorting to arms and handling soldiers. Once during the conflict between the Chu and Han regimes, he assisted Liu Bang in vanquishing Xiang Yu (232-202 BC), a famous ancient militarist.

A drawing of Han Xin

Han Xin was versed in literary and military arts as a kid. Yet since his parents passed away, he led a poor life. What's worse, he had no proficiency at how to earn money. Therefore he failed to get any fish, he had to endure hunger. There was an old woman on the river bank, known as "Old Laundry Woman", who often washed clothes for money. Seeing Han Xin severely weakened from hunger, she took pity on him, sharing the food with him. Han Xin felt grateful to her, saying, "You treat me generously. I must repay your kindness well in the future." Unexpectedly upon hearing this, the old woman turned angry and snapped at him, "You are a man. You can't feed yourself. I see you are pitiful, so I just gave you something to eat. Without repayment on my mind!" Han Xin felt ashamed and then left right away. However, Han Xin never forgot the kindness of the old woman. As soon as he was conferred Prince of Han, he personally paid her a visit and gave her a thousand pieces of gold.

《三字经》在中国可谓家喻户晓，里面有一句话："窦燕山，有义方；教五子，名俱扬"，讲的是五代晚期渔阳（今天津蓟县）人窦禹钧很会教育子女，成为当时人们的表率的事情。其实，他并没有什么高招，只不过要求孩子们学习刻苦勤奋，为他们聘请名师，而且让他们遍读家中万卷藏书。他的五个儿子后来都有成就，曾做过朝廷高官，当时人们把窦家的五兄弟称为"燕山窦氏五龙"。

后来逢年过节，人们便把画有"五子夺魁"的年画赠与亲朋好友，表达他们希望亲朋好友的子女能有所作为的美好祝愿。画中表现的是窦禹钧的大儿子回家后与兄弟们嬉戏的情景。

窦禹钧的五个儿子中，要数长子、次子和第四子最为有名。长子窦仪在北宋时期任工部尚书，还曾负责编定《刑统》。次子窦俨官至礼部侍郎；四子窦称死后亦被追授工部尚书。

五子夺魁

Five Factitive Sons of the Dou's Family

A famous story about Dou Yujun was mentioned in the *Three-Character Classic*, one of Chinese classic texts, which reads: "Dou Yanshan owned a very effective educational technique, taught by which his five sons all passed the Imperial Examinations." Dou Yujun lived in Yuyang (today's Jixian County, Tianjin) during the late Five Dynasties (907-960), and was famous for his classical Chinese poetry. He educated his children well and his methods became the example for people around the whole nation to follow. In fact, Dou Yujun had no unique skill; he just encouraged his sons to study hard and hired a learned tutor to teach them. In addition there was a rich collection of books in Dou's family, and the five sons were unconsciously influenced by what they constantly heard and saw. When they grew up, they all turned out well: they passed the Imperial Examinations one after another and were all assigned to different high positions.

Later, during the Spring Festival, people would present New Year paintings based on the five sons of the Dou's family as gifts to friends and relatives to express their hope that their children could do something successful in the future. The picture indicates the scene that the eldest son is frolicking with his young brothers after he returns home.

Among Dou's five sons, the eldest, the second and the fourth were the most outstanding. The eldest son, Dou Yi, was appointed Minister of Works during the Northern Song, and was once in charge of making criminal laws. The second son Dou Yan was Vice-Minister of Rites, and the fourth son Dou Cheng was made Minister of Works after his death.

米芾是北宋有名的书画家，诗章行文奇险，不蹈袭前人旧辙；书法得东晋王献之笔意，势若飞龙走虎，与苏轼、黄庭坚、蔡襄合称“宋四家”。米芾画的山水人物多用水墨点染，善长绘画云烟出没、林木掩映的山川景色，功力深厚，风格独创，自成一家。

米芾性情古怪，放荡不羁，神态潇洒，仪表轩昂。米芾酷爱奇石，家中收藏众多，仍然四方寻觅。有一次，他出外游玩，见到一块形状奇特怪异的巨石，欣喜若狂，不禁整理衣冠，伏首大拜，口中还念念有词。这幅画描绘的便是此情景。从此，米芾拜石，传为佳话。

米芾拜石

Mi Fu Bowing to the Stone

A portrait of Mi Fu

Mi Fu (1051-1107) was a famous poet, calligrapher and painter in the Northen Song Dynasty. His poems, novel and original, were extracted and read repeatedly by Wang Anshi (1021-1086), a politician, thinker and writer of this period. As to calligraphy, he was reputed as one of the Four Greatest Calligraphers in the Song Dynasty, together with Su Shi, Huang Tingjian and Cai Xiang. His style arose from that of calligraphers in earlier dynasties, but with a unique mark of his own seeming like imposing dragons and tigers. Mi Fu was also skillful at landscape painting, displaying a kind of artistic circumstances of cloud circling around and trees then setting off.

Mi Fu was of eccentric character, unconventional and uninhibited. Dressed in the style of the Tang Dynasty (618-907), he was always crowded round wherever he went. Mi Fu had a strong affinity for stones. Though there was a rich collection at his home, he still searched around for wonderful and unique stones. Once while he was going for an outing, he found a stone of peculiar-looking shape. Wild with joy, Mi Fu straightened his clothing and respectfully bowed to the stone. This became an often-told story. The painting just shows this scene.

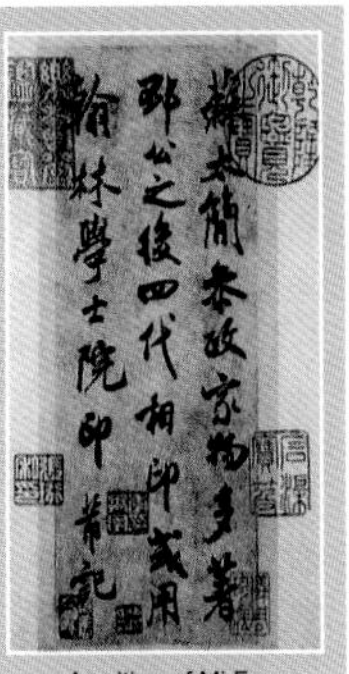

A writing of Mi Fu

这幅画取材于陶渊明的名作《归去来兮辞》。陶渊明自幼博览群书，有远大的政治抱负。在社会动乱、政治黑暗的年月里，他不断尝试革新，却不断失望、终至绝望，最后终于"不为五斗米折腰"，弃官隐居。《归去来兮辞》就是在他辞官后所作，他把自己13年的仕途生活看作是失路之人走过的一段"迷途"，委婉曲折地表现自己的痛苦和对社会的不满；而后又以明快的笔调写了归途上的愉快心情，作者通过对田园生活的描绘充分抒发了悠闲惬意的情感和对当时社会的反抗。这篇文章音节和谐、文字优美、感情真挚、意境深远，乃千秋佳作。

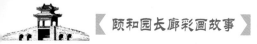

归田乐

Pastoral Pleasure

A portrait of Tao Yuanming

This painting is based on Tao Yuan Ming's renowned masterpiece *Lyrical Ballad of Returning to Nature*.

Tao Yuanming (about 365-427), also known as Tao Qian, was a great man of letters from the Eastern Jin Dynasty (317-420). He came from a notable family which had descended into poverty; however, he read widely during his childhood and grew up to be a man having great political ambitions. During years of social instability and political corruption, he tried again and again to fulfill his ambitions; however, he failed over and over, and eventually he grew disappointed. Clinging to his principle – never bowing for five bushels of grain (the term "five bushels of grain" is often used to describe wealth, power and officialdom) – he deserted his official post, and lived in seclusion.

The piece was written after he resigned. He took his 13 years of political life as the wrong path that a stray person had passed by and euphemistically expressed his agony at that period and his discontent toward society. Then he described his happy feeling on the way returning to his hometown in a delightful manner and the leisurely and comfortable sentiments for a pastoral life, which could be perceived as a kind of resistance to the social reality at that time. The ballad, well-rhymed, literarily beautiful, genuine in feeling, and profound in meaning, is one of the best in Chinese literary history.

程颢（1032～1085年）是北宋时期的一位大哲学家。他曾和弟弟程颐就学于周敦颐，同为北宋理学的奠基者。他们的学说后来为朱熹（南宋思想家）所继承发展，并称“程朱理学”。程颢一生潜心于理学研究，可也常陶醉于自然美景。

他的七言绝句《春日偶成》就写出了他对大自然的热爱和自己恬逸的心情。“云淡风轻近午天，傍花随柳过前川。时人不识余心乐，将谓偷闲学少年。”这首绝句景物描写朴实生动，表达自然亲切，就像一幅笔墨清新的图画，因而画工们便用明丽的色彩把它搬到了颐和园的长廊上。

时人不识余心乐，将谓偷闲学少年

People Don't Know My Pleasure, and Presume I'm Pretending to Be a Youth at Leisure

Cheng Hao (1032-1085), a great philosopher from the Noerhern Song Dynasty, used to learn from Zhou Dunyi (1017-1073) with his brother, Cheng Yi. Later they all became the founders of the Neo-Confucianism. Their doctrines were inherited and developed by Zhu Xi (1130-1200, a famous philosopher in the Southern Song Dynasty). Cheng Hao lived to study the philosophy of reasoning all his life; however, he was often touched by the beauty of nature and from time to time wrote about it.

His poem *Occasional Observation on a Spring Day* expressed his love for nature and his leisurely attitude towards life. The poem goes,

The clouds are light and the slight breeze blows,
I stroll along the creek in flowers and willows;
People don't know my pleasure,
And presume I'm pretending to be a youth at leisure.

A Portrait of Cheng Hao

It was a sunny and mild noon, and the poet strolled amongst flower beds and willows by the mountain, he felt comfortable and spiritually happy. However, he was afraid that people would not understand his pleasure, and took it as he behaving like a presumptuous youth who just sat idling around. The poem offers vivid descriptions of the landscape as well as his natural and gentle sentiment. It is like a freshly painted picture, thus later artists interpreted it with ornate color on the Long Corridor in the Summer Palace.

这是一幅写意画，取材于南宋诗人僧志南的一首绝句："古木阴中系短篷，杖藜扶我过桥东；沾衣欲湿杏花雨，吹面不寒杨柳风。"诗中描写的是春天晴时雨的景色：杏花如簇，杨柳轻扬，湖岸绿阴，小船隐约。作者虽已年高，雅兴不减，扶杖过桥，尽赏春光。微风拂面，不觉其寒；细雨蒙蒙，沾衣欲湿。景色的描写清新、秀丽，表达的心情自然、轻快，颇如一幅古人绘制的小品，确是一篇佳作。

诗作的后两句是传诵千古的名句，尤为精彩。作者把吐芳的杏花、初绿的杨柳与和煦的风、无声的雨联系起来，虽没有一个"春"字，却准确精炼地勾勒出春天和暖美丽而宜人的景象。而用"沾衣欲湿"和"吹面不寒"来描述春雨和春风，真是惬意十足啊！

:吹面不寒杨柳风:

A Fresh Breeze Blows and Carries the Aroma of the Willow Trees

This painting of sensation is based on a well-known poem composed by a Southern Song Dynasty (1127-1279) monk poet, Zhinan. The poem goes,

Under the umbrageous trees I tie my small boat,
Then with my stick I cross the bridge to the east;
The apricot-flowers rain wets my clothes,
A fresh breeze blows my face and carries the aroma of willow trees.

The poem seeks to portray the fickle spring weather in East China in which sunshine may alternate with drizzle in a matter of minutes. This happens about the time when the apricot is in bloom. A fantastic landscape is clearly described in this poem: an old monk who was travelling down streams anchored his small boat under an old tree and got on shore. He was old and weak, but in high spirits. He is not stopped by the rain, crosses the bridge using his stick and gets a full view of spring. The breeze blows over, and the rain wets his clothes, but he doesn't feel the coldness. The scenic description of the poem is fresh and beautiful, and the sentiment is natural and delightful, which makes it a masterpiece of this genre.

In Chinese poetry, "apricot-blossom rain" means a rain of early Spring and "Spring-willow wind" implies a breeze of the same season. In Chinese verses, these two expressions are more lively and charming than a gentle breeze and a fine rain.

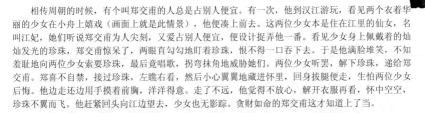

相传周朝的时候，有个叫郑交甫的人总是占别人便宜。有一次，他到汉江游玩，看见两个衣着华丽的少女在小舟上嬉戏（画面上就是此情景），他便凑上前去。这两位少女本是住在江里的仙女，名叫江妃，她们听说郑交甫为人尖刻，又爱占别人便宜，便设计捉弄他一番。看见少女身上佩戴着的灿灿发光的珍珠，郑交甫惊呆了，两眼直勾勾地盯着珍珠，恨不得一口吞下去。于是他满脸堆笑，不知羞耻地向两位少女索要珍珠，最后竟唱歌，拐弯抹角地威胁她们。两位少女听罢，解下珍珠，递给郑交甫。郑喜不自禁，接过珍珠，左瞧右看，然后小心翼翼地藏进怀里，回身拔腿便走，生怕两位少女后悔。他边走还边用手摸着前胸，洋洋得意。走了不远，他觉得不放心，解开衣服再看，怀中空空，珍珠不翼而飞。他赶紧回头向江边望去，少女也无影踪。贪财如命的郑交甫这才知道上了当。

江妃

Jiang Fei

It's said that in the Zhou Dynasty there lived a man named Zheng Jiaofu. Using his smooth tongue, he often profited at others' expense. Many an honest person was hurt because of him. His neighbors all scolded him.

One day, Zheng came to a river and saw two girls in splendid attire playing in a boat. He then went forward and got astonished at two sparkling pearls dressed respectively on them. He stared at the pearls so greedily that he couldn't wait to swallow them. He used all his lures to shamelessly coax the pearls away from them. Afterwards he began to sing, and cajole the girls by all means. The two girls, however, generously gave him the pearls. Overjoyed, Zheng, holding the pearls in his hands, promptly ran away for fear that two girls would be regretful; and then nestled them in his arms. After a short distance when he undid the clothes to admire his pearls, however, he found they had disappeared. And Zheng didn't realize he was cheated until he saw that the two girls also disappeared once he turned back and looked toward the river.

The two girls mentioned above were called Jiang Fei, the divine spirits of the river. When they heard that Zheng was out for small advantages, they had plotted to play a trick on him.

姜维，文武双全，智勇足备，堪称当世之英杰。诸葛亮率兵讨伐魏国的时候，本想用计谋攻下天水关，却被姜维识破；半夜又遭姜突袭。诸葛亮爱惜人才，欲将姜维收归己用。

探知姜维母亲居住冀城，诸葛亮命魏延引军诈取冀城。姜维听说，领兵去救；魏延诈败奔走，放姜维入城。此时，诸葛亮却派人假扮姜维、夜间攻打天水关，并散布谣言说姜维已经降蜀。守军皆以为姜维已经投降。两军混战一夜，直到天亮蜀军才撤走。随后，诸葛亮率兵攻打冀城。姜维在城上见蜀军搬运粮草，忙引兵劫粮，中了蜀军的埋伏，抵挡不住，只得杀条路奔天水关而来。城上守军见是姜维，只当是又来攻城，一阵乱箭射下，姜维只好撤走。行至茂林之处，杀声四起，数千蜀兵拥出，截住去路。姜维人困马乏，见前后无路，只得下马投降。

天水关诸葛亮收姜维

Jiang Wei Going over to Zhuge Liang

Jiang Wei was a man both of civil and military competence and profound wisdom and courage. Once Zhuge Liang was leading the Shu army against the Wei State to seize Tianshui Pass, which unfortunately his enemies had anticipated. It was Jiang Wei who saw through Zhuge Liang's stratagem. Zhuge Liang led the Shu army into the pass again, and this time, his army was ambushed. Like knows like. Zhuge Liang tried to summon Jiang Wei to surrender because of his military capability and resourcefulness.

Having heard that Jiang Wei's mother was living in Ji City, Zhuge Liang dispatched Wei Yan to pretend to attack the city. Upon hearing the news, Jiang Wei led his army to reinforce Ji City. Wei Yan met Jiang Wei, pretended to be defeated, and let him enter the city. At the same time, Zhuge Liang sent someone disguised as Jiang Wei to lead the Shu army in their attack of the Tianshui Pass. Seeing "Jiang Wei" holding his spear on his horse, asserting his strength and power, the defense troops in the pass thought he had surrendered to the Shu army. The two armies had a long fierce fight throughout the night, and by dawn, the Shu army had retreated. Then Zhuge Liang led the Shu army in a siege against Ji City. Jiang Wei saw the Shu soldiers carrying grain and fodder outside the city, so he rushed to seize the grain. But it was a decoy; his men were ambushed. Unable to hold on, he retreated toward the Tianshui Pass. The defensive army, however, seeing Jiang Wei coming, thought it was another attack. They shot arrows at Jiang Wei, and did not let him in. Thus, Jiang Wei had no choice but to escape. When he was passing by a forest, there appeared thousands of Shu soldiers, blocking the way. Weary as were both horse and rider, there was no chance of successful resistance, and Jiang Wei had to surrender.

陷空山上有一个老鼠精，她见唐僧仪表堂堂，便用尽办法抢来成婚。悟空等三人找到妖精的洞穴—无底洞，悟空遂变作小虫，飞进去打探，留下八戒和沙僧把守洞口。看见女妖正在劝唐僧与她喝酒成亲，悟空变作一只飞虫落入酒⼟¬中，被女妖看见，泼了出去。悟空大怒，变成一只老鹰，掀翻桌子，搅乱了酒席。悟空又变回小蝇，飞到唐僧耳边，低声告诉唐僧他的计谋。

唐僧依计行事，请女妖到花园散步，并摘下一个桃子递给女妖。女妖以为唐僧回心转意，欢天喜地地吞食下去；片刻，肚子疼痛难忍。原¬来桃子是悟空变的。女妖只好放出唐僧。刚出洞口，唐僧又被捉走。悟空又进洞中，没找到师父，却见到托塔李天王和哪吒牌位。悟空便找玉帝。玉帝命李天王父子收服老鼠精，放出唐僧。

无底洞

Bottomless Cave

A mouse spirit dwelled in the Pitfall Mountain. Seeing Tang Seng was handsome, the mouse spirit captured Tang Seng as her husband. The three brothers traced the monster to a deep and bottomless cave. The Monkey King then turned into a fly and entered the cave, leaving his two brothers guarding the entrance. He saw the she-devil forcing his master to drink and marry her. Then he transformed into a tiny insect and flew under the bubbles in wine cup of the monster, waiting for her gulping him down into her belly. However, the she-devil saw the insect and flicked it away. The Monkey King flew into a rage, and immediately turned himself into an eagle and swooped down on the spirit. The dinner table was overturned, and the spirit was gravely shocked. Then the Monkey King turned back into a small fly, flew to Tang Seng, and whispered some words into his ear. Tang Seng then invited the spirit to take a walk in the garden. He plucked a peach for her, and the spirit was happy. When she was just biting, the peach, however, rolled straight down her throat into her stomach. In fact, the peach was changed by the Monkey King, who was inside her belly now, tearing her stomach, ripping her guts, and shouting, "Let my master go, and I will spare your life."

The spirit had to set Tang Seng free. Just outside of the cave, the Monkey King jumped out of the spirit's mouth, and began to hit her with his cudgel. Bajie and Monk Sha also came to help, leaving Tang Seng unprotected. The spirit spotted the chance and took Tang Seng away again. The Monkey King entered the cave a second time, but couldn't find his master. He saw sacrificial altars for the Heavenly King Li and Prince Nezha. So he turned to the Jade Emperor for help, who then sent the Heavenly King Li to subdue the spirit, who actually was his foster daughter, and rescue Tang Seng.

“八卦”最早起于殷周之际，是当时占卜算命的工具。到了战国秦汉时代，它发展成为一种具有神秘主义色彩的哲学思想，并被人们记录成书，取名《周易》。

“八卦”指的是用“-”和“- -”两个符号组成八种简单的图形，分别表示天、地、雷、风、水、火、山、泽八种自然现象，并认为“天”、“地”是世间万物的本源。这种思想具有朴素唯物论的观点，但基本上属于唯心主义世界观。到了北宋，周敦颐将其进一步发展，提出完整的“太极图说”，表达了阴阳轮转，相对统一的哲理，从而为后来的宋、明理学奠定了理论基础。这幅画画的是周敦颐在濂溪讲学的情景。

八卦图

The Graph of Eight Diagrams

The *Bagua* (Eight Diagrams) was created during the years between the Shang and Zhou dynasties, which at that time, was used for fortune-telling and prophecy. From the Warring States Period through the Qin Dynasty to the Han Dynasty, it was developed into a school of mysterious philosophy and was recorded in the *Classic of Changes*. The Eight Diagrams are composed of signs such as “-” and “--,” which constitute eight different simple graphs symbolizing eight natural items or phenomena – the Heaven, the Earth, the thunder, the wind, the fire, the water, mountains, and the swamp, and this school of philosophy takes Heaven and Earth as the origin of the world, which reflects some simple ideas of materialism while its basic value is still mentalism.

In the Northern Song Dynasty, Zhou Dunyi further developed it into the *Explanation of the Diagram of the Supreme Ultimate*, which elaborated the shift between *Yin* (the negative) and *Yang* (the positive) as well as the philosophical reasoning of relative generalization, thus founding the theoretical basis of the Neo-Confucianism which was popular in the Song and Ming dynasties. The scene in this painting is that of Zhou Dunyi giving a lecture and the graph in the middle is the Graph of Eight Diagrams.

Bagua (Eight Diagrams)

贾岛，中唐时期著名诗人，曾出家做过和尚，后又还俗。他生平很不得志，只作过小官，其诗篇虽然题材狭窄，情调凄苦，但写作态度异常认真。也有一些诗写得自然、清新，比如这首《寻隐者不遇》，就是一首流传很广的杰作。

这首诗的全文是："松下问童子，言师采药去，只在此山中，云深不知处。"这四句诗，第一句写向童子问话，第二、三、四句写童子的答话。在问答的话中写出了古松参天、山如云海的景象，以白云比喻隐者的高洁，以苍松比喻为隐者的风骨，从侧面表现了隐者放迹山林的不羁生活和旷达的性格。简练的文字使事、人、景跃然纸上。

松下问童子

Asking a Disciple Under a Pine

Jia Dao (779-843), a celebrated poet during the Mid-Tang Dynasty, once became a monk and then returned to lay life. He only managed to achieve a low-ranking official position in his life, and never achieved his loftier ambitions. Though his poems were of neither broad themes nor bright strain, he had an extremely earnest attitude toward composing. His works were criticised as thin by Su Shi, a great poet from the Northern Song Dynasty (960-1126).

A portrait of Jia Dao

Yet some of the poems displayed a kind of natural and fresh set of circumstances, like the poem below titled *Searching for a Recluse without Success*, a masterpiece that spread throughout the country.

Beneath a pine I asked a disciple where his master is,
I was told that he went to gather herbs,
Though he must be somewhere in the mountains,
I was unable to find him as mist weathered on the hilltops.

The poem, integrating the matter, persons and scene together in brief words, reveals in profile the recluse's uninhibited life and broad-minded character by description of the tall pine and mist-weathered mountains, which became the theme for other creative works. This picture is based on the poem.

麻姑是中国道教中的神话人物，东晋道教学者、著名炼丹家葛洪曾在《神仙传》中对麻姑有出神入化的描写。相传，农历三月初三是住在昆仑山上的神仙西王母的寿辰。每当寿辰之日，她都要设蟠桃会，宴请众仙。八方神仙，四海龙王，天上仙女都赶来为她祝寿。百合、牡丹、芍药、海棠四位花仙采集了各色鲜艳芬芳的花卉，邀请仙女麻姑和她们同往。麻姑用灵芝草酿成仙酒，带到蟠桃会，献给了西王母。因此，过去民间为妇女祝寿时，常常绘“麻姑献寿”的图画相赠。

据传，麻姑原是建昌（江西省南城县）人，她勤劳美丽，后得道升天。汉桓帝时，曾投胎转世于一个普通人家。她掷米成珠，分给贫苦百姓。麻姑曾对人说，她亲眼看见东海三次变为桑田，“沧海桑田”的成语就出自于此。唐朝代宗年间，颜真卿曾为麻姑山撰文立碑，不幸被雷火击毁。

麻姑献寿

Magu Presenting a Birthday Gift to the Queen Mother of the West

Magu is a legendary Taoist immortal associated with elixir of life, and symbolic protector of females in Chinese mythology. Ge Hong, a Taoist philosopher and alchemist of the Eastern Jin Dynasty introduced her stories in his work, *Biographies of Divine Immortals*. The third day of the third lunar month was supposed to be the birthday of the Queen Mother of the West who lived on the Kunlun Mountains in the far west. And every year on this day, she would invite immortals to attend her Peaches of Immortality. The four flower fairies – lily, peony, fragrant peony, and caval vine – collected brightly-colored and aromatic flowers and invited the fairy Magu to go with them. Magu then brewed a kind of immortal wine with special fungus, brought it to the fest, and presented it to the Queen Mother. Traditionally in ancient times when celebrating a woman's birthday, people often presented a picture painted with “Magu Presenting Her Birthday Gift”.

It's said that Magu was born in Jianchang (present-day Nancheng County, Jiangxi Province). Diligent and charming, she cultivated herself according to a religious doctrine and became an immortal. During the reign of Emperor Huan (132-167) of Han, she was reborn into a common family. In this reincarnation, she threw rice grains into the air and changed them into pearls, and distributed among the poor, providing relief to them. She once told people she had witnessed the blue ocean turning to mulberry fields for three times, from which derived the Chinese of Canghai Sangtian (blue ocean, mulberry fields), meaning gerat changes over the course of time. Yan Zhenqing (709-785), a great calligrapher during the Tang Dynasty, once erected a stele for her in Linchuan, Jiangxi Province, which was later destroyed by lightning.

曹操平定了北方的割据势力后，又亲率83万大军准备渡江消灭江南的孙权和刘备，进而统一全国。这一日，天气晴朗，风平浪静。曹操乘船巡视长江，命人在船上置酒设乐，款待诸将。曹操坐大船之上，左右侍者数百人，文武众官依次而坐。此时天色将晚，长江一带，如横素练。曹操见南屏山色如画，东视柴桑之境，西观夏口之江，南望樊山，北觑乌林，四顾空阔，心中欢喜，命左右行酒。饮至半夜，曹操取槊立于船头，满饮三爵，对诸将道："我持此槊，破黄巾、擒吕布、灭袁术、收袁绍，深入塞北，直抵辽东，纵横天下，颇不负大丈夫之志也。今对此景，甚有慷慨。我当作歌，你等和之。"遂赋诗一首，即著名的《短歌行》。开头几句"对酒当歌，人生几何；譬如朝露，去日苦多"，尤为脍炙人口。

宴长江曹操赋诗

Cao Cao Composing a Poem at a Feast at the Yangtze River

After suppressing various separatist forces in northern China, Cao Cao gathered an army of 830,000 men led by himself, and marched to the Yangtze River, intending to annihilate Liu Bei and Sun Quan and thus unify China. On a clear day, no harsh wind blew, and the river water was smooth. Cao Cao in a ship was looking through the defense and the army deployment along the Yangtze River. He ordered a feast and a concert on the ship to entertain his fellow generals. The night was about to fall, and the river at dusk looked like a silver belt. On the ship, Cao Cao was accompanied by hundreds of generals and staff, and officials took their seats according to rank.

Cao Cao appreciated the beauty of picturesque Nanping Mountain; he looked east to the land of Chaisang, west to the river by Xiakou, south to the Fanshan Mountain, and north to Wulin. What a broad country! Delighted, he ordered to drink. The feast went on well into the night. Then Cao Cao took a Shuo (a short-spear-like weapon), standing on the deck, and after drinking three full cups of wine, he said to his followers, "This is the Shuo that defeated the Yellow-Turban Rebellion, caught Lü Bu, destroyed Yuan Shu, and subdued Yuan Shao. It even went deep into the northern border area crushing my enemy at Liaodong and stretched out over the South China, all of which has fulfilled my heroic ambitions. At this moment, in such a wonderful place, I'd like to sing a song, in which you shall accompany me." Then he chanted a self-composed poem, *A Short Song*, which is one of his most celebrated poems. The first lines enjoy great popularity: We should sing before wine, for life is full short and has few satisfactory days; Life goes as the dew drops, flying swiftly away.

相传有一种毒草，叫水莽草。人误食以后，会中毒致死,变成水莽鬼；只有再去毒死别人，找到替身，才能转世投胎。时值仲夏，少年祝生走到途中，口干舌燥，见路边有个茶棚，便走了过去。一老太太捧茶相奉。祝生刚要喝，嗅到一股怪味，放下碗。老太太忙向里屋呼唤：“三娘，拿杯好茶！”话音刚落，一位姿容艳丽的少女端茶而出。祝生顿时魂消意乱，再闻那茶，只觉得芳香无比，一饮而尽。过后就觉得心痛难忍，倒地而死。原来祝生吃了水莽草，而那个少女就是误食水莽草而死的寇三娘。祝生死后，变成了水莽鬼，把寇三娘抓了回来，结成夫妻。祝生有个老母亲，儿子死后，生活非常困苦，终日饮泣。祝生听到母亲的哭声，心里很难过，说服了寇三娘，两人一起回到人间，服侍母亲，直到老母寿终正寝。

水莽草

Shuimang Plant

It’s said that people who ate Shuimang Plant, a kind of poisonous herb growing by the river bank, by mistake would be poisoned and die, then turn into Shuimang devils. And such devils were unable to be born again unless they poisoned some one else by the Shuimang plant to take their place.

On a hot summer day, a young man named Zhu felt thirsty and walked into a tea shed. An old woman then walked up and gave him a cup of tea. He was about to drink when he caught a whiff of a nasty smell, and put the cup down. Seeing this, the old women shouted, “Sanniang, bring a nice cup of tea!” A charming girl walked out and Zhu was hypnotized by her beauty. The tea she brought smelled fragrant and Zhu drained the cup. After a while he felt a sharp pain in his heart and died. Actually what Zhu had drunk was Shuimang-Plant-Tea; that girl died from it several years before and was looking for a replacement. Zhu felt ashamed of his infatuation of beauty and resentment that the girl cheated him. No sooner had Zhu died than he caught Sanniang back. The two got married.Zhu hated this kind of vicious circle and refused to poison anyone else.

After Zhu’s death, his old mother led a hard life and wept tears all day long. One day Zhu felt very sad when hearing his mother’s crying; he persuaded his wife to attend his mother. The two then returned to the world and led a happy life through their hard work. They took care of the old woman until she died. The God of Heaven was moved by the couple’s deed and promoted them into the world of immortals.

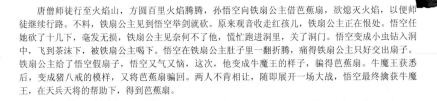

唐僧师徒行至火焰山，方圆百里火焰腾腾，孙悟空向铁扇公主借芭蕉扇，欲熄灭火焰，以便师徒继续行路。不料，铁扇公主见到悟空举剑就砍。原来观音收走红孩儿，铁扇公主正在恨处。悟空任她砍了十几下，毫发无损，铁扇公主见奈何不了他，慌忙跑进洞里，关了洞门。悟空变成小虫钻入洞中，飞到茶沫下，被铁扇公主喝下。悟空在铁扇公主肚子里一翻折腾，痛得铁扇公主只好交出扇子。铁扇公主给了悟空假扇子，悟空又气又恼，这次，他变成牛魔王的样子，骗得芭蕉扇。牛魔王获悉后，变成猪八戒的模样，又将芭蕉扇骗回。两人不肯相让，随即展开一场大战，悟空最终擒获牛魔王，在天兵天将的帮助下，得到芭蕉扇。

孙悟空三调芭蕉扇

The Monkey King Borrowing the Plantain Fan Three Times

On their way to the West, Tang Seng and his disciples arrived at the Flaming Mountain, where fires raged for hundreds of miles. The only way to get across the mountain was to borrow a Plantain Fan from the Princess Iron Fan, which could put out the fire. Knowing that the Princess Iron Fan was the wife of Bull Demon King, his sworn brother, the Monkey King volunteered to borrow the magic fan. However, since Kwan-yin caught her only son, the Red Boy, the princess had been longing to get her revenge on the Monkey King, but didn't know where to find him; now the Monkey King was just standing in front of her. Her face went bright red and evil anger flared up in her heart. Without a word, she swung both of her swords and hacked at the Monkey King's head. The Monkey King let her poke a dozen times but remained unhurt. Realizing she would never be able to kill him, she brought out her plantain fan and with a single wave blew the Monkey King right out of sight. The Monkey King borrowed a Wind-fixing Pill from a Bodhisattva and came back. He turned into a fly, and got into the princess' body. He pulled her liver and hit her heart, which brought extreme pain to the her. She rolled all over the ground, and had to give her fan to the Monkey King. The Monkey King took the fan and went to the Flaming Mountain. However, when he flapped the fan, the fire grew fiercer. Apparently, the fan was a fake one. He was furious and resentful, and decided to seek the Princess Iron Fan again. This time, he turned himself into the Bull Demon King and easily got the fan. But the real king came back and played a trick back on the Monkey King: he changed into Bajie, recouping the fan. Then the two had a good fight. Just as they were becoming locked in the struggle, the real Bajie came. He joined in the battle and defeated the bull, who tried to escape but was stopped by heavenly generals dispatched by the Buddha. The couple had to surrender and give the real fan to the Monkey King.

东吴大将周瑜心胸狭窄，一心想除掉胜过自己的诸葛亮。赤壁之战时，周瑜请诸葛亮前来议事，借口军中缺箭，令他十日内督造10万支箭。诸葛亮却说十日必误大事，三天便可完成，并立下军令状，若完不成任务，甘受重罚。周瑜暗中吩咐士兵不给诸葛亮准备制箭材料。

然诸葛亮找来鲁肃，向其借船20艘，每船配士卒30人，船两边束满草人。待到第三日四更时分，20艘船用长索相连，列队往北岸进发。时江中大雾漫天，不见对面。近曹寨，船上士卒擂鼓呐喊，曹操怕重雾有伏，只命弓弩手乱箭射之。而诸葛亮和鲁肃坐船中酌酒取乐。日出雾散之后，船两边的草人上早已箭满，每船足有五六千支。待曹操知道中计后，诸葛亮早已收船率兵远去，追之不及。诸葛亮回到岸上交付周瑜。周瑜自叹不如诸葛亮神机妙算。

草船借箭

Zhuge Liang Borrowing Arrows with Straw Boats

During the Battle at Chibi, Zhou Yu invited Zhuge Liang to have a meeting; making an excuse of lack of arrows, he asked Zhuge Liang to supervise the production of 100,000 arrows within 10 days. Zhuge Liang, however, said it would be devastating for the battle if it took 10 days to produce such a number of arrows, and he promised he could do it within three days. Then they signed an agreement that if Zhuge Liang failed to complete the task in time, he would be severely punished. After that, Zhou Yu surreptitiously ordered his soldiers not to supply the materials used to produce arrows to Zhuge Liang.

Zhuge Liang turned to Lu Su, an advisor for Sun Quan, and borrowed 20 boats, with 30 soldiers and numbers of straw-made men on each boat. On the early morning of the third day, the 20 boats connected in a long chain moved toward the north shore of the Yangtze River. It was seriously foggy on the river, and one person could scarcely see another. On approaching to the camps of the Cao Cao's army, soldiers on the straw boats began to hit drums and shout. Cao Cao was afraid that there would be an extra, unseen, ambush force in the heavy fog; he just ordered his archers to shoot, but did not send troops to confront them. Meanwhile, Zhuge Liang and Lu Su were sitting inside a straw-boat, drinking and having fun. Until the sun rose and the fog faded away, the straw-made men on Zhuge Liang's boats had been covered with arrows, and there were 5,000 to 6,000 arrows on each boat. It was too late for Cao Cao to realize it was a trick; Zhuge Liang and his boats had already escaped by then. Zhuge Liang turned his achievement over to Zhou Yu, and Zhou Yu had nothing to say but sigh because he was less prominent than Zhuge Liang.

这幅画是根据晚唐诗人杜牧的《清明》一诗写意而成的。全诗如下："清明时节雨纷纷，路上行人欲断魂。借问酒家何处有，牧童遥指杏花村。"

杜牧（803～852年）有雄才谋略，好谈军事，为人刚直不阿，敢于论列大事，指陈时病，政治上是一位有见识、有胆量的进步人士。可是他一生仕宦不得意，始终未能施展抱负。他的诗、赋和古文都极负盛名，尤以诗的成就最高，和李商隐齐名，并称"小李杜"。他的七绝诗高度凝练、清新自然，如这首《清明》诗，信手写来，绝无斧凿之痕，却别有一番风趣。

:牧童遥指杏花村:

A Shepherd Boy Pointing to the Xinghua Village

The painting is based on the poem *Tomb-Sweeping Day* composed by Du Mu, which goes,

Continuous rain on Tomb-Sweeping Day,
Sad pedestrians on the way;
I enquired where the nearby tavern was,
A shepherd boy pointed to the Apricot-Blossom Village in the distance.

A portrait of Du Mu

Du Mu (803-852), a poet during the late Tang Dynasty, was known for his extraordinary talent for running the country. He loved talking about military affairs and his personality appeared straightforward and righteous; he often boldly criticized social injustice and deficiencies; however, he was not lucky enough to fulfill his ambition since his political status was barely satisfactory throughout his life. He expressed his feelings in literature.

His works like poems, lyrical essays and articles are widely appreciated, among which his achievement in poetry is particularly remarkable. He is on a par with Li Shangyin and together they are generally considered the two top poets in the late Tang Dynasty, and often mentioned as the Little Li-Du, in contrast to the Great Li-Du, Li Bai and Du Fu. His verses with seven characters in a line are concise, natural and vivid, such as the one above, which gives readers a sense of truth but with a special sort of sentiment.

宋朝时候，荆州有一个叫秦香莲的妇女，勤劳肯干，为丈夫陈士美辛苦攒下赴京赶考的费用；可是陈士美一去三年，杳无音信。秦香莲在家里奉养公婆、抚育儿女。不料连年灾荒，公婆病死。因为无法生活，秦香莲领着儿女，到京城寻找丈夫。她打听到陈士美已经中了状元，并且被招为驸马。香莲又气又恨，带着孩子到驸马府找陈士美。陈士美不但不与香莲母子相认，还把他们赶出府去。秦香莲在街上遇见宰相王延龄，便拦轿控告陈士美。王延龄同情秦香莲的遭遇，便给她出了个主意，叫她假扮成艺人随他去给陈士美祝寿。在堂上，秦香莲弹起琵琶，哭诉自己的身世和家庭的苦难，希望能感化陈士美，使他回心转意。画面中画的就是此情景：白髯老者是王延龄，中间的是陈士美。但是陈士美把王延龄骂出府，又派人去暗杀香莲母子。

秦香莲

Qin Xianglian

There lived a scholar named Chen Shimei. He married a tender and industrious lady Qin Xianglian who supported the whole family without a complaint. Relying on Qin's earning, Chen went to the capital city to take part in the Imperial Examinations, while Qin stayed at home, taking care of her parents-in-law, raising children, as well as waiting for his back. Three years later, Chen Shimei got first place in the Imperial Examinations. The emperor, fond of Chen Shimei's talent and appearance, married his daughter to him. At that time, Chen Shimei just coveted riches and honor, having his parents, wife and children out of his mind. Due to the famine for years, Chen's parents died and Qin Xianglian had no method to make a living. She then, with her children, trudged to the capital to look for her husband. However, seeing Qin Xianglian and his children, Chen Shimei not only disavowed all responsibility for them, but also denied their relation, driving them away. Qin Xianglian had to bring a lawsuit against Chen Shimei. No officials dared to hear the case. The upright courtier Wang Yanling took sympathy on her and gave her a piece of advice.

On Chen Shimei's birthday party, Qin Xianglian disguised as a singer, played the Chinese lute at the party. She poured out their past love and the miserable experiences, in hope that Chen Shimei would be moved and come around. The picture shows this scene. In the picture the older man with white-beard is Wang Yanling and the man sitting in the middle is Chen Shimei. Chen Shimei, however, drove Wang Yanling out of his residence and dispatched someone to assassinate Qin Xianglian and their children.

曹操欲取荆州，不料关羽先发制人，挥师攻打曹军驻守的襄阳，随后围住樊城。曹操闻之，急命大将于禁、庞德率七路大军营救樊城。然关羽早接到消息，亲自迎敌。两军相对，激战一日，未分胜负。第二日，两军对垒，关羽中箭，回到营中，坚守不出。于禁、庞德便移军下山扎寨，等待时机。适逢连日大雨，襄江水势甚急，关羽心生一计。他令人预备船筏，收拾水具，又差人堵住各处水口；时机到时，一齐放水淹没魏军。这夜，四面大水骤至，曹军惊慌失色，抱头鼠窜，淹死无数。关羽统大军乘船杀来，生擒于禁，怒斩庞德，大获全胜。

水淹七军

Guan Yu Flooding Seven Divisions of the Enemy

Cao Cao planned to seize Jingzhou, while Guan Yu, who in the charge of Jingzhou, attacked the enemy first, seizing Xiangyang, and then surrounding Fancheng, both cities being under Cao Cao's administration. Knowing the situation, Cao Cao dispatched Yu Jin and Pang De, two well-known generals to lead an army of seven divisions to save Fancheng. Guan Yu had already received the news before the enemy arrived, and led his army to confront them. The two armies fought for an entire day, but neither was able to claim victory. The next day, they fought again. During the battle, Guan Yu was shot, and had to order a retreat. He stayed in his camp because of the injury, and simply ordered his soldiers to defend the camp but not to fight a battle. Yu Jin and Pang De moved their army to camp by the mountain, waiting for better opportunities. Guan Yu learned that they camped by the mountain and the water of the Xiangjiang River which had become turbulent because of the recent heavy rains, ordered his soldiers to prepare boats and sort out water-proof equipment, and he sent his men to build dams to accumulate the water and flooded Cao's army.

That night there came a great storm. In his camp, Pang De heard loud noises as if hundreds of thousands of horses were running toward his army. As he rode out, then he saw the rolling waters coming in from every side. Soldiers of the seven divisions fled in disorder, and many were drowned. Yu Jin, Pang De and several other officers sought safety by rushing up the hills. Then Guan Yu leading his army rushed in to attack Cao's army. As Guan Yu came round onboard a large boat, Yu Jin surrendered immediately; however, when Pang De was brought to Guan, he refused to give in and cursed and swore at the surrendered soldiers. Guan Yu then had him beheaded.

细柳19岁嫁给丧偶的高生，前妻留一子高福。后来，细柳又生一子高怙。高生不久身亡，细柳和两个儿子相依为命。大儿高福不用功读书，经常逃学，细柳让他和牧童一块干活。没几天，高福熬不住，逃走，以乞食为生。邻人看见都责怪西柳狠心。高福在外生计困难，回家跪求母亲让他读书。细柳说，如果他肯挨一百棍就答应，高福情愿挨打；细柳见他悔过，没打他，反而让他继续读书。高福从此判若两人，刻苦读书，博取功名。高怙大脑迟钝，细柳让他务农，他经常逃工；细柳让他经商，他又把本钱赌光。后来，高怙去洛阳贩货，他因用细柳给他的假银逛妓院而入狱，受尽磨难。细柳让高福把他救出来。回来后，高怙悔恨交加，改邪归正。邻人这才明白，细柳让孩子在磨难中锻炼是真正地爱孩子。

细柳

Xiliu Teaching Her Children

Xiliu, a beautiful girl, married Mr. Gao at the age of 19, who had just lost his wife and had a son named Gao Fu. The couple loved and respected each other very much. Shortly afterwards Xiliu gave birth to a son, and called him Gao Hu. Yet before long, Mr. Gao died, leaving two sons for Xiliu to care for.

Gao Fu was often truant from his studies. Having used up all her efforts to instruct Gao Fu, Xiliu then sent him to pasture. Gao Fu could not stand the suffering and ran away, living upon by begging foods. All neighbors called Xiliu a heartless woman. Finally, Gao Fu went back home and asked Xiliu to allow him to return to school. Xiliu told that he could if he was ready to take a beating of 100 strokes. Hearing this, Gao Fu was willing to accept the punishment. Aware of his genuine repentance for his errors, Xiliu didn't beat him. Since then, he seemed another man, studying hard and gaining for himself the reputation of being a scholar. While the younger son Gao Hu was a slow-minded child, so Xiliu asked him to work on the farm. But he was so lazy that he often neglected work. Xiliu then asked him to engage in trade, but he used up all his money gambling. Later he, using the excuse of selling goods with businessmen to Luoyang, asked Xiliu for a large sum of money. And this time all the money was used in a whorehouse. When he paid for the bill, he was put into jail for using fake silver. In jail he suffered greatly. One day Xiliu said to Gao Fu, "I gave the fake silver to your brother on purpose, intending to make him repent just like you had to. Now you go and get him out of prison." Back home, Gao Hu knelt down before his mother, bitterly remorseful. He finally gave up evil. Fellow villagers then realized that Xiliu loved her children by chastening them in tribulation.

唐僧师徒行至火焰山，方圆百里火焰腾腾，孙悟空向铁扇公主借芭蕉扇，欲熄灭火焰，以便师徒继续行路。不料，铁扇公主见到悟空举剑就砍。原来观音收走红孩儿，铁扇公主正在恨处。悟空任她砍了十几下，毫发无损，铁扇公主见奈何不了他，慌忙跑进洞里，关了洞门。悟空变成小虫钻入洞中，飞到茶沫下，被铁扇公主喝下。悟空在铁扇公主肚子里一翻折腾，痛得铁扇公主只好交出扇子。铁扇公主给了悟空假扇子，悟空又气又恼，这次，他变成牛魔王的样子，骗得芭蕉扇。牛魔王获悉后，变成猪八戒的模样，又将芭蕉扇骗回。两人不肯相让，随即展开一场大战，悟空最终擒获牛魔王，在天兵天将的帮助下，得到芭蕉扇。

孙悟空三调芭蕉扇

The Monkey King Borrowing the Plantain Fan Three Times

On their way to the West, Tang Seng and his disciples arrived at the Flaming Mountain, where fires raged for hundreds of miles. The only way to get across the mountain was to borrow a Plantain Fan from the Princess Iron Fan, which could put out the fire. Knowing that the Princess Iron Fan was the wife of Bull Demon King, his sworn brother, the Monkey King volunteered to borrow the magic fan. However, since Kwan-yin caught her only son, the Red Boy, the princess had been longing to get her revenge on the Monkey King, but didn't know where to find him; now the Monkey King was just standing in front of her. Her face went bright red and evil anger flared up in her heart. Without a word, she swung both of her swords and hacked at the Monkey King's head. The Monkey King let her poke a dozen times but remained unhurt. Realizing she would never be able to kill him, she brought out her plantain fan and with a single wave blew the Monkey King right out of sight. The Monkey King borrowed a Wind-fixing Pill from a Bodhisattva and came back. He turned into a fly, and got into the princess' body. He pulled her liver and hit her heart, which brought extreme pain to the her. She rolled all over the ground, and had to give her fan to the Monkey King. The Monkey King took the fan and went to the Flaming Mountain. However, when he flapped the fan, the fire grew fiercer. Apparently, the fan was a fake one. He was furious and resentful, and decided to seek the Princess Iron Fan again. This time, he turned himself into the Bull Demon King and easily got the fan. But the real king came back and played a trick back on the Monkey King: he changed into Bajie, recouping the fan. Then the two had a good fight. Just as they were becoming locked in the struggle, the real Bajie came. He joined in the battle and defeated the bull, who tried to escape but was stopped by heavenly generals dispatched by the Buddha. The couple had to surrender and give the real fan to the Monkey King.

每逢端午节，人间的雄黄药酒就会令白娘子和小青无法忍受。这年又逢端午节，清早小青就到深山去了，然许仙要白娘子陪他看龙船，白娘子因已怀身孕，推托。谁知许仙听说妻子怀孕，高兴地搀着她上楼，并烫了一壶雄黄酒，要白娘子喝下。白娘子硬着头皮喝了一口，可是酒一落肚，她便瘫软在床。许仙忙泡茶送到床前，床上没有白娘子，却盘着一条白蛇。许仙大叫一声，栽倒在地。日落时分，小青回家，看到此景，急忙推醒白娘子。白娘子又急又悔，前往昆仑山去盗灵芝仙草救丈夫。白娘子带着仙草正要离去之时，不想被守护仙草的白鹤仙和鹿仙发现。双方打得难解难分之时，南极仙翁正好经过。白娘子哭着跪求仙翁给她一株灵芝救丈夫。仙翁善心大发，点头答应。白娘子急忙回到家中，把灵芝熬成药汁，喂给许仙。半个时辰后，许仙苏醒过来，白娘子和小青才松了一口气。

盗仙草

Lady White Stealing the Immortal Herb

During the Dragon Boat Festival (the 5th day of the 5th lunar month), Lady White and Xiaoqing could not bear the strong odor of the arsenic wine, and they used to hide in the mountain. This day, Xiaoqing had already gone to the mountain early in the morning, while Xu Xian asked Lady White to accompany him to watch the dragon boats. Lady White made an excuse that she was pregnant in order to put off her husband's request. However being happy to hear this, Xu Xian walked Lady White upstairs, heated a bottle of wine, and pretentiously asked his wife to drink it up. In order not to cause Xu's suspicion, Lady White was obliged to have a sip, which paralyzed her. Xu Xian hurried to get a cup of tea for her, but back to the bed, only found a coil of white snake. He gave out a shout and died. By nightfall, Xiaoqing had come back. Seeing the scene, she woke Lady White up.

Lady White was anxious and repentant, and in order to save her husband, she went to Kunlun Mountain to steal the immortal herb. When she got the herb and was about to leave, the crane elf and the deer elf, the guards of the herb, discovered her. In the ensuing fight, the Immortal Father of Antarctica came out from behind a rock. In tears, Lady White came over to him and begged for a piece of immortal herb to save her husband. Moved by her sincerity, the Immortal Father agreed. After returning home, Lady White boiled the herb into some syrup, and fed it to Xu Xian. An hour later, Xu Xian woke up, and the sisters were finally relieved.

中国古代，有不少贫寒的知识分子，深受孔子“学而优则仕”思想的影响；通过读书、科举邀取地位、声望、财产，成为一条捷径和正途，惹得“人人皆有觊觎之心，不忍自弃于盗贼奸宄”。人们从孩提时代就接受这样的教导：“天子重英豪，文章教尔曹；万般皆下品，惟有读书高。少小须勤学，文章可立身；满朝朱紫贵，尽是读书人”；“十年寒窗无人问，一举成名天下知”。

他们毕生刻苦治学，希冀通过科举考试，改变生活境遇，摆脱清贫、苦难的命运，取得仕途的成功，跻身于达官贵人之列。即使穷到身无分文，他们也不愿卖书来换一点粮食，民间流传的“穷不卖书留子读，老来栽竹有人砍”的谚语即是这种思想的反映，这幅画也是根据这句谚语写意而成的。

Keeping Books for Later Generations and Never Selling Them

In ancient China many poor scholars were subjected to the influence of the Confucianism: studying and taking examinations became a shortcut to achieve social status, fame, and prosperity. Everybody wanted to try. In their childhood, common people were educated as following:

“The Son of Heaven recognizes the hero; the articles teach you people how to please the Imperial Majesty. The worth of other pursuits is small; the study of books excels them all! Study hard in youth. The articles will help you find a secure job; all of the highest officials are intellectuals.” “Ten years’ hard study for being a mandarin may be miserable and seem fruitless; but once one succeeded in passing the exam, they would immediately become famous all over the world.”

They yearned to become high officials by passing the Imperial Examinations. These people, though very poor, usually had a rich collection of books. Some of them would even endure hunger and poverty rather than sell their treasured books to get food. They fantasized that they could obtain the success of an official career after passing the Imperial Examinations by diligent study, thus changing their life circumstances and getting away from the destiny of distress and hardship.

The idiom “never selling a book even in poverty but keeping it for the next generation”, like “planting trees in old age just to let someone else cut it down”, is an excellent reflection of this kind of thought, which is also indicated in the picture.

梁山好汉“活阎罗”阮小七自与众弟兄分手后，改名萧恩，和女儿桂英相依为命，在江边打鱼为生。时因天旱水浅，鱼不进网，加上萧恩年迈体衰，生活困难，欠下了乡宦丁员外很多渔税。

一天丁府派恶奴前来催讨，萧恩说，眼下没钱，改日把渔税送到府上去，可是恶奴狗仗人势，不依不饶，恰好被萧恩的好友、梁山好汉“混江龙”李俊及“卷毛虎”倪荣遇见。二人大怒，一齐为萧恩打抱不平，恶奴见状，连滚带爬地逃离开去。丁员外闻报，随即派一帮家奴至萧家强行索取税银，并动手打人。萧恩忍无可忍，怒将来人打跑。萧恩见丁家人欺人太甚，至官府报案。岂知县令和丁家早已狼狈为奸，不分青红皂白，痛打萧恩40大板，还命他连夜过江向丁员外赔礼请罪。是夜，萧恩暗藏戒刀在身，与女儿以献珠赔礼为名进入丁府，杀了丁员外，远走他乡。

打渔杀家

A Fisherman Killing an Oppressor

Having departed from his brothers in the Liangshan Marsh, Ruan Xiaoqi changed his name to Xiao En, and lived on fishing with his daughter, Guiying. Due to drought, the river became shallow, thus they couldn't catch enough fish to sustain their life. They lived in poverty, and owed the local officials lots of tax.

One day, a local bully surnamed Ding sent a servant to urge them to pay their tax. Xiao En said he didn't have money, and promised to take the tax to the official's house as soon as he had. But the servant, with the backing of his master, continued to press him, having no intention to leave before getting the money. Xiao En's intimate friends, Li Jun and Ni Rong, arrived at that moment. They were furious at the scene, and helped resist the servant. The villainous servant was scared, and fled away.

Knowing the result, the bully sent a group of civil servants to Xiao En's home to get the money by force. The servants beat Xiao En heavily. In such a situation with no reason to hold back, Xiao En had to fight, and the servants fled away under his fierce resistance. He went to launch his grievance to the county government, but the county magistrate had already collaborated with the Ding family. Xaio En was flogged 40 hits and was ordered to apologize to the Ding family that evening. At the night, under the guise of donating pearls for an apology, Xiao En came to Ding's home along with his daughter. He then slayed the bully and fled away with his daughter.

在中国民间人民普遍认为狐狸狡猾、残忍而妖媚，具有妖性。但是在蒲松龄的《聊斋志异》里狐狸有了更多的形象。全书400余则故事中涉及狐狸的就有86篇，大多是以美丽善良的少女形象出现，惹人怜爱，表现出作者对封建礼制的反抗和对女性的新认识。《彭二挣》中就描绘了一只顽皮的狐狸。

有一次，韩公甫和同乡彭二挣一起去城里买东西。他们骑着毛驴、驮上空口袋，一前一后边走边聊。走着走着，韩公甫不见后边答话，回头一看，彭二挣不知去向，只有一头空驴跟在后面。又听见一阵阵的呼救声从驴背上的口袋里发出。他急忙跑过去，用刀子割开口袋，见彭二挣正缩在里面。韩问他是怎么进去的，二挣自己也莫名其妙，却只说他家里常闹狐仙，经常不知不觉地就被狐仙藏起来。韩公甫一听，笑着说，这准是狐仙在和二挣开玩笑呢。

彭二挣

Peng Erzheng

In Chinese mythology, fox had been considered a kind of crafty, cruel but charming creature, which were capable of acquiring human forms, magical powers, and could even achieve immortality. Those women who disregarded the feudal code of ethics were often called fox spirits because of their low social statue in feudal period. The best known Chinese stories written about fox-spirits are those written by Pu Songling, in his novel: *Strange Tales from Make-Do Studio*. A total of 86 tales mentioned foxes, most of which are those of fox-spirits appearing as beautiful young girls, who express their feelings frankly and bravely pursue the improvement of women's status. The author extols and longs for true love between men and women. This kind of ideal held great progressive significance at the time. The author also portrays fox spirits appearing in male form, and of different characters. Here is a joky fox.

Once, two men named Han Gongfu and Peng Erzheng, went into a town together. They chatted along the way. When all of a sudden, Han found that Peng disappeared, leaving the donkey followed behind. Han heard Peng's voice calling for help, and apparently proceeded from inside one of their bags strapped across the donkey's back. Han then opened the tightly-sewed bag. Peng was actually crouched in the bag, although the bag did not seem to be at all displaced by his weight. Han then helped him out and asked, "How did you get in?" Peng himself was puzzled, but shared, "The fox spirits often play tricks on me and my family. And we are always hid by them unconsciously." Han laughed and said to Peng, "Do not fear; just now it was a joke the fox spirit played on you."

白娘子与许仙结成夫妻后，开了一个药店“保和堂”。这一年，城里闹瘟疫，人们纷纷到保和堂看病、抓药，而到寺中烧香叩头的人越来越少。这气坏了金山寺的老和尚法海。他原是西天的一只乌龟，学了法术，跑到金山寺。为了使百姓都敬仰他的法力，法海散布了这场瘟疫，没想到被白娘子搅了局。法海恨得咬牙切齿，于是就设计骗许仙七月十五日到金山寺烧香。

许仙一到金山寺，便被法海扣在寺中。当听说妻子是一条白蛇妖怪后，许仙不肯回家，白娘子便带上小青来到金山寺。两人见到法海苦苦哀求，无济于事。法海举杖就砍，白娘子和小青拔剑相争。白娘子怀有身孕，渐渐支持不住，败下阵来。回到杭州西湖边上，白娘子和小青，来到断桥亭，正好碰上回杭州的许仙。善良的白娘子念夫妻恩情，宽恕了许仙。三人重归于好，到许仙姐姐家安身。

断桥亭

The Broken-Bridge Pavilion

After Lady White and Xu Xian got married, she used magic to help Xu open an herbal medicine shop called Bao He Tang to make their living. They lived a happy life together and soon Bai became pregnant. It was a year of plague. The people in the city all went to Bao He Tang to get themselves diagnosed and buy drugs, and the number of people who went to the temple for blessings fell dramatically, which maddened the old monk, Fahai, at Jinshan Temple. Originally, he was a tortoise in West Heaven. After mastering certain skills, he moved into Jinshan Temple, and it was he who created the plague, with the aim of making folks believe in his power. His conspiracy was broken by Lady White, and for revenge, he tricked Xu Xian into coming to Jinshan Temple on July 15, and held him there under a pretext of lies.

The monk asked Xu Xian to become a disciple of his and revealed that his wife Lady White and Xiaoqing were not humans but snake monsters. Scared, Xu Xian did not dare to come back home, so he stayed at the temple. Lady White and Xiaoqing went to the temple to plead for Xu's release, but Fahai refused, and hit them with his stick. Lady White and Xiaoqing had no choice but to fight back. However, they were defeated soon because Lady White was pregnant, and went back to West Lake. One day, they happened to meet Xu Xian at the Broken-Bridge Pavilion, who had eventually gone back to Hangzhou. The good-hearted Lady White forgave Xu Xian's betrayal, and the three became reconciled again. They settled down in the house of Xu Xian's elder sister.

这首诗是盛唐诗人王之涣（688～742年）所作。王之涣出身于名门望族，才高气盛，豪放不羁。因不满官场黑暗，愤然辞官，寄情山水15年。王之涣早年精于诗文，乐工多引为歌词，名动一时。他常与王昌龄、高适、崔国辅等名诗人交游，擅五言诗，以描写边塞风光的最为著名。

《登鹳雀楼》这首诗前半部分描写落日、山川、黄河、大海的壮丽风景，后半部分表达了如能极目千里，看到山的那边、海的那边，就要再登高一步。诗作被人们视为一种追求崇高的精神世界的象征。

登鹳雀楼

At the Guanque Mansion

Wang Zhihuan (688-742) was a high-profile, open-minded, and prominent Tang Dynasty poet. He was brought up in a family that loved poetry and music, which contributed much to his keen interest in the art during his childhood. After serving as a local official for a brief period, he left his position and began to travel among China's beautiful mountains and rivers for 15 years. In his early years, he wrote many excellent poems and essays, and musicians loved incorporating his words into their own lyrics, which brought him fame. He was often in the company of Wang Changling, Gao Shi, Cui Guofu and other prominent poets, and his Wu Yan poems (a genre of poems that have five Chinese characters in each line), especially those describing landscapes in the border areas, were among the best. Wang Zhihuan had written many poems on this topic, but unfortunately only six of his poems survived to this day.

The poem *At the Guanque Mansion* is his most famous work. This five-character quatrain has been widely read and praised by generations of Chinese, which reads:

The sun sinks behind the mountains; the Yellow River empties into the oceans.
If you want to widen you sight; Come to the upper storey by climbing one more flight.

The first two lines describe the grand beautiful view of the sunset, the mountains, the Yellow River, and the sea, while in the following two lines the author ingeniously transits from a portrait of natural destiny to a philosophical theory of life, expresseing an idea that if one wants to obtain a broader vision, one should climb to a higher place. The pursuit of spiritual nobility is often perceived as its symbolic significance.

祝鸡公是晋朝洛阳人。他以养鸡为业，终生与鸡相伴为命。相传，祝鸡公很会养鸡，他养的鸡，不但体态健美、啼鸣洪亮，而且每只鸡都有一个很好听的名字。只要祝鸡公一叫鸡名，那些鸡便拍翅，应声而来。白天，鸡群在山岭田野间觅食、嬉戏；晚上，就像鸟儿一样在树上栖息。古书上还记载着这样一个有趣的故事。一次，祝鸡公得到一颗神鸡生的蛋。他十分喜爱，精心侍弄，孵出来一只小鸡。那小鸡浑身紫色，可以日飞万里。在坚实的翅膀下，还生着一对明亮的千里眼。祝鸡公大喜，给它起名叫“目羽鸡”。后来，祝鸡公的名声越来越大，方圆几百里的农人都来向他学习饲养方法。他总是热心地向人们传授自己的技术和经验。祝鸡公去世后，人们为了纪念他，便用他的姓“祝”呼唤鸡，这个习惯一直延续到今天。

祝鸡公

The Zhu Father of Chickadees

In the Jin Dynasty, there was a man, called Zhu Father of Chickadees by locals, living in Luoyang (in present-day Henan). He made a living on raising chicks, and they were his life companions. It was said that he was good at raising chicks. All chicks he raised were healthy and beautiful, and had nice loud voices. They also had a fancy name. So long as he called the names of his chicks, they would all flap their wings and come over to him. His chicks freely searched for food and played in the mountains and fields in the day time, and during the night, they rested in trees like flying birds.

There was an interesting story in an ancient book. Once, Zhu Father of Chickadees received an egg produced by an immortal hen. He was very fond of the egg, and took good care of it. The egg then hatched a chick that grew purple feathers and could fly ten thousand miles a day. Under its strong wings, there was a pair of bright eyes which could cover a thousand miles. The Father was pretty happy, and named his holy chick, the Wing-Eyed Chick.

Later, his reputation became more and more widespread. Local farmers over an area of several hundred miles all came to learn his method for raising chicks. The Father was always kind enough to teach them his ways and experience. After his death, folks used his surname, Zhu, to call upon chicks, in his memory, and the ritual continues in China to this day.

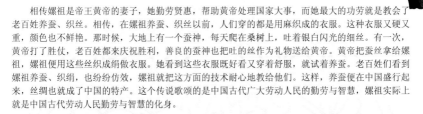

相传嫘祖是帝王黄帝的妻子，她勤劳贤惠，帮助黄帝处理国家大事，而她最大的功劳就是教会了老百姓养蚕、织丝。相传，在嫘祖养蚕、织丝以前，人们穿的都是用麻织成的衣服。这种衣服又硬又重，颜色也不鲜艳。那时候，大地上有一个蚕神，每天爬在桑树上，吐着银白闪光的细丝。有一次，黄帝打了胜仗，老百姓都来庆祝胜利，善良的蚕神也把吐的丝作为礼物送给黄帝。黄帝把蚕丝拿给嫘祖，嫘祖便用这些丝织成绢做衣服。她看到这些衣服既好看又穿着舒服，就试着养蚕。老百姓们看到嫘祖养蚕、织绢，也纷纷仿效，嫘祖就把这方面的技术耐心地教给他们。这样，养蚕便在中国盛行起来，丝绸也就成了中国的特产。这个传说歌颂的是中国古代广大劳动人民的勤劳与智慧，嫘祖实际上就是中国古代劳动人民勤劳与智慧的化身。

嫘祖养蚕

Lei Raising Silkworms

It was said that Lei was the wife of the Yellow Emperor in the remote antiquity. She was hardworking, capable, and virtuous, and helped the Yellow Emperor deal with state affairs. One of her great contributions was discovering silk. According to the ancient legend, prior to Lei's raising silkworms and producing silk, people wore hemp-made clothes which were hard and heavy and the color was ugly. There was a silkworm elf on the Earth at that time, who threw up white sparkling silk on mulberry trees every day.

Once, the Yellow Emperor won a victory, people all came to celebrate, and the kind silkworm elf donated his silk to the Emperor. The Emperor presented the silk to his wife. In terms of its gentleness and lightness, Lei weaved it into *Juan* (a kind of thick, loosely woven raw silk fabric), and then made it into clothes. The clothes were so nice-looking and comfortable that they inspired her to try to raise silkworms. It was said that when the silkworms produced cocoons, she picked out some big ones and dropped them into the steaming water. The threads started to separate from the cocoons. She wrapped them around her figer, and got the soft and lovely silk. Then she invented the silk reel, by which she produced thread strong enough for weaving. People all began to imitate her and raise silkworms and weave *Juan*, and Lei patiently taught her experience to them. Thus, the silkworm raising business became popular in China, and silk also became a special product of China. The legend showed the diligence and wisdom of the ancient Chinese people, and Lei became the symbol of their virtue.

这诗句出自李白的《月下独酌》。李白平生非常喜欢月亮，对明月有着深厚的感情，写了大量歌咏明月的诗篇。

诗的大意是：春光明媚，花好月圆，伴月偕影，开怀畅饮，酒助诗兴，月下徘徊，吟咏诗句。诗人把月和影当作是忠诚的朋友，在寂寞之中，它们给他以安慰和欢乐；诗人欲离开知音难寻的黑暗世界，飞往太空仙境。

这首诗委婉地表达了诗人对当时腐朽政治的忿懑心情。李白的笔下，月亮纯洁、光明，不仅是美好事物的象征，也成了诗人理想的寄托。诗人在人间，净土难寻，知音稀少；在邈远的太空，却发现了可结永好的朋友。

举杯邀明月

Proposing a Toast to the Moon

Li Bai is considered a successor of the optimistic romanticism of Qu Yuan, who was the great poet and statesman of the Warring States Period. He endowed his poems with an unbridled enthusiasm, a grand and powerful style, bold imagination, a hue of overstatement and lifelike, buoyant language. Li Bai loved the moon, for which he had formed a unique and profound fondness. He wrote many poems in praise of its beauty, and always cherished a deep feeling for the moon. This painting depicts the scene in one of his most famous poems: *Drinking Along by Moonlight*, which is a good example of some of the most famous aspects of his poetry – a very involuntary poem, full of natural imagery.

The background of the poem is that on a spring night, flowers were blossoming and the moon was full, and the poet, accompanied by the moon and his own shadow, drank to the fullest. The sense of drunkenness aroused his poetic feelings, and he chanted the poem from the bottom of his heart under the moonlight. He imagined the moon and his own shadow were his loyal friends, and they brought the lonely poet comfort and happiness. However, it's a pity that the moon could not drink with him, and the shadow just knew to follow him round. What's worse, when he was drunk, they three would be apart again. How could they enjoy a permanent renuiting? There was only one way: leaving the dark world to fly to Heaven.

The poem indirectly reflected Li Bai's anger and resentfulness at the corrupt politics of his time. The moon was bright and pure, which represented all his hopes and aspirations. In the secular world, the poet could hardly find a clean place or a soul mate, while in the remoteness of space he found a friend whose friendship would last forever.

老子，姓李名耳，是春秋时期著名的思想家。他被尊为道家学派的始祖；在道教中，也是一个很重要的神仙，被称为太上老君。老子主张“无为”。相传老子曾经是孔丘的老师，孔丘经常去向他请教，学习做人的道理。青出于蓝而胜于蓝，渐渐地，孔丘在一些地方超过了老子。老子觉得再这样下去，于孔丘、于己都不利，于是离开故地，到西方去。老子骑着一头青牛，来到了函谷关（今河南灵宝西南）。守官听说老子来了，立刻带着人出来迎接。老子来到关上，守官请他给文武官员和士兵们讲学。可是，老子讲得太深奥，大家都听不懂，守官只好请他把所讲的写下来。老子连夜写了五千多字，第二天早上，他把这些交给守官后，骑上青牛出了函谷关，一直往西走去。据说，老子写的这五千多字就是留传后世的《道德经》。

老子出关

Lao Tzu Crossing the Pass

Lao Tzu (60-470 BC), named Li Er, was a famous philosopher in the Spring and Autumn Period, and is considered as the founder and patriarch of Taoism, in which he popular known as Senior Lord Taishang (Absolutely Superior). His main proposition was “non-action,” which has exerted important influence on China’s politics, philosophy and culture for several thousand years.

It was said that Lao Tzu had once been Confucius’ teacher. Confucius learned a lot from him, especially about the correct philosophy of life. Gradually, the prominent student surpassed his teacher in some areas, and Lao Tzu thought it was not good both for Confucius and himself; so he decided to leave and go west. Riding on a green ox, he arrived at Hangu Pass (today’s southwest of Lingbao, Henan Province). The official in charge, learning Lao Tzu was coming, hurried to stop him. Lao Tzu was invited to give a speech to the officials and soldiers in the pass, but his ideas were too profound to be understood. Then the chief official asked him to write down what he just had said, so that they could have a careful study about his philosophy later. Lao Tzu wrote a piece of over 5,000 characters overnight, and the next morning, he handed it over to the chief, and left. Having crossed the pass, he continued to go west. According to old sayings, the piece, which he had written overnight became known as the *Tao-te Ching* (also *Classic of the Way and Virtue*), a Taoist masterpiece that has been studied generation after generation by scholars and one of the most widely translated Chinese work.

暮春时节，大观园里群芳尽谢，微风一吹，残花落瓣满地滚动。黛玉见此情景，便一人肩扛花锄，手提花帚，打扫落英。在园中，正好碰见宝玉在看《西厢记》。两人正在嬉闹，袭人跑来叫走了宝玉。黛玉便回潇湘馆去。走到一堵院墙外，忽听笛韵悠扬，歌声婉转，原来是戏班正在排练《牡丹亭》。黛玉停下脚步，细细倾听，又见眼前残红遍地，顺水飘流，落英缤纷，随风而去，不觉牵动心肠，想到寄人篱下的凄苦以及和宝玉受到压抑的爱情，触景生情，潸然落泪。这时，香菱路过这里，便接过黛玉手中的花帚，把她送回了潇湘馆。

《牡丹亭》艳曲警芳心

The Peony Pavilion Breaking a Delicate Heart

In late spring, flowers in the Grand View Garden began to wither; and when the breeze came, petals spread all over the ground. Seeing this, Lin Daiyu carried a small hue and a broom, and set out to collect these petals and bury them into a "grave". She happened to meet Jia Baoyu who was reading *the Romance of the West Chamber* in a garden. She laid down her gredening tools and began to read, and then frolicked with Baoyu. At this time, Xiren, one of Baoyu's maids, came to call Baoyu away. With Baoyu gone and other girls evidently all out, Daiyu suddenly feel lonely and depressed, and had to back to her Bamboo Lodge.

On the way, when she was passing a wall, she heard a melodious flute playing and poignant singing. It was a troupe rehearsing drama. Daiyu stopped, and quietly listened to it. She was an emotional girl, and the drama lyrics moved her to the depth of her being. The petals, which fell all over the ground and were trampled by feet or dropped on the stream and were carried away by water, aroused her sorrow for her life experience: losing both her parents during childhood, taking shelter in the house of others', as well as suppressing her love with Baoyu. And she could't help weeping. At that moment, a maid named Xiangling passed by, she helped Daiyu carry the broom, and walked her to the Bamboo Lodge.

A drawing of The Peony Pavilion Breaking a Delicate Heart

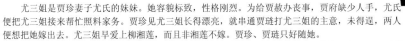

尤三姐是贾珍妻子尤氏的妹妹。她容貌标致，性格刚烈。为给贾赦办丧事，贾府缺少人手，尤氏便把尤三姐接来帮忙照料家务。贾珍见尤三姐长得漂亮，就串通贾琏打尤三姐的主意，未得逞，两人便想把她嫁出去。尤三姐早爱上柳湘莲，而且非湘莲不嫁。贾珍、贾琏只好随她。

一日，贾琏碰到柳湘莲，向他说了婚事，湘莲一口应允，解下“鸳鸯剑”作信物。尤三姐见到剑喜出望外。几个月以后，湘莲见到宝玉问起尤三姐的来历，当他听说三姐竟然在宁国府中，便找贾琏退婚。尤三姐知道湘莲一定是把她当作下流人物，一手把剑递给湘莲，一手按住剑柄，自刎身亡。湘莲悔恨不已，放声痛哭。他浑浑噩噩行至一座破庙前，看见门前坐着一个道士。湘莲抽出宝剑，断发出家。

尤三姐自刎

You Sanjie Committing Suicide

You Sanjie was the younger sister of Jia Zhen's (Jia Baoyu's cousin) wife. She was attractive and open-minded in appearance but strong and pretentious in character. It was during Jia She's (Grandmother Jia's eldest son) funeral that she came to help deal with daily chores. Jia Zhen was attracted to her, and collaborating with his cousin Jian Lian, they tried to get her, but failed. Then the two intended to marry her to another man. However, You Sanjie, who had already fallen in love with Liu Xianglian (an actor), swore that she would not marry anyone other than Liu. Having learned of her determination, Jia Zhen and Jia Lian had to follow her choice.

One day, Jia Lian met Liu Xianglian, and proposed to him in You Sanjie's stead. Liu accepted the proposal, and asked Jia Lian to give his Mandarin Duck Swords to the lady as proof of his love (Mandarin Ducks are a cultural symbol of Chinese long-term love). On seeing the sword, Sanjie was ecstatic. A few months later, Liu Xianglian met Jia Baoyu, and asked after the origins of Sanjie. When Liu Xianglian learned Sanjie was staying in the notorious Jia's mansions, he went to cancel the engagement. Sanjie knew that he must have heard some gossip in the Jia's mansions which led him to believe her a shameless wanton, and suddenly cut her throat with the Mandarin Duck Swords when she handed them to Liu Xianglian. It was all over in a moment. In great repentance, Liu Xianglian passed out. He never thought she was so chaste. Waking up, he found himself in front of an old temple, and a Taoist sitting by the gate. Liu cut off his hair with the swords, and became a Taoist for the rest of his life.

刘备、张飞夜劫曹寨，不料兵败，各自奔走，关羽守城。曹操一直想使关羽归顺自己，便采纳了谋士程昱的计谋。次日，曹操令刘备手下降兵混入城去，作为内应。又使夏侯惇引诱关羽出战，然后诈败而走。关羽引兵退到土山上歇息之时，被曹兵团团围住。

此时，曹操部将张辽上山，劝关羽投降，一不负桃园结义之盟誓，二可保刘备的两个夫人的安全，三则待有了刘备音信后，和刘备共扶汉室。关羽听了，提出三约：一是只降汉帝，不降曹操；二是赡养刘备的两位夫人；第三，若知刘备去向，便当辞去。这三者缺一不可，若曹操能从，他即归降。张辽回报曹操，曹操应允，待关羽甚厚——赐宴席、赏美女、封公侯，但这些都未能动摇关羽对刘备的感情。后来，关羽打听到刘备的下落，便毫不犹豫地前去投奔。

屯土山关公约三事

Three Conditions of Guan Yu's Compromise

Liu Bei and Zhang Fei launched a night attack on Cao Cao's army, but were defeated, and had to escape, leaving Guan Yu in charge of the city's defense. Cao Cao had been longing to summon Guan Yu to surrender. The next day, according to his counselor Cheng Yu's scheme, Cao Cao ordered Liu Bei's former soldiers to enter the city serving as spies; then he dispatched Xiahou Dun, a famous general, to challenge Guan Yu and pretend to be defeated, seducing Guan and his main force out of the city. After Guan Yu and his troop retreated onto a hill to rest, they were totally surrounded by Cao Cao's troops.

The following morning, when Guan Yu planned to break through, Zhang Liao, one of Cao's generals, came over and tried to persuade Guan Yu to surrender, and elaborated three reasons: one was that it did not break the brotherhood promise made with Liu Bei and Zhang Fei; the second was that it would ensure the safety of Liu Bei's two wives; and the third was that after he learned Liu Bei's whereabouts, Guan Yu could still help him to restore the Han Dynasty. Guan Yu responded with a compromise of three articles: first, in name, he subordinated to the Emperor of the Han Dynasty not Cao Cao; second, Liu Bei's two wives were to be suitably provided for and should only be looked after by him; third, all three would leave to seek Liu Bei once they found out his whereabouts. The three above should be all implemented simultaneously. Zhang Liao reported to Cao Cao. Cao eventually approved. He showered Guan Yu with many gifts, sent him beauties and promised high posts, but never changed his loyalty to Liu Bei. Later, as Guan Yu learned Liu Bei's whereabouts, he left for him without hesitation.

陷空山上有一个老鼠精，她见唐僧仪表堂堂，便用尽办法抢来成婚。悟空等三人找到妖精的洞穴一无底洞，悟空遂变作小虫，飞进去打探，留下八戒和沙僧把守洞口。看见女妖正在劝唐僧与她喝酒成亲，悟空变作一只飞虫落入酒土¬中，被女妖看见，泼了出去。悟空大怒，变成一只老鹰，掀翻桌子，搅乱了酒席。悟空又变回小蝇，飞到唐僧耳边，低声告诉唐僧他的计谋。

唐僧依计行事，请女妖到花园散步，并摘下一个桃子递给女妖。女妖以为唐僧回心转意，欢天喜地地吞食下去；片刻，肚子疼痛难忍。原¬来桃子是悟空变的。女妖只好放出唐僧。刚出洞口，唐僧又被捉走。悟空又进洞中，没找到师父，却见到托塔李天王和哪吒牌位。悟空便找玉帝。玉帝命李天王父子收服老鼠精，放出唐僧。

无底洞

Bottomless Cave

A mouse spirit dwelled in the Pitfall Mountain. Seeing Tang Seng was handsome, the mouse spirit captured Tang Seng as her husband. The three brothers traced the monster to a deep and bottomless cave. The Monkey King then turned into a fly and entered the cave, leaving his two brothers guarding the entrance. He saw the she-devil forcing his master to drink and marry her. Then he transformed into a tiny insect and flew under the bubbles in wine cup of the monster, waiting for her gulping him down into her belly. However, the she-devil saw the insect and flicked it away. The Monkey King flew into a rage, and immediately turned himself into an eagle and swooped down on the spirit. The dinner table was overturned, and the spirit was gravely shocked. Then the Monkey King turned back into a small fly, flew to Tang Seng, and whispered some words into his ear. Tang Seng then invited the spirit to take a walk in the garden. He plucked a peach for her, and the spirit was happy. When she was just biting, the peach, however, rolled straight down her throat into her stomach. In fact, the peach was changed by the Monkey King, who was inside her belly now, tearing her stomach, ripping her guts, and shouting, "Let my master go, and I will spare your life."

The spirit had to set Tang Seng free. Just outside of the cave, the Monkey King jumped out of the spirit's mouth, and began to hit her with his cudgel. Bajie and Monk Sha also came to help, leaving Tang Seng unprotected. The spirit spotted the chance and took Tang Seng away again. The Monkey King entered the cave a second time, but couldn't find his master. He saw sacrificial altars for the Heavenly King Li and Prince Nezha. So he turned to the Jade Emperor for help, who then sent the Heavenly King Li to subdue the spirit, who actually was his foster daughter, and rescue Tang Seng.

杨玉环天生丽质，姿容绝艳。16岁时被选进王府，做了妃子，很快被唐玄宗召入皇宫，立为贵妃。玄宗经常和贵妃游于骊山宫，每次贵妃都要在华清池沐浴。出浴的贵妃皮肤嫩而柔滑，妩媚百生。

后来，安禄山、史思明叛乱，唐玄宗带着贵妃，率文武百官弃京出逃。大军行至马嵬坡，文武百官不肯前进，非要唐玄宗赐死杨贵妃。玄宗无奈，只得挥泪赐绢贵妃，请她自缢。安史之乱平息后，玄宗重回长安，他整日沉浸在对贵妃的思念和感伤之中，最终忧郁而死。贵妃沐浴华清池的情节，在玄宗与杨贵妃的爱情悲剧故事中，占着十分重要的位置，所以，成为民间艺人和画家偏爱的题材。

贵妃出浴华清池

Lady Yang Bathing in the Huaqing Pool

Concubine Yang Yuhuan was one of the Four Beauties in ancient China. Her beauty was naturally attractive. She was selected as a concubine at the age of 16, and soon was summoned to the imperial palace by Emperor Xuanzong of Tang (reigned 712-756), becoming the Honorable Concubine. Emperor Xuanzong and Concubine Yang used to stroll in the Lishan Palace (in today's Shaanxi Province), and each time, Concubine Yang would take a bath in the Huaqing Pool inside the palace. It was said that she was at her most beautiful state when she got out of the pool – her skin was fresh and smooth, and her figure was plump and well-proportioned, as if she was a lotus shooting out of the water and the beauty was too hard to describe by words.

Later, An Lushan and Shi Siming rebelled against the court. Emperor Xuanzong was forced to escape from the capital Chang'an along with Concubine Yang and the officials of the court. But when they came to the Mawei Slope (in the west of present-day Xingping County, Shaanxi Province), the army was reluctant to carry on the journey – they thought it was Concubine Yang who were responsible for the country's upheaval, and they petitioned the emperor to kill her. The Emperor had to endow his concubine with a piece of white brocade, and in tears, he asked her to strangle herself. After suppressing the rebellion, Emperor Xuanzong returned to the capital, but at the thought that his favorite concubine could no longer bathe in the Huaqing Pool, he missed her greatly. He died in depression and loneliness in the end. Because Concubine Yang bathing in the Huaqing Pool was the main ingredient in the tragic love story between Emperor Xuanzong and his concubine, many folk artists and painters frequently incorporated it into their works.

苏武（前140～60年）是汉武帝时的中郎将，统领皇帝的侍卫。公元前100年，匈奴政权新单于即位，汉朝皇帝为了表示友好，派遣苏武出使匈奴。不料被扣留。单于想让苏武臣服于匈奴，辅以朝政，派人向苏武游说，并许以高官厚禄，苏武严辞拒绝。劝说无用，单于就用酷行逼迫苏武屈服。严冬大雪纷飞，单于命人把苏武关入地窖，断食绝水，苏武渴了就吃雪，饿了就啃破皮带和羊皮碎片。见苏武仍不肯屈服，单于就把他流放到荒无人烟的西伯利亚的贝加尔湖一带去牧羊。苏武每天拿着这根使节棒放羊，日夜期盼有一天能够拿着使节棒回到自己的国家。19年后，匈奴和汉朝和好，苏武最终回到自己的国家，百姓倾城而出，潸然泪下。

苏武牧羊

Su Wu Shepherding in the Wild

Su Wu (140-60 BC) was a commander of royal guards during the reign of Emperor Wu of Han (reigned 141-87 BC). In 100 BC, a new Chanyu (chief of the Hun Regime) came to the throne. In order to show friendliness, Emperor Wu dispatched a team of envoys led by Su Wu to pay a visit to the Hun Regime. Unfortunately, they were detained. Chanyu wanted Su Wu to subordinate to his regime and help him deal with national affairs. He promised a high rank and rich rewards, and sent many people to persuade Su, but Su Wu firmly refused.

A portrait of Su Wu

Having learned that those persuasions did not have an effect on Su, Chanyu intended to force him to submit. He had Su Wu locked in a cell and did not give him water or food, while Su Wu ate snow when he was thirsty and bit his leather belt and clothes when he was hungry. His stubbornness further angered Chanyu, who later exiled him to be a shepherd by Lake Baikal in the Siberian wilderness. Every day, Su Wu shepherded with his envoy stick, and expected some day in the future, he could carry this stick to his motherland. 19 years passed, the Hun and the Han established a friendly relationship, and Su Wu was eventually able to return to his motherland. When he arrived at the capital, all the residents went out to welcome him in tears.

相传宋朝时，有个叫王华的人，为人老实厚道。有一天，王华见一群人围着一个老头。那老头高喊："谁买我做爹，将来能富贵。"周围的人有的嘲笑，有的谩骂，有的用石头砸他。王华见老人穿得破旧，很可怜他，便拨开众人，挤上前去，恭恭敬敬地对老头叫了一声："爹"，然后就带着老人回家了。一到家，王华就亲自伺候老人梳洗、换衣；然后又把孩子叫出来，让他们认了爷爷。王华每次打鱼回来，总要拣出最鲜最嫩的鱼留给老人；媳妇在家做饭，也总是把最好的东西端给老人吃。画中就是王华夫妇在家里服侍老人的情景。一天，老人交给王华一块写得密密麻麻的白绫，让他带着老婆孩子按白绫上写的地址去找他，说完老人就走了。王华一路寻找打听，最后来到了都城开封。进了皇宫，他才知道那个老人就是宋太祖赵匡胤的弟弟赵光义。善良的王华过上了荣华富贵的生活。

王华买父

Wang Hua Buying a Father

It was said that in the Song Dynasty (960-1279), there lived an honest and kind fisherman, Wang Hua, who lost his parents in his childhood. One day, on his way home after selling his fish, he saw an old man in a crowd yelling, "Anyone who buy me as his father will be rich in the future." People surrounding him poured scorn at his words. They began to abuse the old man, and some even threw stones at him. Seeing such a piteous scene, Wang Hua had sympathy for the old man; he got into the crowd, went over to him, and humbly called him, "Father." Then he took the old man home. He helped the old man wash and dress up, and called upon his kids to recognize the old man as their grandfather.

Each time after fishing, Wang Hua always left the freshest and most delicious fish for the old man, and on the dinner table, his family always fed the best food to the old man too. The scene in this painting is about the couple serving the old man at their home. Thus a few months went by. One day, the old man gave Wang a piece of white brocade, on which lots of characters were written. He told Wang to look for him along with his wife and kids according to the address written on the brocade, and then he went away. Afterwards, Wang Hua and his family probed their way to the capital city, Kaifeng (in today's Henan Province), and then to the royal palace. Eventually, they found that the old man was Emperor Taizu's brother, Zhao Guangyi (later Emperor Taizong of Song, reigned 976-997), who was now a noble prince. The good-hearted Wang Hua eventually led a wealthy life.

这幅画是根据唐代诗人杜甫的《客至》一诗画的。画中那个持笤帚的就是杜甫。杜甫忧国忧民、诗艺精湛，有"诗圣"的尊号，与李白齐名。诗歌内容多是描述社会动荡、政治黑暗和人民疾苦。他将博大精深的思想内容和细致入微的表现方法相结合，形成了"沉郁顿挫"的独特风格。他的许多脍炙人口的诗篇，成为历代画师们的创作题材。杜甫隐居在成都草堂时，交游冷淡。有一天，崔县令路过这里，特地来看望他。杜甫喜不自禁，欣然挥笔写了这首诗。大意是这样的：江村的生活，无比寂寞，除了群鸥，难得贵客临门。满是花草的小路，从来不曾为了迎接客人打扫过，今天为您敞开茅屋的大门。远离市镇，没有很好的酒菜，如果您愿意和邻居小酌，就让我隔着篱笆招呼他过来一起共饮。诗写出了杜甫的喜悦心情和平日清寂、简朴的生活。

：花径不曾缘客扫，蓬门今始为君开：

The Flowery Path Has Never Been Swept for the Arrival of Guests; While My Humble Door Is Opened Broadly for You Now.

The person holding a broom in the painting is Du Fu (712-770). Du Fu, as a famous patriotic poet, was always concerned about the country and the people. His character was noble, and his mastery of poetic composition was excellent. He was enshrined as the Sage of Poetry, rivaling Li Bai in China's literary history. He lived in the period when the prosperity of the Tang Dynasty began its decline, and his poems were mostly about social upheaval, political corruption, and the plight of the downtrodden. With profound significance and delicate expressions, he formed a unique style of Rhythmic Profundity. Many of his famous poems have become the source of artistic creation in paintings.

He used to live in a farmhouse in the suburbs of Chengdu, Sichuan Province, and had few acquaintances. One day, the magistrate paid a visit to him. He was so delighted that he wrote this poem. The probable meaning of the poem is that living in a village by the river, the poet felt extremely lonely and took the gulls as his companions; so it had been unnecessary for him to clean up his path, which was covered with flowers and grass. But today, he opened the gate of his farmhouse broadly for the arrival of the magistrate. Far from the town, he had no delicacies to offer; and if the noble guest wanted to have a drink with his neighbor, he would be delighted to invite him to hold a humble dinner. The poem reflects Du Fu's delightfulness as well as his simple and lonely daily life.

故事与《三碗不过冈》相连。约行了四五里路，武松见一棵大树被刮去了一块树皮，上面写着两行字，大意是景阳冈有老虎伤人，过往客商应结伴成队过冈。武松不以为意，只当是酒店老板的诡计，欲骗客人去他的酒家借宿。日落时分，武松提着哨棒，大踏步来到冈上，行至一个破庙，在庙门上看到了官府的告示，才相信冈上确实有老虎。这时武松想转身回酒家，又怕店主人嘲笑武松胆小，非英雄好汉。于是继续行路，走了一阵，酒力发作，武松踉踉跄跄地找了块石头，准备仰身躺下。

忽然一阵狂风呼啸，一只猛虎跳了出来，武松大吃一惊，酒也醒了。看到猛虎朝自己扑过来，武松翻身，闪到老虎背后；老虎侧身一掀，武松向旁边一让，躲了过去；老虎逮不着武松，急了，竖起尾巴一剪，武松飞身跳开。一连三次，老虎扑了空，力气也消了一半。武松趁老虎刚翻过身来，举起

武松打虎

Wu Song Beating the Tiger

The story is followed by the *Three Bowls of Wine and You Can't Cross the Ridge* at page 70. Wu Song didn't believe what the tavern owner told him and left for Jingyang Ridge. Soon after Wu Song saw a sign posted on a tree, which read, "Travelers are advised to go in groups over this mountain, especially at night, as the tiger here have taken several lives. Please don't take risk of your life." Wu Song reasoned that it must have been written by the tavern owner who tried to scare customers into spending the night at his tavern. So he didn't pay attention to it and simply continued on his way.

At sunset Wu Song reached an old temple and on the door there was an official announcement posted about hunting for tiger. Just then Wu Song realized and believed that there was indeed a tiger on the ridge. However he still wasn't willing to return to the tavern for fear that the owner would laugh at him a coward. After walking on for a moment, Wu Song felt too drunk to continue, so he found a stone, left his cudgel beside, clambered onto its flat surface and prepared to have a sleep.

Just then, a gust of wind whistled and a mammoth tiger jumped at him. At this sight Wu Song was shocked and awaken, and managed to dodge behind the tiger, which leapt again but fanned the air. Wu Song evaded it successfully. The tiger flew into a rage. With a thunderous roar, the tiger swept toward Wu Song with its tail. Wu Song jumped to avoid the attack. After several scary moments, the tiger effectively exhausted most of its strength. Before the tiger turned around, Wu Song seized the opportunity, lifted his cudgel, and hit toward its head with all his strength. However, he hit a branch of an old tree instead of the tiger. And the cudgel was snapped in two. The tiger then

哨棒，对准虎头劈了下去，不料却打在了树上，老虎性急，朝武松又扑了过来，武松扔掉半截哨棒，一个箭步跳到老虎背上，左手揪住老虎的顶花皮，右手攥拳猛打。直到老虎的眼、嘴、鼻、耳都迸出鲜血，趴在地上，没了力气，武松方才罢手。

这时武松也筋疲力尽，坐在青石上歇一会，便朝冈下走去。正走间，又遇两只“老虎”，武松定睛一看，原来时两个披着老虎皮的猎人，因老虎已伤害多条人命，前来埋伏、捕猎，当猎人听武松说老虎已经被他打死的时候，半信半疑。武松随后领着猎人上山见了老虎的尸体，猎人方才相信。当众人得知武松赤手空拳打死了老虎时，无不高兴欢呼。武松为众人除了害，被誉为“打虎英雄”，名声大震。

武松打虎

launched another attack. Wu Song threw away the bits of his cudgel and jumped on to the back of the tiger. With his left hand, he grabbed the skin of the tiger's head and struck out at its eyes, mouth, nose and ears with his right hand. The tiger struggled frantically, but later lay prostrate on the ground and expired. Wu Song didn't stop swinging until the tiger's eyes, mouth, nose, and ears blooded heavily and eventually died.

Wu Song also felt very tired after this, and took a rest on the stone. Then Wu Song continued to walk down toward the foot of the ridge so as not to be hit by more tigers. Just then he met two "tigers" and he gazed. In fact, they were two hunters in tiger's clothing. Because the tiger had already taken many lives, they came to ambush and hunt for it. When asked if Wu Song had seen the tiger, Wu Song replied that the tiger had been beaten to death by him. The hunters did not believe it until Wu Song led them to see the tiger's corpse. When everyone was informed that Wu Song had single-handedly killed the tiger, they were all happy with cheers. They deemed Wu Song as their heroes for his brave and beneficial deed for people.

文王见武吉没来投案，掐指一算，得知他已投河自尽，便不再追究。有一次，周文王外出打猎，在溪边却遇见武吉。他十分诧异，下令将武吉拿下；武吉以实情相告。文王听说有此奇人，又惊又喜。虽然文王手下有不少文臣武将，可是他认为还缺少一个能够统筹全局的人帮他筹划灭商大计。文王忙令武吉带路去找子牙。在和子牙的谈话中，周文王发现子牙是一个眼光远大、学问渊博的人。他上通天文，下知地理，对政治、军事各方面都很有研究，特别是对于当时的政治形势，分析得头头是道。文王恳切地希望子牙能帮助他治理国家，并邀请他和自己一同上车，回到都城。子牙果然没有辜负文王期望，在文王去世后，他辅佐文王的儿子周武王灭了商朝，建立了周朝。

文王访贤

King Wen Visiting a Prominent Leader

King Wen was also a famous Chinese ancient fortune-teller; he believed that Wu Ji made a hole in the water and leading his army left the city. Although many brilliant generals and ministers followed him, he felt none of them could oversee from a general perspective and help him make a major strategy to destroy the Shang Dynasty; so he always held onto a need to visit the prominent thinkers.

One day, King Wen went hunting. To his surprise, he saw Wu Ji at the river bank several days later and ordered his soldiers to catch Wu Ji on the spot. Wu Ji then told the truth to King Wen, who was pleasantly surprised when he heard about the talent of Ziya. He instantly realized that Ziya might be a great genius and would be helpful to his career, so he released Wu Ji and asked him to lead the way to find Ziya. By a stream, King Wen encountered Jiang Ziya.

In their conversation, the King found Ziya was a man of broad vision and profound knowledge and was learned in astronomy and geography, and had done detailed studies in politics and military strategy; especially contemporary politics which he analyzed clearly in a quite reasonable way. King Wen sincerely asked Jiang Shang to help him deal with state affairs, and took him on his carriage to the capital city. King Wen made Ziya Prime Minister, and he never failed to live up to King Wen's expections, and his loyalty and farsightedness in governing spread his fame throughout China. In the fourth year after King Wen died (1046 BC), Ziya assisted King Wu, the son of King Wen, to overthrow King Zhou of Shang and established a new dynasty – the Zhou Dynasty (1046 -256 BC).

书生刘彦昌赴京赶考，途经圣母庙，见圣母像美貌非凡，触动情思，在圣母的飘带上写下了自己爱慕之情的诗句。圣母为刘彦昌的衷情所动，遂不顾天条禁令，下凡与刘彦昌结为夫妻。一年之后，圣母生下男婴，取名沉香。夫妻恩爱，生活美满。圣母的哥哥二郎神闻妹妹与凡人结合，残忍地将圣母压在华山脚下，拆散了这个幸福美满的家庭。霹雳大仙见沉香可怜，救走沉香，教他武艺，并传授法术给他。15年后，沉香长大成人，霹雳大仙便把圣母的遭遇告诉沉香。沉香知道自己的身世后，悲痛万分，执意要去华山救母，大仙给他一把开山神斧。沉香先到二郎庙找舅舅二郎神，苦苦哀求舅舅放了母亲。二郎神非但不肯，还举起三尖两刃刀向沉香砍来，沉香抡起神斧，二人对打起来，最终打败了二郎神。沉香来到华山脚下，举起神斧，猛劈过去，华山顿时裂开，母子相会，夫妻团圆。

劈山救母

Chenxiang Leveling a Mountain to Rescue His Mother

A scholar named Liu Yanchang went to the capital city to attend the Imperial Examinations. He stopped by the Temple of the Holy Mother, and was attracted by the Holy Mother's extraordinary beauty, falling in love with her. He wrote some poetic sentences in the temple, which showed his admiration of her. The Holy Mother was moved by his deep love, went to the secular world, and married him. One year later, they gave birth to a boy named Chenxiang. The family lived in peace and happiness.

Yang Jian, a Chinese God with a third true-seeing eye in the middle of his forehead, who was the elder brother of the Holy Mother, was furious to learn his sister married a mortal being. He brutally trapped the Holy Mother under Huashan Mountain, and destroyed the happy family. The Great Immortal of Thunder lamented Chenxiang's pitiful situation; he took him as his disciple, and taught him martial arts and witchcraft. 15 years later, Chenxiang grew up. The Great Immortal of Thunder told the unfortunate experience of the Holy Mother to him. On learning his origin, Chenxiang was agitated, and he was determined to go to Huashan Mountain and save his mother. His master gave him a giant ax to level the mountain. Chenxiang went to the Temple of Yang Jian at first, and he sincerely begged his uncle to release his mother. Yang Jian, however, not only did not approve his nephew's application, but also attacked him with his Three-Point Double-Blade Knife. The two had a good fight, and eventually Chenxiang defeated his uncle. Then he went to Huashan Mountain, and leveled with his giant ax. The family finally had a happy reunion.

蒋干是曹操手下的谋士，自荐过江劝降周瑜。周瑜闻讯，猜出蒋干来意，亲出迎接并设盛宴款待。席间，周瑜吩咐，只准共叙朋友旧交，若有人提起周瑜与曹操的双方战事，即刻斩首。”蒋干听了，面色如土。周瑜又传令奏乐，开怀畅饮，喝得酩酊大醉。宴罢，蒋干扶着周瑜回到帐中，周瑜朦胧睡去。蒋干见周瑜鼾声如雷，便摸到桌前，拿起一叠文书偷看起来。正翻着，忽见里面有一封书信，细看却是曹操的水军都督蔡瑁、张允写给周瑜的降书。蒋干看罢，大吃一惊，慌忙把信藏在衣内。清晨，蒋干回到曹营向曹操禀报。其实，周瑜知道曹军中只有蔡、张二将精通水战，便设下反间计，欲借曹操之手除此二人。曹操果真上当，杀掉了蔡、张二将。待曹操省悟过来，为时已晚。结果，赤壁一战，曹操水军一败涂地。

蒋干盗书

Jiang Gan Stealing a Letter

Jiang Gan, a counselor to Cao Cao, recommended himself to persuade Zhou Yu to surrender. On learning it, Zhou Yu easily perceived his intention, went out to welcome him, and held a feast to entertain Jiang. During the banquet, Zhou Yu order, “Today we meet only as friends and speak only of friendship, and if anyone shall begin a discussion of the questions at issue between Cao Cao and us, he would be slew.” Jiang Gan was scared at hearing that, and his face turned gray.

After the banquet, Zhou Yu pretended to be drunk and showed Jiang Gan around his camp. The he fell asleep. Jiang Gan could not sleep peacefully and he crept out of bed, sneaked to Zhou Yu’s desk, and browsed through Zhou’s documents. Then he saw a letter addressed to Zhou from Cai Mao and Zhang Yun, both being Cao Cai’s marine force commanders. Jiang read the letter and was shocked when he found out that Cai and Zhang were planning to kill Cao Cao and surrender to Zhou Yu. He hurried to hide the letter inside his clothes.

In the early morning, Jiang Gan snuck back to the Cao army encampment, and reported the important military secret to Cao Cao; the latter ordered the two generals to be executed immediately. However, it was actually a trick set by Zhou Yu aiming to push Cao Cao to kill them – the two generals excelled in commanding marine battles. Cao Cao fell into the trap, but when he realized the situation, it was too late. This resulted in the failure of his marine forces in the Battle at Chibi.

这是关于西晋文学家张翰避祸保身、托辞退隐的故事。张翰，吴郡（今江苏苏州）人，为人处事，纵任不拘。他曾作过朝廷的命官，但看到政治黑暗，想到家乡的美味—莼（一种蔬菜）羹和鲈脍（鲈鱼片），便弃官回乡。回到家乡后，张翰或举杯饮酒，或挥毫作文，或浪迹名山，或寻访渔樵。

他的故事流传很广，许多文人在文章、诗词中都曾从不同的角度引用过张翰这个典故。唐朝诗人李白在《秋下荆门》一诗中表达自己是离乡远去，不是像张翰那样为了想吃家乡的鲈鱼脍而回家乡。南宋杰出的爱国词人辛弃疾在一首《水龙吟》中抒发自己恢复中原的意愿不能实现，一腔忠愤。但他不愿意学张翰那样忘情时事，为了“莼羹鲈脍”而弃官返乡。而宋代诗人戴复古的诗句“功名未必胜鲈鱼”最准确地表现了张翰回乡的本来意义。

：功名未必胜鲈鱼：

The Official Title Is Not Worthier Than the Weever Chips

This is a story about Zhang Han who made an excuse about resigning so as to avoid trouble and protect himself from dark rule and wars in the Western Jin Dynasty (265-316). Zhang Han, a native of Wujun (present-day Suzhou, Jiangsu), used to be an official in the court, but the prevalent political corruption disappointed him. He missed the delicacies of his hometown – the Chun (a sort of vegetable) skilly and weever chips (local delicacies), so he resigned and went back to his hometown. From then, he drank wine, composed essays, traveled to famous mountains, and visited fishermen and woodsmen. He had never sought fame but rather wanted to live his life to the fullest.

His story was widespread in literary circles, and “Going home to eat weever chips” became a literary allusion. Many men of letters cited his story into their works showing various perspectives. Li Bai (701-762), the most renowned poet in the Tang Dynasty (618-907), expressed in his poem *I Went down to Jinmen in Autumn*, his feelings of leaving from his hometown, not like Zhang Han’s going back to his hometown because of missing the “weever chips”. Xin Qiji (1140-1207), a famous patriotic lyrical poet in the Southern Song Dynasty (1127-1279), expressed his loyalty to the country and the resentment for being unable to recover some lost territories in central China as well as his unwillingness to act on national affairs after Zhang Han, who missed “the Chun skilly and the weever chips” and left national business untended. The sentence, “The official title is not worthier than the weever chips,” by Dai Fugu (1167-?), a poet in the Song Dynasty, is probably the most accurate expression of the purpose of Zhang Han’s resignation.

丝竹，是我国民间弦乐器和竹管乐器的总称，包括笛、萧、二胡、琴、琵琶等；亦可泛指音乐。

东晋著名的政治家谢安，做官之前曾在东山（今浙江上虞县南）隐居。朝廷几次召用，他都不去就职，每天只是带着乐器游玩于山水之间。他走到哪里，音乐丝竹之声就响到哪里。因此，人们把他带着乐器游玩的事，叫做“东山丝竹”。

直到40岁时，谢安出山从政。383年，前秦苻坚率军南侵。谢安指挥弟弟谢石、侄子谢玄等领兵8万拒敌于淝水，以少胜多，大破前秦90万大军，夺得了著名的“淝水之战”的大捷，保卫了东晋王朝，可谓名噪一时。但后来谢安却因皇族猜忌相争，被剥夺了实权，抑郁而死。谢安一生，爱好文学，是当时很有名气的文士。所以“东山丝竹”的典故也就不胫而走，被人们传为佳话。

东山丝竹

The Si Zhu of the East Mountain

Si Zhu (literarily, the silky bamboos), was a general address for Chinese folk music instruments, including stringed instruments and flutes, such as the flute, the two-stringed Chinese fiddle, the *qin*, *pipa*, and the vertical bamboo flute.

Xie An (320-385), a famous politician in the Eastern Jin Dynasty, used to live in seclusion in the East Mountain (south of the present-day Shangyu County, Zhejiang Province). Reluctant to take an official position, he took musical instruments and travelled among rivers and mountains, and wherever he went, there was always music playing, which folks called the Si Zhu from the East Mountain.

When Xie An was 40, he eventually set out to serve the country. In 383, Fu Jian (reigned 357-385), the founder of the Former Qin State, leading his 900,000 soldiers, invaded southern China. Xie An, prime minishter then, dispatched his younger brother, Xie Shi, and his nephew, Xie Xuan, to confront the invaders by Feishui River. Their much smaller army of just 80,000 defeated the enemy, presenting Fu Jian from destroying the Eastern Jin Dynasty and uniting China. The Battle at Feishui River was a well-known case that a smaller defeated a larger army in China's history. Later, however, Xie An was involved in the tussles among the royal powers; he was deprived of political power, and died from depression. Xie An loved literature all his life, and was a reputable man of letters then. His story, the Si Zhu from the East Mountain, has been widely shared among Chinese people.

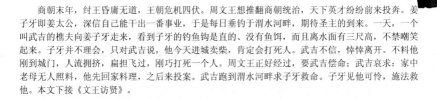

商朝末年，纣王昏庸无道，王朝危机四伏。周文王想推翻商朝统治，天下英才纷纷前来投奔。姜子牙即姜太公，深信自己能干出一番事业，于是每日垂钓于渭水河畔，期待圣主的到来。一天，一个叫武吉的樵夫向姜子牙走来，看到子牙的钓鱼钩是直的、没有鱼饵，而且离水面有三尺高，不禁嘲笑起来。子牙并不理会，只对武吉说，他今天进城卖柴，肯定会打死人。武吉不信，悻悻离开。不料他刚到城门，人流拥挤，扁担飞过，刚巧打死一个人。周文王正好经过，要武吉偿命；武吉哀求：家中老母无人照料，他先回家料理，之后来投案。武吉跑到渭水河畔求子牙救命。子牙见他可怜，施法救他。本文下接《文王访贤》。

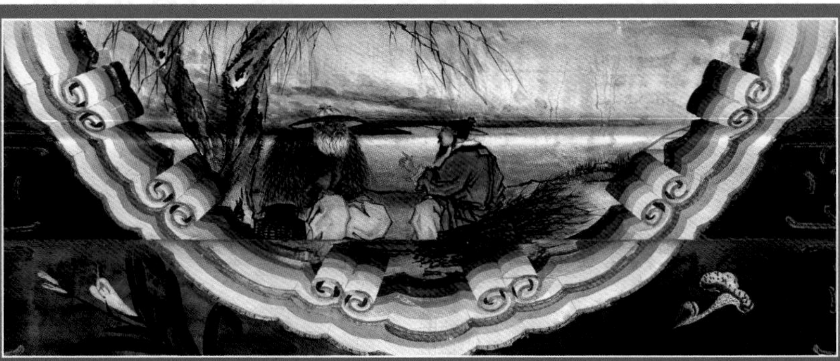

姜太公钓鱼

Lord Jiang Casting a Line

Toward the end of the Shang Dynasty (1600-1046 BCE), the country was going to rack and ruin due to the pruriency and barbarity of King Zhou of Shang (the last king of the Shang Dynasty). A state named Zhou, by the Weihe River, began to rise. The king of Zhou State was Ji Chang, namely King Wen of Zhou. He was waiting for his chance to overturn King Zhou of Shang and many people were willing to follow him. Jiang Ziya, i.e. Lord Jiang, believing that he could hew out a career, fished by the river every day to wait for wise and able king's coming. One day a woodsman named Wu Ji walked toward Ziya and couldn't help laughing when he saw the way of Ziya's fishing: the fishing hook was actually not a hook at all but was straight, without bait and hanging about a meter high over the water surface. However Ziya said, "I fish here just expecting the wise and able king to arrive rather than the quality of the fish." Wu Ji figured Ziya was just bragging; he did not believe a word he said. Ziya saw through Wu Ji's thoughts and said, "You're wrong; I forecast that you'll kill a person when you sell your wood in the city." Wu Ji walked away unhappily.

It was heavily crowded in the city. And a person actually died from the force of Wu Ji's iron shoulder-pole just when King Wen passed by. Then Wu Ji was taken into custody and required to repay the life for the dead person. Wu Ji knelt down to implore, "I should die, but my old mother is at home with nobody taking care of her, so please allow me to attend to her first and then I'll give myself up." The king agreed. At the thought of Ziya's words, Wu Ji rushed to the bank to beg for help. Taking sympathy on Wu Ji, Ziya then created a small miracle to help Wu Ji escape death. The following story is *King Wen Visiting a Prominent Leader* at page 148.

岳飞（1103～1141年）是我国南宋时期杰出的军事家，著名的民族英雄。这一年，朝廷举行武考，岳飞应考。小梁王文武双全，有权有势。考试这天，岳飞和小梁王两人先比试文才，主考张邦昌命岳飞作“枪论”；小梁王作“刀论”。岳飞即刻而就；而小梁王左涂右改，胡乱交卷。接着比射箭，张邦昌怕岳飞再赢，便暗中差人将箭靶移至200步以外，可岳飞一连九发射中靶心，全场无不震惊，吓得小梁王不敢比弓法。最后是马上比武。可岳飞心里犯了难：小梁王是贵胄，怕万一失手，伤了他，担待不起。因此，比武场上岳飞并不还手。几个回合后，岳飞跳出阵，要求立下“生死文书”，不论哪个受伤，对方都不偿命。主考同意。岳飞心中没了顾忌，杀得小梁王闪闪躲躲。忽然，岳飞一枪，反手直刺小梁王的心窝，小梁王当场毙命。全场高声喝彩。

岳飞枪挑小梁王

Yue Fei Spearing the Prince of Liang

Yue Fei (1103-1142), born in Tangyin, Henan Province, was one of China's greatest generals and patriotic heroes who fought for the Southern Song Dynasty (1127-1279) against the Jin armies. According to legend, Yue's father was drowned in a flood when Yue Fei was just an infant. Fortunately, he and his mother survived in a water vat. After years of practice, Yue was skilled in archery and 18 branches of *Wushu* (martial arts). Then he participated in the imperial military exams. After defeating all competitors, Yue Fei met Chai Gui, the Prince of Liang.

Yue Fei won in the archery competitions by shooting a succession of nine arrows through the bull's eye of a target, although the examiners quietly moved the target farther, from 100 paces to 240 paces. Then Yue Fei fought a duel with the Prince of Liang. In the beginning, Yue Fei was seen parrying all the time without striking back because he was a commoner, and didn't dare to offend the prince. Examiners suggested the two sides make a blood pledge: the winner would not be punished even if he hurt or killed his opponent. Yue Fei's misgivings were driven out, he suddenly became a tiger. On horseback, Yue easily unmounted the Prince of Liang and then speared him through the heart.

Overcome with shock, the examiners broke their promise and arrested Yue Fei, which made all the other examinees extremely angry. Led by Yue's sworn brothers, the examinees were threatened with rebellion if they did not release Yue. The examiners had to set him free. Yue Fei was forced to flee the city but obtained a great reputation.

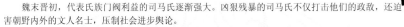

魏末晋初，代表氏族门阀利益的司马氏逐渐强大。凶狠残暴的司马氏不仅打击他们的政敌，还迫害朝野内外的文人名士，压制社会进步舆论。

文坛中的代表人物阮籍、嵇康、阮咸、山涛、向秀、王戎、刘伶七人，虽有济世扶贫、清明政治的远大抱负，但在腐败黑暗的现实面前，不仅理想破灭，自身安全也无保障。这七位朋友志同道合，情趣相仿，他们以庄子精神为寄托，每当苦闷之时，就相约畅饮，然后带上琴、棋、书、画和食物，躲进山后竹林，抚琴吟诗，放情肆志，借酒消愁，放浪形骸，企图以此逃避严酷的社会现实。人称“竹林七贤”。但是，他们并没有真正消沉下去。他们写下大量反抗司马氏黑暗统治的诗文。

竹林七贤

The Seven Sages of the Bamboo Grove

In the early Jin Dynasty (265-420), the Sima Family, representative of the aristocratic class, gradually grew more and more powerful. The ruthless family not only undermined their political opponents in court, but also attacked renowned men of letters throughout the country so as to suppress the progressive public opinion. There were seven representative figures in literary circles at that time, Ruan Ji, Ji Kang, Ruan Xian, Shan Tao, Xiang Xiu, Wang Rong, and Liu Ling.

The seven were all talented and ambitious, stressing the enjoyment of ale, personal freedom, spontaneity and a celebration of nature. But the corrupt social reality not only crushed their dreams, but also forced on them an unstable and unsafe life. They were all good friends with similar tastes and interests. In their resentfulness, they gathered together, took musical instrument, the chess board, books, and food, and hid in a bamboo grove behind a mountain near the house of Ji Kang in Shanyang (in present-day Xiuwu, Henan). They played the musical instrument and composed poems, got drunk, and tried every means to please themselves so as to stay away from the dark social reality. This was contrasted with the polotics of court. Folks called them the Seven Sages of the Bamboo Grove. However, they did not really fall into depression; they wrote many poems and essays criticizing the court and the administration, using them as weapons in the struggle against the brutal rule of the Sima Family.

The Seven Sages have been remarked to be influential in Chinese poetry, music, art and overall culture.

颐和园苏州街 SUZHOU STREET

STORIES BEHIND THE LONG CORRIDOR PAINTINGS IN THE SUMMER PALACE

《颐和园长廊彩画故事》

关羽得知刘备下落后，便按当初与曹操约定，保护着刘备的家眷，前往投奔。不料路上遭到曹兵重重阻拦与围困。各处守将都想活捉关羽，向曹操献功。关羽经东岭杀了守将孔秀；过洛阳斩了韩福和孟坦，连夜向汜水关行来。汜水关守将卞喜听说后，在关前镇国寺埋伏下刀斧手，假借宴请之名，将关羽诱至寺中，欲生擒关羽。寺内有个和尚是关羽的同乡，得知卞喜的诡计，便借送茶的机会，暗示关羽。关羽会意，命左右持刀紧随。在卞喜动手之前，关羽早已拔出剑来，一口气砍倒了数个刀斧手。卞喜见势不妙，绕廊而逃，关羽紧追不舍。卞喜取出流星锤朝关羽掷来。关羽躲过飞锤，一刀把卞喜斩成两段。谢过和尚之后，关羽护送刘备的家眷继续赶路。一路上，关羽过了五个关口，斩杀六员大将，从此名扬天下。

汜水关关羽斩卞喜

Guan Yu Killing Bian Xi at the Sishui Pass

The scene in this painting is about one of the episodes that Guan Yu broke through five passes and killed six generals. Having found out the whereabouts of Liu Bei, Guan Yu escorted Liu's family to join him, but they were blocked by Cao Cao's troops on the way. Local generals along the way all intended to kill or capture Guan Yu, so that they could get rewards and promotions from Cao Cao. Guan Yu had killed Kong Xiu, defender of Dongling Pass, and Han Fu and Meng Tan, generals in charge of Luoyang's defense, and he hurried his way through the night to Sishui Pass (north of present-day Xingyang, Henan Province). Then Bian Xi, the general guarding Sishui Pass, laid an ambush in the Zhenguo Temple near the pass. Having won Guan's trust, Bian Xi invited Guan Yu to a feast in the temple, with the purpose to take him captive.

Fortunately, a monk in the temple, who was from the same county as Guan Yu, knew Bian Xi's trick and hinted the danger to Guan Yu while serving tea to him. Guan Yu got it, and ordered his followers to carry swords and closely escort him. Before Bian Xi's killers took action, Guan Yu gained the initiative by striking the first blow. He killed several soldiers of Bian Xi, and the latter realized the situation was disadvantageous, and tried to escape out the veranda. Guan Yu went after him. Bian Xi threw a bola at Guan, but missed. Guan Yu caught up with Bian Xi and cleaved him into two halves. Then Guan Yu thanked the monk, and continued his journey. On the journey, he smashed through a total of five passes and killed six warriors, and his ferocity and capability became well-known throughout the country.

倪瓒是元朝著名的画家，擅长风景山水画。他博取各家之长，融会贯通，创出自己的独特风格。他画疏林坡岸、浅水遥岭等平远风景，以真、幽、淡为宗旨；画墨竹，又贯孤高自赏之神。他的画以简洁沉着的笔触，似嫩而苍的格调，开创了水墨画的新天地，称雄一时，与黄公望、王蒙、吴镇并称“元四家”。

相传倪瓒很爱干净，史书上说他“好洁成癖”，竟传为一时佳话，效仿者众多。倪瓒爱画梧桐，书房四周种植了梧桐树。为了保持树身洁净，他每天早晨都叫书童端水洗树，直到树干被擦洗得洁白无瑕，他才离开。这幅画讲的就是这个故事。

好洁成癖

An Inveterate Habit of Cleanliness

Ni Zan (1301-1374), a great painter of the Yuan Dynasty and a native of Wuxi, Jiangsu Province, excelled in painting landscapes. During the early years he learnt panting with artists from different schools. He drew together their strongest points by completely understanding their meaning, and went on to create his own special style.

The sparse wood, sloped banks, shallow water and remote mountains he drew aimed at natural and pleasant ambience; the ink bamboo indicated the verve of proud self-admiration and a cynical attitude toward the world. Therefore, his work was judged as “superior artistic work” in posterity. His paintings, with a simple and direct style and delicate pattern, created a new world for wash painting. He became one of the well-known “Four Greatest Landscape Painters of the Yuan Dynasty” (The other three were Huang Gongwang, Wang Meng and Wu Zhen).

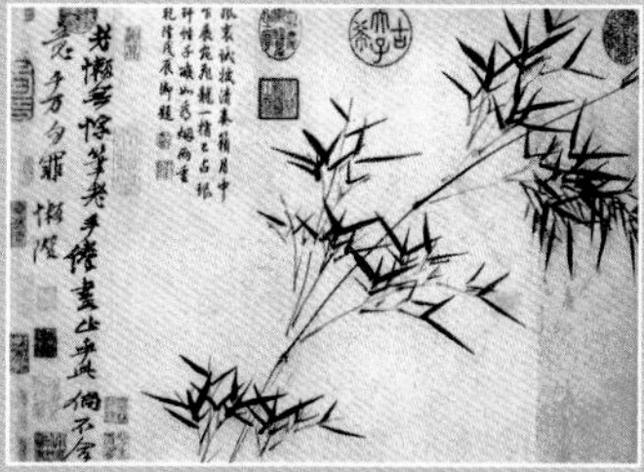

A painting by Ni Zan

According to historical records, Ni Zan was a bit obsessed with cleanliness, which became well-known at that time and was constantly imitated by people. Ni Zan liked painting the Chinese parasol tree. Every morning he asked his disciple boy to wash the trunk clean and he stood beside it and inspected personally. He wouldn’t leave until the trunk was clean. Though he was sneered at, he didn’t mind and continued to live his life the same.

一次，刘备领兵讨伐袁术，行前张飞自告奋勇留守徐州。刘备怕张飞酒后鞭挞士卒，又不从人谏，细细叮咛一番，才出发。送走刘备后，张飞随即摆下宴席，请守城官员议事。张飞两次到曹豹面前劝饮，曹豹第一次硬着头皮喝了一盅，第二次再三推辞，张飞酒醉性起，硬是叫军士把曹豹打了五十鞭。曹豹怀恨在心，写了一封密信给女婿吕布，让他趁张飞酒醉，刘备、关羽在外之机，领兵来袭徐州。

吕布带兵杀进徐州城，曹豹早已打开城门，张飞酒醉未醒，不能力敌，顾不上刘备的家眷，带着败兵逃跑，见了刘备，张飞忙跪倒在地，报告了曹豹与吕布里应外合，徐州失陷的经过。这幅画描写的就是此情景。万分悔恨之下，张飞拔剑就要自刎。刘备连忙将其抱住，苦苦劝慰，兄弟抱头大哭。

失徐州张飞赔罪

Zhang Fei's Apology for Losing Xuzhou

Once, Liu Bei received an imperial edict to attack Yuan Shu (?-199) in Huainan (in presend-day Anhui Province). Before Liu Bei left, Zhang Fei recommended himself to be in charge of Xuzhou. Liu Bei, knowing Zhang Fei's character, was afraid he would be unjust and lash soldiers when he got drunk, and he also knew that Zhang was too stubborn to take any advice from his advisors, so he gave detailed instructions to Zhang before setting out. Zhang Fei promised to Liu that he would abstain from drinking wine.

Seeing Liu Bei off, Zhang immediately held a feast and made a decision to abstain from drinking after this party. He invited all officials in Xuzhou and made each of them drink. When Zhang toasted Cao Bao, one of officers, for the second time, he refuesd. Zhang Fei was drunk, so he became furious and ordered Cao Bao to be severely beaten up.

From that moment on Cao Bao hated Zhang Fei. He conspired with Lü Bu, his son-in-law, to attack Xuzhou when Zhang was drunk and Liu Bei and Guan Yu were absent. When Lü Bu's troop arrived, Cao Bao opened the city gate for them, while Zhang Fei, who was too drunk to fight, escaped with his troops, even having no time to take Liu Bei's family. Lü Bu successfully seized Xuzhou. Meeting Liu Bei, Zhang Fei hurried to kneel down and reported how Cao Bao had collaborated with Lü Bu and occupied Xuzhou, the scene of which is well described in this painting. Being extremely repentant, Zhang Fei took out his sword and tried to commit suicide. Liu Bei hurried to hold him back and consoled him. The two brothers cried on each other's shoulder.

攻打樊城时，关羽右臂中箭落马。众将急忙将关羽救回，拔出臂箭发现箭头带毒，毒已入骨。将士们劝关羽回荆州治疗，关羽不肯。将士们只好便派人四处寻访名医。华佗听闻，特地赶来为关羽治伤；此时关羽正在与人对弈。看过伤势，华佗建议关羽找个僻静之处，将胳膊束起、以被蒙头，再开始手术。关羽却要求当场手术。他命人设宴后，将右臂伸给华佗，继续下起棋来。华佗切开皮肉，用刀刮骨。在场的人吓得用手捂着眼。再看关羽，一边喝酒，一边下棋，若无其事。过了一会，血流了一盆，骨上的毒刮完，关羽的胳膊伸弯自如，好像从前一样。关羽连声称赞华佗是神医。而华佗却夸关羽神勇。

刮骨疗毒

Scraping the Poison off the Bone

A portrait of Guan Yu

Guan Yu had been struck in the right arm by an arrow when he attacked the city of Fancheng. The arrow was promptly removed but poison smeared on the arrowhead had already seeped deep to the bone. All his subordinate generals proposed that he retreat for treatment, however, Guan Yu was unwilling to abandon the offensive campaign. So his subjects had to send for physicians to the camp to treat the poisoned arm.

One day, Hua Tuo, a famed physician then, came by boat to the camp especially to cure Guan Yu, who was engaging in a game of chess. When asked how to heal the wound, Hua, after examining the wound suggested Guan that he should select a privated room, insert his injured arm in a ring fixed to a pillar, and then cover his head with a quilt. However, Guan Yu requested that the surgery be performed on the spot, while he continued the game. Then he held out his right arm to Hua Tuo, and the surgeon performed. Hua cut open the flesh and scraped off the residual poison on the surface the bones. Everyone present didn't even dare to have a peek while Guan ate and drank, talked and laughed, as if he did not feel any pain. Within moments, the treatment was completed. Hua Tuo applied some herbal medicines to the wound and sewed it up. Guan Yu then stood up and laughed, and praised the skills of Hua Tuo, for his arm could move freely just like before but felt no more pain. Hua Tuo replied, "I have spent my life in the art, but I have never seen anyone as brave as you. You are amazing!"

陆绩是三国时期吴国人。他六岁那年，随父亲陆康去九江拜访父亲的朋友袁术。袁术叫人拿橘子给他吃，陆绩却偷偷藏了三个；临走告辞时，橘子不小心掉在地上。袁术笑着问陆绩：在别人家做客，为什么却怀揣着橘子回去？陆绩跪着回答道，因为橘子很甜，想拿回去给母亲吃。袁术惊叹陆绩年纪尚小却这么孝顺。他敬母的行为和率真的天性，也使在场的人都深受感动，大家不禁交口称赞。

孙策占据江东后，有一次对幕僚说道：定邦安国需要用武力去征服、平定。陆绩当时年龄尚小，未能列席，便在远处大声叫道："昔日管仲辅佐齐桓公，先后九次会集诸侯，使天下一切得到匡正，齐桓公也因此成就霸业。孔子也曾说过，如果远方的人不归附，修正文德便会使他们前来归降。可是如今你们却崇尚武功。即使是我这样年幼无知的小孩子，听了也难以安心啊！"

陆绩怀橘

Lu Ji Hiding Oranges in His Clothes

Lu Ji was a filial son in Jiujiang, Jiangxi Province. Once he followed his father to pay a visit to Yuan Shu, a friend of his father. Yuan Shu entertained them with oranges. Lu Ji ate several small ones, which tasted sweet. So he put three big and round oranges into his pockets, which, however, fell onto the ground when Lu Ji bowed down to bid farewell to the host. Yuan Shu then asked, "As a guest in my home, why did you take away the oranges?" Lu Ji hurried to kneel down, answering, "My mother likes oranges very much and your oranges taste delicious, so I want to bring her some to taste. Please forgive me!" Yuan Shu and the guests present couldn't help praising, "What a filial son!"

After Sun Ce, a warlord during the late Eastern Han Dynasty who managed to lay down the foundation of the later Eastern Wu, occupied Jiangdong area (the region in the south of the Yangtze River), he said to his aides and staff, "The only way to pacificate China is to conquer by force of arms." Lu Ji was too young to participate the discussion, but he happened to hear it, and shouted in the distance, "Guan Zhong, prime minister of the State of Qi during the Spring and Autumn Period, helped Duke Huan of Qi held a total of nine peace conferences with all vassal kings. During his term of office, the state of Qi became much stronger and Duke Huan of Qi gained hegemony among the states. And Confucius once said, 'If remoter people are not submissive, all the influence of civil culture and virtue are to be cultivated to attract them to be so.' Now I know you are martial persons. Even a child like me is greatly perturbed!"

北宋末年，朝廷腐败无能。金国兴起后，举兵南侵，占了都城汴梁（今开封），掳走钦宗（1100~1161年）、徽宗（1082~1135年）。岳飞拒绝各种势力的劝诱，和母亲、妻子在家苦守清贫。

为了警醒儿子永远做个忠臣，一日岳飞的母亲命其摆设香案，祭拜完天地祖先，岳母便在岳飞的脊背上，用毛笔书写、绣花针刺就了“精忠报国”四个字，然后涂以醋墨，使永不褪色。这时南宋高宗（1107~1187年）继位，召岳飞进京受职。岳飞领兵大败金兵，力图恢复中原。不料奸臣秦桧私通金国，最后把岳飞害死在风波亭。岳飞虽死，可是岳母训子报国的故事和岳飞的英雄事迹却流传千古。

岳母刺字

Mother Yue Tattooing Her Son's Back

By the end of the Northern Song Dynasty, the court was corrupt and incapable of managing the national affairs. The Jin State began its rise and invaded the Song territory; they took the capital Bianliang (today's Kaifeng, Henan Province), and carried away Emperor Qinzong (1100-1161) and Emperor Huizong (1082-1135). Yue Fei, as a prominent figure at that time, resisted various temptations and pressure from authorities, and remained poor staying at home with his family.

In order to encourage her son to be a loyal and incorruptible minister throughout his life, one day, Mother Yue asked Yue Fei to set up the incense altar to hold a ceremony. After making sacrifices to Heaven and Earth, and Yue clan's ancestors, she picked up the brush and wrote out on his spine the four Chinese characters: Jing Zhong Bao Guo, which means "serving the country with the utmost loyalty". Then she bit her teeth and tattooed them with a needle. Having finished, she painted the charaters with ink mixed with vinegar so that the color would never fade.

After Emperor Gaozong (1107-1187) had established the Southern Song Dynasty, Yue Fei was summoned to the capital Lin'an (today's Hangzhou, Zhejiang Province) to take an official position. He led troops, defeated the Jin army, and did his utmost to recover the lost territories in central China. Unfortunately, the cunning and corrupt minister, Qin Hui, who was a secret collaborator with the Jin Dynasty, set traps against Yue Fei, and finally killed him at the Fengbo Pavilion. Although Yue Fei died, his heroic deeds to serve the country were spread, which have been inspiring generations of Chinese people.

唐德宗元年（779年），书生张生赴京赶考。一日，他行至普救寺，与已故的相国之女崔莺莺偶遇，一见倾心。他不想再谋取功名，便借寺中西厢房住下。莺莺和母亲此时也寄居寺中一座宅子里。

一天，乱贼率兵围寺，欲抢莺莺为妻。老夫人情急无奈，亲口许诺，谁有办法打退乱贼，便将女儿许配给他。张生借助好友之力，解除了危难。岂料老夫人食言赖婚，害得张生寝食难安，相思成病。原来莺莺也早已爱上了张生，迫于封建礼教，不敢表露爱意。在红娘热情相助之下，两人结为夫妻。然老夫人知道后，逼迫张生赴京应试。最后张生考中状元，与莺莺重新团聚。

西厢记

The Romance of the West Chamber

During the first year of Emperor Dezong's reign (799) in the Tang Dynasty, a scholar named Zhang Sheng went to attend the Imperial Examination. He stopped by the Pujiu Temple to worship Buddha and get his blessings, where he encountered Cui Yingying, the daughter of the passed-away prime minister. He fell in love with her at first sight, and having no motivation for the examination any more, he lived in the west chamber of the temple. Yingying and his old mother temporarily took shelter in a house on the west side of the temple, while escorting the coffin of Yingying's father back to their native town. Zhang was eager to express his feeling, however, Yingying had always been under her mother's watchful eye.

One day, a band of bandits, on hearing Yingying's beauty, attacked the temple and intended to seize Yingying. Her old mother, in such urgent circumstances, claimed that if anyone could defeat the bandits, she would marry her daughter to him. Zhang solved the crisis with his friends' help, but the old mistress broke her promise, with the excuse that Yingying was already betrothed to the son of a high official in the court, which saddened Zhang, who was depressed and later became sick. Yingying, however, who had already fallen in love with Zhang, did not dare to express her feelings directly to Zhang, in terms of the harsh and rigid feudal ethic value at that time. Fortunately, with the help of Hongniang, who was Yingying's maid and served as a match maker between the two, they eventually became a couple. When she discovered this, Yingying's mother reluctantly consents to a formal marriage on one condition: Zhang must pass the Imperial Examination. To the joy of the young lovers, finally, Zhang was listed as first and was appointed to a high-level position. He reunited with Yingying and the two married.

天女散花是佛经中的一个故事。相传如来佛的得意弟子维摩诘善于教导人们领会深奥玄妙的道理，但常常假托病由，自己在家学道。

一天，如来佛在西天莲花宝座讲经解法，忽见瑞云东来，遥知维摩诘患病，于是，派众弟子前去问候。他断定维摩诘必定会借机宣经释典，便派天女前去检验弟子们的学习情况。天女手提花篮，飘逸而行，来到尘世，低头下望，见维摩诘果然正与众人讲学。天女随即将满篮鲜花散去，弟子舍利弗满身沾花。众人十分诧异，天女说道，只有那些修道成功的人，才不会沾满花瓣。舍利弗自知法术相差甚远，从此更加努力学习。

天女散花

Celestial Maid Scattering Flowers

This story originates from the Buddhist scriptures. Vimalakirti, a disciple of Tathagata, is by some considered to be the first Zen Buddhist Master aside from the Buddha himself and is the subject of the *Vimalakirti Sutra*. He was adept in inducting people to understand profound theories and always spent time learning sutra by himself at home. One day, Tathagata explained the sermon of the sutra on the lotus seat when he saw a propitious cloud wafting near. Guessing that Vimalakirti fell ill, Tathagata sent Bodhisattvas, with many disciples, to visit him. According to Vimalakirti's usual practice – never miss a chance to lecture sutra to others, Tathagata dispatched the celestial maid to follow them to examine their self-cultivation.

The celestial maid, dressed in colorful clothes and lifting a flower basket in her hand, levitated on the cloud and finally reached the human's world. When she saw Vimalakirti was preaching, the celestial maid lifted the basket and the fresh flowers were immediately sprinkled down. All of a sudden, the sky was full of fresh and colorful blossoms falling down in riotous profusion and pervading the air with fragrance.

Only Sariputra was covered by flowers. The disciples felt surprised and then looked up while the celestial maid explained, "The flowers fell onto the disciples who don't fully understand the sutra; those who really have achieved it won't be covered with the flowers." Hearing this, Sariputra determined to double his efforts to learn Buddhism. Later, Sariputra became an Arhat renowned for his wisdom and is depicted as one of the most important disciples of the Buddha, who declared Sariputra to be the second only to himself in transcendent knowledge.

刘备三顾茅庐，请诸葛亮出山相助，拜为军师。不久，曹操派夏侯惇带兵十万攻打刘备驻地新野。然刘备只有三千军马，遂请诸葛亮商议。诸葛亮第一次指挥战斗，恐众将不服，向刘备求得剑印。他命关羽在左，张飞在右去博望坡埋伏，赵云引兵诱敌，刘备为后援，准备用火攻曹军。

众将不知孔明韬略，疑惑不定，张飞更是不服气。孔明道："剑印在此，违命者斩。"众将才领命而去。

博望坡道路狭窄、树木丛杂，待曹军行此，刘备等人放起火来。曹兵突陷火海，顿时慌乱起来，自相践踏，死伤无数。刘备大获全胜。关羽、张飞等众将见诸葛亮用兵如神，从此对他心服口服。

博望坡诸葛亮初用兵

Zhuge Liang Achieving First Success in Bowang Hillside

After Zhuge Liang became Liu Bei's military counselor, soon they heard that Xiahou Dun, one of Cao Cao's warriors, was leading an army of 100,000 troops against them. Liu Bei had just 3,000 men. He consulted Zhuge Liang on how to resist the powerful Cao army with such a small number of troops. Zhuge Liang was afraid that his ideas might not be accepted by the generals because it was the first time he had commanded a battle, so he asked Liu Bei to give him a seal of office and sword of authority. So Liu Bei gave him both. He then ordered Guan Yu to ambush his soldier to the left of Bowang Hillside, while Zhang Fei to the right; he used Zhao Yun to lure the enemy, and left Liu Bei as the reinforcement in the rear; he planned to attack the Cao army with fire.

The generals, however, were not sure how capable Zhuge Liang would be and became suspicious about what he was playing at. Zhang Fei was especially displeased. Zhuge Liang simply replied, "I have the sword and seal, and anyone who doesn't follow my orders will be executed." The generals had to accept his directions.

Bowang Hillside was a place where the road was narrow and the forests were lush, so when the Xiahou Dun and his soldiers marched through there, Liu Bei's troop set a fire. Cao's troops were thrown into confusion and trampled each other down. Many perished. Xiahou Dun dashed through the fire and smoke to escape. Thus, under Zhuge Liang's command, Liu Bei's army achieved victory. From then on, Guan Yu, Zhang Fei and other generals began to admire Zhuge Liang for his military insight.

传说王母娘娘有七个美丽的仙女。小妹七仙女不甘天宫的寂寞，私自下凡来到人间。巧遇卖身葬父的孝子董永。这幅画描写的就是他们相会的情景。

七仙女美丽善良；董永憨厚淳朴，两人一见钟情，在老槐树下喜结良缘。婚后，七仙女为了使董永卖身的工期从三年减至百天，特邀众姐妹相助织锦。最终工期期满，董永离开地主家，朝自己家中走去，欣闻此时七仙女已怀有身孕，可谓是喜上加喜。夫妻俩男耕女织，相亲相爱，过着平凡而幸福的生活。然好景不长，天帝得知七仙女与凡人成亲，大发雷霆，特派天神传旨：七仙女午时三刻即返回天廷，否则便将董永碎尸万段。七仙女为了使丈夫免遭毒手，只好与董永忍痛分离，哭诉相约，第二年老槐树下把子交。说罢，飘然而去。董永悲痛欲绝，昏厥在地。

天仙配

The Marriage Between the Mortal and the Fairy

The Queen Mother of the West had seven fairy maids. The Seventh Fairy, the youngest one, could not bear the lonely life of Heaven. A girl with plenty of pluck, she sneaked into the world. She encountered Dong Yong, a filial young man, who was selling himself into slavery to a landlord in order to have his dead father buried. The scene in this painting is about their encounter.

The girl was beautiful and kind-hearted, while the boy simple and honest. The two fell in love at first sight, and got married under an old locust tree. After the wedding, the Seventh Fairy asked all her sisters to help weave brocades so that she could subsidize her husband to reduce his term of service to the landlord from three years to 100 days. At the end of the hundred days, husband and wife left the landlord's place and set out for their own home. On their home, the couple came to the locust tree and thanked it. Since then, Dong tilled the land and the Fairy wove cloth; they lived an ordinary but happy life. Soon after, the Seventh Fairy was pregnant, which added to the happiness of their life.

But it did not last long. The Emperor of Heaven, learning of the fairy's marriage with a mortal being, was furious. He sent a heavenly guardian to announce his decree: the fairy should return to Heaven by three o'clock in the afternoon, or Dong Yong would be smashed. Fearing her husband might get punished, the fairy had to leave him and promised to turn over the son to Dong Yong the next year under the old locust tree. Then she was forced to return to heaven.

这幅画是根据李白的诗《示金陵子》写意而成。李白（701~762年），唐代浪漫主义诗人，一生酷爱游览名山大川，写下了不少赞美大好山河、描绘自然风光的诗篇。他的诗构思奇特、气势瑰丽、风格豪迈、语言清新。

李白61岁高龄时，孤身一人来到金陵（今南京）游玩。晚上，他坐在窗前，对着秋花明月，吟歌抚琴。歌声如泣如诉，催人泪下，竟招来一个年轻美貌的少女。孤独的诗人便收留了她，并一起渡江西去。李白坐在船头，眼望浩瀚的江面，轻舟披着晚霞顺流而下，身边这位女子就像空中一朵彩云飞落在自己身旁。李白心悦，不禁雅兴横生，教女子唱起楚歌。他还不由得想到，如果穿上南朝谢灵运发明的登山鞋，与这位女子携手共行，浪迹于山水林泉之间，将是多么惬意。

：随人直渡西江水：

Crossing the River to the West

This painting is based on a sentiment expressed in Li Bai's poem *To the Lady of Jinling*. Li Bai (701-792) was a romanticist in the Tang Dynasty (618-907). As a statesman, Li's ambition had failed; he thus turned to alcohol and supernatural worship for consolation; as a Taoist, he had always been pursuing a free and unrestrained life. Both these two elements – the gloom of failed ambition and the cheer of a free mind – found their way into his poetry, earning him the name "Poet Immortal". He is often regarded, along with Du Fu, as one of the two greatest poets in China's literary history. Nearly 1,100 of his poems remain today. Li Bai loved traveling among the famous mountains and grand rivers, and wrote many poems extolling the beauty of nature. His aspiration for poems was unique; his style was open, grand and ornate; and his poetic language was fresh and vivid.

When he was 61, he went to Jinling alone. One night, he sat by the window, playing the fiddle and singing for the flowers and the moon of autumn. His singing was elaborate and touching, which attracted a beautiful girl's attention. She visited him, and the lonely poet kept her as his companion. Later, they crossed the river to the west together. Li Bai, sitting on the bow and watching the broad river as well as the small boat driven by water in sunset, felt as if the girl beside him was a piece of colorful cloud hanging about near by but unreachable and certainly untameable. Delighted, he taught the girl to sing many songs. He also could not help imagining that it was pleasant if he had put on the mountain climbing shoes invented by Xie Lingyun, and traveled along with the girl among the beautiful mountains and rivers.

孔融刚正不阿，敢于直言，后因触犯曹操被杀。孔融还是当时著名的文学家，擅长写散文，是“建安七子”之一。

相传孔融四岁的时候，父亲带回家一些梨让孩子们分着吃。孔融最小，哥哥、姐姐都让他先挑。孔融拿了最小的那一个，大家都很奇怪。父亲问他为什么，他答道：因为他最小，所以吃最小的一个。从此，孔融谦虚礼让的美德传播开来，受到人们的称颂。后代也把这个故事写进启蒙课本，以教育孩子礼貌让人。后来，孔融步入仕途，虽权重位高，仍保持这一美德。一次孔融被敌兵围攻，在危急之时，城外一人挺枪跃马，杀入敌阵，帮孔融解开重围。原来，孔融一直照顾此人的老母，老母感其恩，命儿子前来搭救。

孔融让梨

Kong Rong Selecting the Smallest Pear

Kong Rong (153-208), a governer during the end of the Eastern Han Dynasty and Three Kingdoms Period, was upright and frank, but unfortunately, he offended and humiliated Cao Cao on multiple occasions and was eventually executed by Cao. Kong Rong was expert at prose, and was ranked among the Seven Scholars of Jian'an, a group of representative litterateur of his time. However, most of his works were lost during the Song Dynasty (960-1279), and only 36 articles were found and compiled during the Ming Dynasty (1368-1644).

A well-known story commonly used to educate children even nowadays on the values of courtesy and fraternal love involves Kong Rong giving up the larger pears. It's said that when Kong Rong was four years old his father brought some pears home. Because Kong Rong was the youngest in the family, his sisters and brothers asked him to select first. Kong Rong, however, took the smallest one, which surprised everyone. When his father asked him the reason, he said, "I'm the youngest and I should take the smallest one." Thereafter, Kong Rong's virtue of modesty was edited into the textbooks to educate children to follow Kong Rong's lead. Kong Rong kept this virtue even though he became a powerful official later. He respected the old and loved the young, thus enjoying popular support among the people. Kong Rong was once besieged by his enemy. At the critical moment, a warrior pushed forward into the enemy's battle array, broke through the tight encirclement and saved Kong Rong. Actually Kong Rong often sent food and clothes and visited the warrior's aged and lonely mother, who asked his son to save Kong Rong when she heard of the enemy's siege.

黛玉从此一病不起，丫环紫鹃、雪雁日夜守护，可是黛玉的病情还是日益加重。这天，黛玉刚一坐起，就是一阵咳嗽，紫鹃劝她躺下，黛玉只是用手指着床边的箱子。原来她是想要那块宝玉送的手绢，那是宝玉不守家规，被贾政毒打一顿后，在床上养伤时，心中惦记黛玉，特地叫丫环给黛玉送来的。黛玉深知宝玉的一片情意，感慨不已，便在手绢上写下了诗句，表达对宝玉的怜爱和对自己身世的感伤。看到手绢，黛玉百感交加，扯过手绢，便狠命撕扯，然而她病体虚弱，喘了一会儿，便叫丫环点上火盆，起身把手绢及平时的诗稿扔在火盆里。

后来黛玉病情恶化，过了几天在宝玉成亲的时候，黛玉便满含悲愤地离开了人世。

林黛玉焚稿断痴情

Lin Daiyu Burning Scripts and Ending Love

Although taking medicine, Daiyu's illness grew worse. During her previous illness, she had always received frequent visits from everyone in the household, from Grandmother Jia down to the humblest maidservant. But now not one relative or servant came, not even sending inquiries. She began to feel her end drawing near, and there was no reason for her to live on.

A drawing of Lin Daiyu Burning Scripts and Ending Love

One day, Daiyu sat up, and coughed severely. Zijuan, her maid, asked her to lie down, but she just pointed at a box by the bed, inside which there was a handkerchief that had been given by Baoyu. Once, Baoyu was seriously beaten by his father for breaking the family rules. When lying on his bed, he could not help missing Daiyu, and sent her a handkerchief. Daiyu knew in the bottom of her heart that Baoyu was deeply in love with her, and being sentimental, she wrote a poem on the handkerchief, expressing her love for Baoyu and her sentimentality over her own pitiful status. Seeing the handkerchief now, however, she felt her heart was broken. She seized it, and tried to tear it to pieces, but she was too weak, and after breathing heavily for a while, she asked her maids to set up a fire basin. Then she threw the handkerchief and all her manuscripts into the basin. Later on Baoyu's wedding day, Daiyu passed away in deep sorrow.

尧是中国传说中一位节俭、朴素、顾民的好国君，在位100年里，为人民做了许多好事。尧老的时候，想把帝位禅让给一个贤能的人。尧的儿子丹朱只知道吃喝玩乐，尧不愿把帝位传让给他，就到处打听天下的贤人。各部落的首领向尧推荐了舜。舜为人至孝，后来因为忍受不了后母的毒打，跑到了山中，过着孤单、愁苦的生活。没多久，山民受舜的德行的感化，不论舜住在哪里，人们都愿意搬到他的附近居住。尧听说后，亲自去访问舜。画中就是尧王访舜时的情景。经过各种各样的观察，尧看到舜果然是个有才干又贤孝的好青年，就决定将国君的位置禅让给这个普通的农民，并把两个女儿娥皇、女英嫁给了他。

尧王访舜

Yao Visiting Shun

Yao was a legendary good emperor in Chinese ancient times, and is said to become the ruler at 20 and died at 119. He led a simple and thrifty life and cared about his people very much. During his 100-year reign, he did many good deeds for his people. Often extolled as the morally perfect sage-king, his benevolence and diligence serve as a model to future Chinese monarchs and emperors.

As Yao gradually aged, it became time for him to select a virtuous and talented successor for the sake of the people's happiness. Yet Yao was reluctant to pass the throne to his son, who just idled away in pleasure. So, Yao inquired about able men everywhere. Afterwards, Shun, who was particularly renowned for his modesty and filial perty, was recommended to Yao. Shun's stepmother, narrow-minded and ferocious, usually maltreated him. Even so, Shun still devotedly took care of his father and stepmother. The vicious stepmother, however, beat Shun mercilessly at home. Thus Shun was forced to put up a shed at the foot of a mountain. He then opened some wasteland and led a lonely and bitter life. The farmers around, influenced by Shun's virtue, emulated him and gave up their high-quality land to others to cultivate. When Shun went fishing, the fishermen nearby also offered the fishery. Wherever Shun lived, people wanted to be his neighborhood. In just a short time this place became a village, which turned into a town the next year and finally developed into a business zone in the third year. When Yao heard of such an able man, he felt very happy and visited Shun in person, which was depicted in this painting. Through various kinds of observation, Yao found Shun actually a talented and virtuous youth. Later Yao passed his throne in favor of Shun and married his two daughters, Ehuang and Nüying, to him.

东汉末年，天下大乱，群雄纷起，南阳太守袁术素有称帝之心。一次，袁术准备起兵攻打驻扎在小沛的刘备，又担心吕布出兵救援，便先派人给吕布送去粮草以拉拢吕布。随后派大将纪灵统兵进攻刘备。刘备兵微粮少，请求吕布支援。吕布考虑再三，想出一个使袁、刘两家都无怨言的办法。

纪灵引兵数万在小沛东南扎营。刘备只有五千余人。吕布也引一支人马在小沛西南下寨。安顿已毕，吕布把纪灵、刘备都请到自己营中，设宴款待他们。二人相遇，正要走开，却被吕布强拉入席。见双方不肯罢兵休战，吕布提戟在手，对纪、刘说道：“辕门离此150步。我若一箭射中戟上的小枝，你两家就此罢兵，如射不中，你们各自回营，安排厮杀。”二人同意。只见吕布挽起袍袖，搭上箭，扯满弓，一箭正中画戟小枝，四下齐声喝彩。就这样吕布化解了一场厮杀。次日，三处军马都散去。

吕布辕门射戟

Lü Bu Shooting a Halberd by the Gate of Encampment

Yuan Shu, a warlord during the late Eastern Han Dynasty and Three Kingdoms Period, had the ambition to become an emperor. Once he planned to attack Liu Bei who at that time stationed his forces in Xiaopei. But he was afraid that Lü Bu would send troops to reinforce Liu, so he tried to bribe Lü Bu by operational ration. Then he dispatched a general Ji Ling to attack Liu Bei. Liu Bei's force was too small to resist Yuan's force, and he turned to Lü Bu for help, just as Yuan worried. Receiving Liu Bei's plea, Lü Bu came up with an idea that could leave no room for complaint from either side.

When Ji Ling and his army camped to the southeast of Xiaopei, Liu Bei was embattled outside the city. At the same time, Lü Bu led an army to camp to the southwest of Xiaopei. After all settled down, Lü Bu invited Ji Ling and Liu Bei to his camp, and held a feast to entertain them. When Ji Ling and Liu Bei met, they were both unwilling to have dinner at the same table, but Lü Bu obliged them to sit down. He tried to persuade the two sides to make peace, but both of them were reluctant to retreat. Then Lü Bu held his halberd, and said to Ji and Liu, “If my arrow hits right at the small branch of the halberd on the gate of the encampment 150 steps off, you two sides can agree to stop the fight; if I fail, you may have your own way.” Ji Ling and Liu Bei agreed. Lü Bu rolled up his sleeves, drew an arrow, and shot the target. All the soldiers cheered. So according to the agreement, the forthcoming fight was avoided, and the next day all the troops decamped.

孙悟空大闹天宫后，玉皇大帝派二郎神带领天兵天将到花果山捉拿他。孙悟空正与二郎神激战时，太上老君暗中投下金钢琢，击中了悟空，把他捉到了天宫。玉帝降旨严惩，但任凭刀砍斧劈、火烧雷击，都伤不到孙悟空。最后太上老君请令，把孙悟空扔进炼金丹用的八卦炉中，想用猛火把他烧死。八卦炉是按天、水、山、震、风、火、地、泽划分的，孙悟空知道其中的奥妙，进去后便钻进"风"的位置上，有风便无火，烧不到他，身体无碍，只是风吹烟起，熏了眼睛而已，这却使悟空炼就了一双能辨别妖魔的"火眼金睛"。孙悟空在八卦炉中烧了七七四十九天，太上老君以为孙悟空早已化成灰烬，下令开炉。谁知孙悟空一跃而起，抡起金箍棒，打倒众天将而去。

The Eight Trigrams Furnace

After the Monkey King created such widespread havoc in the Heavenly Kingdom, the Jade Emperor sent Yang Jian, who had a third true-seeing eye in the middle of his forehead, with heavenly troops to catch him. During the fierce fight between the Monkey King and Yang Jian, the Supreme Lord Lao Zi secretly threw a Diamond Circle at the Monkey. The Monkey King was too preoccupied with fighting Yang Jian to notice this weapon falling on him from heaven. When it struck him, he lost his balance and stumbled, and then was escorted to Heaven. The Jade Emperor passed severe punishments. However, all the punishments, including sword cutting, ax chopping, fire burning, and thunder striking, did not wound the Monkey King.

Finally, the Supreme Lord Lao Zi asked to throw the Monkey into the Eight Trigrams Furnace, which was used to create the golden elixir pills, aiming to burn him alive in the fierce fire. The furnace was divided into eight sections: Heaven, Earth, water, mountain, thunder, fire, wind, and the swamp, and the Monkey King knew its design. After entering the furnace, he squeezed himself into the wind section where there was only wind there could be no fire. So he managed to avoid being burnt, but the wind stirred up the smoke, which agitated his eyes; however, consequently, it helped him develop a pair of "fiery-gaze golden-eyes." Time soon passed, and 49 days later, the Supreme Lord Lao Zi thought the Monkey had already been burnt into ashes, and ordered to open the furnace. However, what he saw was a lively Monkey King, who jumped out of the furnace and kicked it over with a crash. Then the Monkey King brandished his As-You-Will Gold-Banded Cudgel, knocking down all the heavenly generals, and disappeared.

刘备、关羽、张飞在徐州被曹操打散之后，关羽为了寻找刘备，千里走单骑，过五关、斩六将，护送着刘备的家眷，来到古城之下。一打听，守城的是三弟张飞，关羽不禁大喜，忙派人进城通报。不料一队人马杀出城来，只见张飞满脸怒气，持矛冲着关羽便刺。关羽大惊，慌忙闪开，原来张飞误以为关羽背叛刘备，投降了曹操。任关羽怎么解释，张飞就是不信。

正在这时，曹将蔡阳率一队人马追赶关羽，杀奔古城而来。关羽表示愿斩此来将，以表真心。说罢，纵马举刀向蔡阳迎去，手起刀落，蔡阳已人头落地。张飞这才知道错怪了关羽。兄弟相认，各叙前事，百感交集。

斩蔡阳兄弟释疑

Killing Cai Yang to Clear up Suspicion

Having been defeated by Cao Cao in Xuzhou, Liu Bei, Guan Yu and Zhang Fei were seperated and lost touch with each other. In order to find Liu Bei, Guan Yu escorted Liu Bei's family, broke through five passes and killed six of Cao Cao's generals, and then he marched for a thousand miles, and arrived at Gucheng. After learning the general in charge of Gucheng was his sworn brother Zhang Fei, he was delighted, and hurried to send a messenger into the city to tell Zhang to come out to meet him and provide for their two sisters-in-law.

Zhang Fei, holding his serpent spear and leading his soldiers, came out of the city. Guan Yu was very glad when he saw his brother coming, put up his weapons and rode toward him immediately. However, as he approached, Guan Yu saw all the signs of fierce anger on Zhang Fei's face. Without a word, Zhang thrust his spear straight at Guan. Guan Yu was greatly shocked and dodged the attack hurriedly. He shouted to Zhang Fei, "Hey, brother! What's the matter with you? Did you forget our pledge in the peach garden?" Zhang Fei, however, firmly believed that Guan Yu had betrayed Liu Bei, surrendered to Cao Cao and received title and office at Cao's hand. He wouldn't accept Guan's explanation.

Just at that moment, one of Cao Cao's generals, Cai Yang, leading an army, in pursuit of Guan Yu, also arrived at Gucheng. Guan Yu promised Zhang Fei that he would kill Cai Yang to prove his loyalty, and then rode toward Cai Yang. In a few minutes, Cai's head rolled on the ground. Thus, Zhang Fei knew he had made a mistake. The two brothers had a very touching reunion afterwards.

相传很久以前有两个男孩，他们虽不同名同姓，却亲如兄弟。快要成亲时，哥哥才发现新娘却是弟弟的恋人。他很后悔，为了弟弟的幸福，出家做了和尚。而弟弟听说哥哥出家后，跋山涉水，历经苦难，找到了哥哥。弟弟折一支盛开的荷花作为礼物，哥哥手持一个斋盒出迎，两人欣喜若狂，乐极而舞。因“荷”与“盒”同音，旧时百姓不识字，便把二人称作“和合二仙”，取和谐好合之意。“和合二仙”的纹样也成为民间工艺品，如木雕、漆画、砖刻、刺绣、剪纸和木板年画等，常用的题材。

哥哥法名寒山，并在姑苏（今苏州）建了一个寒山寺。后来，弟弟也出家做了和尚，法名拾得。故事流传很多年，各地传说也就有了出入，有的地方把荷花改成喜鹊，这幅画即是按此传说所画。

和合二仙

The Double He Immortals

Long, long ago, there were two boys who, though they were not related, were as close as brothers. When the elder one reached the age for marriage, some fellow villagers acting as matchmakers got him engaged to a girl. On his wedding day, however, the elder one found his bride was the younger one’s sweetheart; he repented, and for his brother’s happiness, he became a monk. The younger one learned his elder brother’s state, looked for him everywhere, and after climbing many mountains, crossing many rives and overcoming many difficulties, he eventually found his brother.

The younger brother plucked a blossoming lotus as a present to meet his elder brother, while the elder one carried a box of food to welcome him. The two were ecstatic about the reunion, and they danced. In Chinese, the lotus and the box are a pair of puns, and they are both pronounced “He”, which also means harmony and reconciling in Chinese. So the image of the brothers became a popular theme in Chinese art, and could be found on woodcarving, lacquer painting, embroidery, paper cutting, new year picture, and so on. Folks in ancient times were illiterates, and they just called them the Double He Immortals.

The elder brother’s Buddhist name was Hanshan, and later, he built the famous Hanshan Temple in Gusu (Suzhou now). The younger brother, following his brother’s example, also became a monk, and his Buddhist name was Shide. Their story has been told for years, and its version differs from one locality to another. In some versions, the magpie replaces the lotus, and this painting is based on the magpie version.

项梁起兵反秦时，韩信去投军，当了一名小卒；项梁失败后，他又跟着项羽，当了个守卫。他几次向项羽献计，都没被重视，于是决定去汉中投奔刘邦。可是通往汉中的惟一的栈道被烧毁，正在焦急之时，韩信碰上一个老樵夫，他急忙上前问路。老樵夫告诉他只有一条去陈仓的路，可很不好走，老虎经常出没，多年没人走了。韩信请老樵夫详细地将路径讲了一遍，并细心地一一记住，谢过老人，向陈仓那条路走去。

然而，这条小路竟成了韩信一生的转折点。韩信投奔刘邦以后，由于萧何的大力推荐，当了大将军，统领三军。他明修栈道，暗渡陈仓，从当年老樵夫指给他的道路，打出汉中，连败项羽，建了奇功。

问路陈仓

Han Xin Probing the Way to Chencang

A drawing of Liu Bang

When Xiang Liang (?-208 BC), a famous leader of uprisings, rebelled against the Qin Dynasty, Han Xin joined the army as a soldier; after Xiang Liang was defeated, Han Xin followed Xiang Yu as a guard. Although on several occassions he had offered his ideas to Xiang Yu, the latter paid no attention to them. Then, Han Xin was determined to turn to Liu Bang. Unfortunately, the only path to Hanzhong (in present-day Shaanxi Province) was destroyed; he was quite anxious but he encountered an old man. He hurried to go over to ask how he could get to Chencang (east of present-day Baoji, Shaanxi Province). The old man told him a way which, however, had not been travelled for years, and there were tigers along the way.

Yet, Han Xin was determined to go. He got the detailed directions, thanked the old man, and hurried on, which proved to be the turning point of his life. After joining Liu's army, through a high recommendation of Xiao He, he became a marshal in command of all of Liu Bang's troops. During the later war against Chu, he ordered to pretend to repair the path, then leading the rest of the army secretly marched on the way out of Hanzhong the old man had told him years ago. His army successfully defeated Xiang Yu, and achieved many great victories. Chencang also became a famous place in China's history after that.

战国时期，群雄争霸。秦国在当时最为强大，它常常仗着自己的优势去侵略别的国家。但实力较弱的国家之间也是纷争不断。有一次赵国准备攻打燕国，燕王非常担心，就请苏代去赵国劝说赵王罢兵。苏代见了赵王，给他讲了一个故事："一只河蚌刚爬上河滩，张开壳儿晒太阳，一只鹬鸟扑过来，啄它的肉。蚌灵敏地合拢起自己坚硬的壳，把鹬鸟的嘴紧紧夹住。鹬说："今天不下雨，明天不下雨，你就会晒死。"蚌说："你的嘴今天拔不出，明天拔不出，你就要渴死、饿死。"鹬和蚌谁也不让谁，结果被渔夫毫不费力地抓住了。"苏代解释道，如果赵王执意攻打燕国的话，两国征战，秦国就会从中获取利益。赵王最终放弃了攻打燕国的计划。"鹬蚌相争，渔人得利"也成为一条成语，用来比喻双方争持不下，让第三者得到了好处。

鹬蚌相争

The Tussle Between a Snipe and a Mussel

During the Warring States Period, conflicts and wars never stopped among the states. Of them, the State of Qin was the strongest, who always invaded other states; however, even among the toparchies, there were ceaseless wars. Once, the State of Zhao planned to launch an attack against the State of Yan. The king of Yan got into a panic and asked Su Dai, a famous lobbyist then, to persuade the king of Zhao to give up the battle plan. Arriving in the State of Zhao, Su Dai came to see the king and told him a story:

A mussel climbed onto the river bank and opened its shells to have a sun bath. A snipe rushed over to peck its flesh. The mussel agilely closed its shells and caught the snipe's beak. The snipe said, "If it does not rain, you will be dry to death." The mussel said, "If your beak cannot get out, you will be thirsty and hungry and die." Thus, the two were in a stand-off, and finally, both were easily caught by a fisherman.

Then Su Dai analyzed: if the king of Zhao insisted on attacking the Yan, he would be locked in a stalemate; thus, the wide community of both states would be extremely exhausted, like the snipe and the mussel; the State of Qin would be happy to take this chance to gobble up both territories, just like the fisherman. Finally, the king of Zhao gave up his original intention. "The tussle between an snipe and a mussel benefits the fisherman" is a Chinese idiom which means the fight between two competitive parties often brings benefits to a third party.

古时候，杭州的西子湖中住着一条善良的白蛇。她化作美貌女子来到人间，取名白娘子。她救下了一条青蛇，即小青，从此二人形影不离。这一天恰逢清明时节，人们纷纷祭坟、踏青。许仙也到庙中烧香、还愿；之后在湖边闲走，观赏风景，忽然天降起雨来，越下越密。许仙赶忙喊来一只小船，匆匆钻进船舱。船夫刚摇了二三下，白娘子和小青便在岸上呼喊船夫，要搭船。许仙叫船夫把船靠岸，请她们入船。白娘子她们一入船，便向许仙道谢。许仙打量着白娘子的容貌，心中连连称赞。白娘子见许仙生得眉清目秀，又知书懂礼，也起了爱慕之意。两人一见钟情，互相倾心。船靠上对岸，雨还是下个不停。许仙让白娘子稍等片刻，便一个人冒雨跑到街上，借了一把伞，返身回到岸边。他撑着伞送了白娘子一程又一程，只因这把雨伞，引出了一段曲折生动、催人泪下的故事。

许仙借伞

Xu Xian Borrowing an Umbrella

In ancient times there lived a well-natured white snake in the West Lake in Hangzhou. One day, it turned into an attractive lady, and came to the secular world. She called herself "Lady White". She saved a green snake (Xiaoqing), and afterwards they became intimate sisters.

It was the Tomb-Sweeping Festival (April 5), and people were busy sweeping their ancestors' tombs and appreciating the beautiful views in early spring. Xu Xian, a poor herbal medicine shopkeeper in Hangzhou, went to the temple to burn incense and make a wish, and then he had an excursion by the lake. Suddenly, it began to rain, and the rain became heavier and heavier. Xu Xian was soon soaked. He hurried to take a small boat, and shortly after the boatman had launched the boat, Lady White and Xiaoqing called for a ride. Xu Xian urged the boatman to stop and get the two ladies.

Once aboard, the ladies thanked Xu Xian, while Xu was stunned by Lady White's beauty. Lady White decided Xu Xian was a handsome and educated young man, and in return, she also began to admire him. The two fell in love. The rain did not stop when the boat reached its destination. Xu Xian asked Lady White to wait for a moment; then he rushed to the street in rain, and borrowed an umbrella. With the umbrella, Xu Xian walked Lady White a long way.

娥皇和女英嫁给舜后，辛勤劳动，操持家务，侍奉公婆。但是舜的父母和弟弟象嫉妒怨恨舜，设下了许多毒计，想要害死舜。娥皇和女英凭着她们的聪明和智慧，使舜一次次地转危为安。有一次，当舜在谷仓上修顶的时候，凶残的父母撤掉梯子，放起了大火。舜焦急万分，伸开手臂向青天呼救。就在他张开手臂，他穿的衣服忽然变成了羽毛；舜化作一只大鸟，冲破烈焰和浓烟，直飞云霄。原来娥皇姊妹预料到诡计，事先给舜穿上一件五彩服，化解了这场灾难。

舜作了帝王之后，娥皇和女英帮助舜为百姓做了许多好事。后来，舜死在巡视南方的途中。娥皇和女英听到噩耗，星夜去奔丧。想起几十年的夫妻恩爱，她们的眼泪像泉水一样奔涌出来，洒在竹子上，留下了斑斑泪痕。之后，人们就把这种斑竹叫做“湘妃竹”，用来纪念这两位善良的中国妇女。

娥皇和女英

Ehuang and Nüying

After marrying Shun, Ehuang and Nüying worked hard to deal with family business and take care of their father- and mother-in-law. However, Shun's parents and his jealous younger brother, Xiang, hated Shun, and they had always aimed to kill him. Their conspiracies were all broken by the wise Ehuang and Nüying, and Shun was repeatedly saved from danger.

Once, when Shun was repairing the top of a barn, his brutal parents took away the ladder, and set it on fire. Shun was anxious, and standing on the top of the barn. Just at the moment he opened his arms, calling for help from the sky, a pattern of the Five-Color Clothes covered his arms, and the clothes suddenly turned into feathers. Shun became a giant bird, and dashed to the sky, leaving the heavy fire and the thick smoke behind. It was Ehuang and Nüying who had already seen through the trick and put this magic Five-Color Clothes on Shun.

After Shun had become an emperor, Ehuang and Nüying assisted him to do much good for the people. Later, Shun died on a journey when he was visiting the South. On learning the sad news, Ehuang and Nüying went to attend their husband's funeral, and they cried and cried. Eventually, their tears, which had been pouring out like a fountain, dropped on some bamboo by the Xiangjiang River, and left marks. For ever after, people called this Xiang Concubine Bamboo in memory of these two Chinese women.

相传管辂是三国时期的一个无事不晓的神卜。一天，他在郊外看见一个少年赵颜正在田中耕作，就停了下来，对其说三天之内必死。赵颜告与父亲。父亲听罢大惊，带赵颜追赶管辂。赶上管辂，父子跪拜于地，再三哭求管辂救赵颜一命。管辂见这种情形，不免动了怜悯之心，泄漏了天机。次日，赵颜带上酒脯杯盘，赶往南山，果然如管辂所说，有两个人正在大松树下的盘石上下棋。赵颜跪下，把带的东西敬上。二人也不推辞，拿来就吃。看他们吃完，赵颜突然哭拜求寿。二人大惊，可是吃了人家的东西，便不好推辞。穿白袍的老者取出簿籍查看，原来赵颜正值十九岁，本应三天之内寿寝；穿红袍的老者在“十”字之前添了一个“九”字，这样赵颜便可以活到九十九岁。添写完毕，二人化作两只白鹤，冲天而去。原来穿红袍的是南斗星，穿白袍的是北斗星。北斗注死，南斗掌生。

赵颜求寿

Zhao Yan Asking for Longevity

It was said that Guan Lu was a holy fortune-teller who could predict anything. One day, he saw Zhao Yan, a boy, plowing in the field; he stopped by, and told him he would die in three days. Zhao Yan told his father; the latter was shocked, and went after Guan Lu along with the boy. Having caught up with Guan Lu, the father and the son knelt down in front of him, and cried and begged him to save the boy, which aroused Guan Lu's sympathy. The holy fortune-teller revealed an unspeakable secret to them.

The next day, as Guan Lu's saying, Zhao Yan, bringing some wine and meat, climbed the south mountain. He saw two persons playing chess by a flat rock under a large pine tree, just as Guan told him. Zhao Yan knelt down, and presented them the food he had brought. The two began to eat while still concentrating on the chess board, while Zhao Yan cried for his life. The two were shocked, but having eaten his food, they could not reject his request. The old man in white took out a book, and checked Zhao Yan's life span – it was true that Zhao Yan, 19 years old at the time, should die in three days. Then the old man in red changed the number to 99, which meant Zhao Yan could live to 99. After that, the two turned into two cranes, and flew away. The two old men were actually the Big Dipper and the Small Dipper. The former was in charge of death, while the latter was in charge of life. It was said that afterwards, Guan Lu had seldom conducted his fortune-telling business for people.

曹操欲扩充军力，准备派人去劝降刘表，孔融便向曹操推荐了朋友祢衡。祢衡，字正平，性情怪僻，颇有奇才。曹操并不把祢衡放在眼里，把他招来，又不以礼相待，祢衡越加不满，骂遍了曹操手下的谋士、战将。因祢衡远近闻名，曹操没有杀他，让他充当鼓吏以辱他。

次日，曹操大宴宾客，令祢衡击鼓为乐。祢衡身穿破衣，上堂击鼓，左右喝其更衣，祢衡当面裸体而立，坐客皆掩面。曹操斥之无礼，然祢衡骂曹操不识贤愚、不读诗书、不纳忠言、不通古今、不容诸侯，欲成霸王之业，却轻人。曹操没有杀祢衡，最后还是派他去荆州招降刘表。

Mi Heng Hitting the Drum and Abusing Cao Cao

Cao Cao wanted to enlarge his force, so he planned to persuade Liu Biao, who was the governor of Jingzhou (in present-day Hubei Province), to join him. Kong Rong (153-208), a litterateur of the time, recommended his friend, Mi Heng, to Cao as the go-between. Mi Heng was an extraordinary man of unique character and capability. However, Cao Cao treated him contemptuously, which caused Mi Heng's dissatisfaction. Thus, Mi Heng began to verbally attacked Cao Cao's counselors and generals, but since he was a celebrity, Cao Cao did not kill him. Instead, he made him a drum master to play at the imperial court in order to humiliate him.

The next day, Cao Cao held a feast, and he ordered Mi Heng to play drum for entertainment. However, Mi Heng arrived dressed in shabby robes. Cao Cao's followers urged him to dress up, but Mi Heng took off his clothes, facing guests naked. All the guests felt this indecent and covered their eyes. Cao Cao reproached him for being impolite, while Mi Heng rebuked that Cao had no sense of distinguishing the prominent and the ignorant; that he did not read classics; that he did not adopt good advice; that he did not know history; that he did not tolerate other lords; and that he despised his followers, while having the ambition to achieve an imperial career. Cao Cao did not kill Mi Heng; he did however later, dispatch him to Jingzhou to persuade Liu Biao to surrender, promising that if Mi could win Liu Biao's support, he would be made a high ranking official.

Eventually, Liu Biao sent Mi Heng to his friend Huang Zu, who was intolerably rude and executed Mi Heng, which was said to be Cao Cao's original plan.

一天，梁山好汉李逵和燕青来到一个庄院投宿；晚上听见庄主夫妇哭泣，无法入睡。二人前去询问，得知这对老夫妇的女儿被梁山头领宋江抢走。李逵不禁大怒，连夜赶回梁山泊。他直奔忠义堂，二话不说，抡开大斧砍倒了堂前“替天行道”的杏黄旗，又冲上堂去，找宋江理论。众头领一看，急忙拉住，问其缘故。李逵把事情说明，宋江却矢口否认。李逵便拉着宋江下山找老夫妇对质。老夫妇一看宋江，都说抢他们女儿的不是这个人。李逵这才知道是有人假冒宋江之名为非作歹。回到山上，李逵向宋江负荆请罪。宋江说，除非李逵下山去把冒充的强盗抓来，才肯饶恕他。李逵一听，赶忙下山去，除掉强盗，救回庄主夫妇的女儿，将功赎罪。

李逵大闹忠义堂

Li Kui Turning over the Hall of Faith and Loyalty

Li Kui, nicknamed Black Whirlwind, is a popular figure among 108 heroes of the Mount Liang in folklore. Although he was fiery-tempered and a bit of a tearaway, he was respected for his unwavering beliefs and filial piety.

One night, he, along with another hero Yan Qing, bedded down at a farmhouse of an old couple. However, he couldn't sleep because he heard someone was weeping and sobbing. Tracing the sound, he found the old couple. On hearing that their daughter had been seized by Song Jiang, head of 108 heroes of the Mount Liang, he was furious. He returned to the Mount Liang overnight, and went directly to the Hall of Faith and Loyalty. With his giant axes, he first knocked down the yellow flag in front of the Hall, which was inscribed with "To Achieve Justice for Heaven", their belief. And then he rushed into the hall and went for Song Jiang. Other generals hurrily stopped him, and asked him why. Li Kui elaborated the evil deed done by "Song Jiang", which Song Jiang firmly denied. Seeing that Li Kui did not believe him, Song asked him to search his house. But Li kui said it would be impossible to find the girl because every man in the fortress was under Song's command. Finally, Song Jiang suggested going to the farmhouse and confronting the couple.

When the old couple saw Song Jiang, they said the person who had gone off with their daughter was not the one in front of them. Then Li Kui realized that someone disguised as Song Jiang and seized the girl. Back in the Marsh, Li Kui pleaded guilty. Song Jiang claimed that Li Kui would be forgiven unless he caught the false "Song Jiang". Li Kui immediately went to search for the bandits. After some adventures, he eventually found the bandits, killed them, and saved the girl.

从前有个叫马子才的人酷爱菊花，只要听说有好的菊花品种就要买回来。一日，他结识了养菊能手少年陶三郎和他的姐姐黄英。恰好姐弟二人想找地方居住，马子才便邀请二人住在家中。陶家姐弟培养的菊花绝美、清香，买花的人络绎不绝。不久，马子才便娶黄英为妻。

一天，陶三郎酒醉后摔倒在地，变成一株菊花。黄英急忙把它拔起放在地上，并拿衣服盖上。天明，马子才见陶三郎依然睡在那里，这才知晓姐弟俩都是菊花精。一次，陶三郎醉酒倒地，和上次一样，又变成一株菊花。马子才照着黄英的办法，把菊花连根拔起来，守在一旁观看。不料过了很长时间，菊叶、根茎都枯萎而死。黄英听说后立刻悲痛地说："你害死我弟弟了。"她立刻赶来，掐一小段根茎，种在花盆里，每天浇水，枯茎渐露新芽，花香如酒。后来人们给这种菊花起名叫"醉陶"。

黄英

Huang Ying

Long ago, there was a man named Ma Zicai who was very fond of chrysanthemums. One day, he made acquaintance with a teenager, Tao Sanlang, and his elder sister, Huang Ying. In the conversation, he knew that both of them were all good at cultivating chrysanthemums and were looking for a quiet living place. Ma Zicai then invited them to live in his house. The chrysanthemums cultivated by the siblings were extremely beautiful and freshly scented, and many people came to buy. Soon after, Ma Zicai married Huang Ying.

One day, Tao Sanlang got drunk, fell down, and turned into a chrysanthemum. Huang Ying hurried to pull the chrysanthemum out of the ground and covered it with Tao's clothes. The next morning, Ma Zicai saw Tao Sanlang was still sleeping in the same place. He realized that the siblings were chrysanthemum elves.

Once, Tao Sanlang got drunk again and fell down, and just like last time turned into a chrysanthemum. Ma Zicai did what Huang Ying had done before, pulled the chrysanthemum out of the ground, and stayed beside it, observing. To his dismay, after a considerable amount of time, nothing astonishing happened, while the leaves and the root of the chrysanthemum began to wither. On hearing this, Huang Ying said sadly, "You killed my brother." She hurried to pluck a little piece of the withering root, and plant it in a flowerpot. She looked after it every day, and gradually, it began to produce new shoots. The fragrance of the new flowers smelled like wine. Later, folks called this sort of chrysanthemum the Drunken Tao.

麒麟是中国古代传说中的一种动物，状如鹿，独角，全身生鳞甲，尾像牛。据说孔子生活的那个时候没有书，孔子常为此苦恼。一天夜里，他迷迷糊糊地看到，有一个地方忽然冒出一股赤红的烟气，聚在一起很久不散。孔子惊醒。他想："莫非是有圣贤出世，要来指点我吗？"他忙叫醒学生颜回和子夏，赶上车，一起去找那个地方。正走着，孔子看见前边的河岸上有个小孩正在拿石头打一只麒麟。孔子急忙下车，朝岸边走去。小孩见有人来，慌忙把麒麟藏在一堆干草中。孔子见麒麟受伤，连忙脱下衣服盖在麒麟身上，又小心地给它包好伤口。麒麟舔着孔子的手，突然吐出三部书来，然后转身跳下河岸，不见了。也许是因为他的"仁爱"，上天派麒麟给他送来三部天书。孔子得到这三部天书之后，整天潜心苦读，渐渐地，他的学问有了很大长进，最终成为名传千古的"至圣先师"。

麒麟献书

A Kylin Contributing Books

A *kylin*, or Chinese, unicorn, was an ancient Chinese legendary animal. It was supposed to look like a deer, and had a single horn and a tail resembling that of the ox, and its body was covered with scale and shell. It was said that there was no books during the age when Confucius lived. Confucius, as the story goes, often felt anxious that he had nothing to study, though he went everywhere to learn from learned people. One night, when falling asleep, his blurry-eye saw red smoke curling up at a certain place in the distance, and the thick smoke gathered into a cloud and did not fade away. He was shocked awake, thinking, "Does this suggest a sage would instruct me?"

He hurried to wake up his students, Yan Hui and Zi Xia. Then they took a carriage to search for the place. On the way, when seeing a child was hitting a *kylin* with a stone on the river bank ahead. Confucius hurried to get off his carriage. The child hastily hid the *kylin* in a pile of straw. Confucius speeded up his pace and went over. Pulling away the straw, he found the *kylin* was wounded. He took sympathy on it, covered it with his clothes, and carefully bound up its wound. The *kylin* licked his hands, and suddenly produced three books. Then it turned around, jumped into the river, and disappeared. Since he got the three holy books, which must be bestowed by Heaven for his benevolence, Confucius studied them day and night, and gradually he had made tremendous progress. Later, he eventually became the most learned sage in China's history.

晴雯是宝玉身边的一个丫环。她心地纯洁，性格泼辣，遇事敢怒敢言。一天，宝玉心中闷闷不乐，偏巧晴雯不小心摔坏了扇子。宝玉大骂其蠢材，晴雯口齿伶俐，连声反驳，气得宝玉浑身乱颤，要把晴雯赶出大观园。恰巧黛玉过来，才解了围。宝玉外出赴宴，晚上回到怡红院。他见凉椅上躺着一个人，以为是袭人，就凑过去坐在一边。哪知是晴雯。宝玉此刻已消了气，知道是自己小题大做，便赔上笑脸，和晴雯说些软话，请她去拿盘果子。晴雯却回答，她连扇子都摔坏了，哪里配端果子；要是再砸了盘子，更要挨骂。宝玉哄道，扇子撕着玩也可以，只是别拿来出气就行。晴雯要过宝玉手里的扇子，几下就把它撕烂。这时，正好有个丫头路过，宝玉把她的扇子也抢过来，递给晴雯；晴雯接过，又给撕了。宝玉一边笑一边说，千金难买一笑，几把扇子，能值多少钱？两人遂和好如初。

撕扇作千金一笑

Tearing up Fans for a Precious Smile

Qingwen was a personal maid to Jia Baoyu. She was good-natured, but had a temper, and she used to boldly criticize to relieve her anger. One day, when Baoyu was gloomy, Qingwen happened to drop his fan and broke it. Baoyu repeatedly abused her as a "moron." Qingwen verbally fought back, which greatly angered Baoyu, who then threatened to drive her away. At this moment, Daiyu walked in and mediated the dispute. Soon after, Daiyu took her leave and Baoyu received an invitation of a party.

When Baoyu came back in the evening, he saw a girl lying on a couch in his courtyard.He thought it might be Xiren, so he went over to the chair and sat by her; but the girl was Qingwen. Baoyu was slightly tipsy and calm down then, and teased, "You are growing more and more spoilt. When you trod on the fan, I only made a harmless little remark. But look at you, launching into such a tirade!" Then he asked her to bring a plate of fruit for him. However, Qingwen answered that she was even unable to hold a fan and how she could get fruit for him; that if she broke the plate, she would be abused even more severely. Baoyu realized her temper was aroused again, and joked that tearing up fans could be fun, as long as one did not throw her anger into them. On hearing this, Qingwen took out Baoyu's fan, and tore it into pieces. Baoyu laughed and encouraged her, "Well done! Try again and make it louder!" Just at the moment, another maid came by. Baoyu got her fan and handed it to Qingwen; the latter laughed and tore it up. Baoyu laughed and said that even a large amount of gold could not buy such a smile and that compared to the cost of the fans was meaningless. Then the two had at last made up.

这一天，贾政要宝玉去陪贾雨村，宝玉讨厌官僚政客，不愿去见。湘云劝宝玉多会会这些官场中人，也好为日后多做打算。不料宝玉听了勃然大怒，还说黛玉从来不说这样的混账话。这时，黛玉走至门外，正好听见宝玉这一席言语，心中不免又喜又惊，又悲又叹：喜的是自己果然没看错人，宝玉正是她知己；惊的是宝玉竟然敢于在众人面前称赞黛玉；叹的是既然互为知己，又何必牵出他和宝钗的"金玉良缘"；悲的是，父母早逝，无人为她做主，而她体弱多病，恐红颜薄命。想到这里，黛玉一面拭泪，一面转身回去。宝玉出屋见黛玉边走边拭泪，赶上去给黛玉擦泪，把自己的一片真心，肺腑之情都倾吐了出来。两人泪眼相对，心中纵有千言万语，却一个字也说不出口。怔了好一会儿，黛玉长叹一声，径直而去。望着黛玉的背影，宝玉站在那里呆呆地发傻。

诉肺腑宝玉痴情

Jia Baoyu Expressing His Infatuation

One day, Jia Zheng asked his son Jia Baoyu to entertain Jia Yucun, a local official who was Lin Daiyu's tutor. But Jia Baoyu said he hated to meet bureaucratic officials and politicians. So Shi Xiangyun, one of Baoyu's cousin, tried to persuaded him, "Be grown-up! You should mix with these officials as much as you can. That will help you to manager your own affairs in future." However, these words appeared to him as nonsense, and he said that only Daiyu was his soul mate.

Daiyu happened to pass by and heard Baoyu's word, which delighted and surprised Daiyu but also distressed and grieved her. She was delighted that she had never misjudged Baoyu, who didn't let her down. She was surprised that Baoyu dared to praise her unreservedly in front of other people. She was distressed that since the two were a perfect match, why Xue Baochai tried to intervene? She was grieved that her parents had died during her childhood, and no one would defend her; besieds, she was sorrowful at her own bad health and she might not have long to live. Then she turned away, tears overflowed.

Baoyu walked out, and saw Daiyu walking and weeping. He hurried to catch up with her in hopes of alleviating her sorrow. Then he verbally expressed his true love from the bottom of his heart. The two gazed at each other and silently shared tears; anything they could say would be lost. After remaining like this for a time, Daiyu let out a heavy sigh and finally walked away. Watching her walk away, Baoyu stood petrified by his own numbness.

曹操刺杀董卓未成，招兵买马，召集各路诸侯起兵共讨董卓。虽刺杀失败，但曹操的胆量已是天下闻名，于是一呼百应，众诸侯纷纷响应，率兵朝汉都洛阳杀来。董卓于是派义子吕布镇守虎牢关。

吕布英勇无敌，连败讨董兵将。张飞见状，圆睁环眼，倒竖虎须，挺丈八蛇矛，飞马冲上前去，酣战吕布。吕、张大战五十回合不分胜负，关羽挥起青龙偃月刀，拍马赶到，前来助战。三人战得难分难解。看到吕布愈战愈勇，刘备担心伤了两位兄弟，一挺双股剑，斜里杀出来，加入战斗。三兄弟围住吕布，如转马灯般厮杀，众人皆看得目瞪口呆。吕布招架不住，冲着刘备虚刺一戟，刘备急忙躲闪。吕布趁机杀出包围，弃城而逃。

图中描绘的便是刘、关、张三人围攻吕布于核心，曹操等兵将在城上一角观战。

虎牢关三英战吕布

The Three Heroes Fighting Lü Bu at the Hulao Pass

Cao Cao started recruiting for his army after he failed to assassinate Dong Zhuo. He called upon local military leaders of different areas to send forces to suppress Dong Zhuo. This was widely supported. Various uprising forces rose in rebellion. Dong Zhuo dispatched Lü Bu to defend the Hulao Pass (also named Sishui Pass, in today's Xingyang, Henan Province), a pass of strategic importance. Lü Bu successively defeated many generals challenging him. Then Zhang Fei galloped out to fight Lü Bu with his Serpent Spear. Seeing the two were drawing after 50 rounds, Guan Yu, wielding his Green Dragon Crescent Blade, dashed out to assist his brother. Later, Liu Bei, could not bear to sit and watch, also joined the battle with his swords. The three brothers galloped in a circle caging Lü Bu, just like a merry-go-round. Unable to face the combined efforts of his three opponents, Lü Bu had no choice but to flee. He then made a feign at Liu Bei, retreated and escaped.

In the painting, Liu Bei, Guan Yu and Zhang Fei are cornering Lü Bu, while Cao Cao and other generals and soldiers are watching the fight.

颐和园石舫 MARBLE BOAT

STORIES BEHIND THE LONG CORRIDOR PAINTINGS IN THE SUMMER PALACE

《颐和园长廊彩画故事》

北宋真宗时，辽国进犯，几次被北宋大将杨延昭打败。这一年，辽国集结人马，在谷口天险处布下“天门阵”，阵内阴霾密布、毒气阴森，宋军多次攻阵均告失败，死伤无数。

杨延昭得知惟有用穆柯寨的“镇寨之宝”降龙木方可破阵之后，便命手下部将孟良、焦赞前往穆柯寨，打算强取降龙木。不料，孟、焦二人被寨主之女穆桂英打败。恰逢杨延昭的儿子杨宗保路过此地。年轻好胜的杨宗保便跃马挺枪，策马向前，和穆桂英打了起来。两人打得难解难分之时，穆桂英拔马就跑，杨宗保紧追不舍，眼看宗保就到跟前，穆桂英取出红落套，回身抛去，杨宗保立即翻身下马，束手就擒。

穆桂英飞索套宗保

Mu Guiying Getting Yang Zongbao with a Lariat

During the reign of Emperor Zhenzong (reigned 998-1022) of Northern Song, the Liao Dynasty (916-1125) invaded central China, but after several attempts, they were defeated by the Song army under the commander-in-chief Yang Yanzhao. This time, the Liao Dynasty summoned a giant army, and deployed the Sky Gate Formation in a dangerous valley, which could reek with poison gas. The Song army was unable to break, and suffered great losses.

Yang Yanzhao invited his brother Yang Yande to help. However, Yande needed a weapon – a battle-ax, the handle of which must be made of “Dragon-Conquering Wood”, a special kind of wood which could only be found near Muke Castle. So, Yang Yanzhao sent his fellow generals, Meng Liang and Jiao Zan, to the Muke Castle, with the intention of taking the Dragon-Conquering Wood by force. But, without too much preparation, the two generals were defeated by Mu Guiying, the daughter of the castle chief. Having grown up in a band of outlaws, she mastered military skills and formed a resoluted and courageous character.

At the moment, Yang Zongbao, the son of Yang Yanzhao, happened to pass by. The presumptuous and competitive young man immediately rushed to fight Mu Guiying. The two had a good fight. Instead of animosity, love sparked between Mu Guiying and Yang Zongbao, so she tried to take him captive. When Mu turned her horse to run way, Yang went in close after her. Seeing the young man was about to catch up, Mu took out her red lariat and threw at him. Yang Zongbao was bound in the lariat, fell off his horse, and ended up caught.

唐僧师徒傍晚来至通天河边，河宽水急，无法渡过，便到河畔陈家庄借宿。庄里的百姓告诉他们：河中住着一个妖怪，每年须用一对童男童女祭祀它，方才风调雨顺；否则它便会兴风作浪。悟空、八戒为救陈家庄百姓，变作童男童女，不料八戒一遇妖怪，心中着慌，现出原形，提钯就打，妖怪见势不妙，钻进河中，不见踪影。

次日，见通天河冰冻且有人行走，师徒四人继续赶路。然而行到河中央，冰突然裂开，唐僧掉进水中，被妖怪捉走。悟空等人潜入河中，打败了妖怪；妖怪却逃回老窝，紧闭大门，不再应战。观音赶来收走了妖怪。这时，游来了一只巨鼋。它原住在河里，被金鱼精霸占了府邸；除掉妖怪，它也得以返回故里。为表感谢，巨鼋驮着唐僧师徒渡过通天河。

通天河

The Tongtian River

Tang Seng and his three disciples came to the Tongtian River by nightfall. Seeing that the river was as turbid and huge as the ocean, they had to take rest in a village by the river, where a Buddhist worship was holding. The villagers told them that there lived a monster in the river. Every year the villagers would hold a sacrifice to him, at which a young boy and a girl had to be offered, then the monster would send timely rain; but if there was no sacrifice it would send disaster. In order to save the villagers, the Monkey King and Zhu Bajie, Tang Seng's two disciples, turned into a boy and a girl, and set out to deal with the monster. Unfortunately, Bajie became nervous while they were confronting the monster, and revealed his original shape. Then he just directly hit the monster with his weapon, a nine-tooth iron muck-rake. The monster understood the dangerous situation, and escaped.

The next day, the river froze and looked thick enough to support a person's weight. Tang Seng and his disciples tried to cross the river. When they walked in the middle of the river, the ice suddenly broke, and Tang Seng sank into the water where the evil monster captured him. The three brothers dived below the surface and defeated the monster; however, the latter hid itself in its residence and never showed again. Hopelessly, the Monkey King had to call on the Kwan-yin Bodhisattva, who successfully subdued the monster. As a matter of fact, it was a goldfish that Kwan-yin raised. After the three brothers rescued their master, Tang Seng, there appeared an gigantic, old tortoise, who uesd to live in the river but was chucked out by the monster. It promised to take the four across the river, as a repay for helping it back home.

明朝时，礼部尚书之子王金龙与名妓玉堂春邂逅，两人情投意合，互为知己。一年后，王金龙几万银两被老鸨骗尽，被赶出来，沦落街头，靠乞讨为生。玉堂春倾囊相助，劝公子用功读书，早日考取功名。

王金龙走后，玉堂春拒不接客。老鸨将其卖给山西富商沈燕林为妾。富商之妻皮氏与人私通，害死亲夫，反诬玉堂春，告到官府。县令接受皮氏钱财，对玉堂春严刑拷打。玉堂春被屈打成招，定为死罪。恰在此时，科举中第、做了八府巡按的王金龙审理此案。几经周折，查明案情，便升堂复审（画面上即是此情景），为玉堂春平反申冤，两人也破镜重圆，结为夫妻。

玉堂春

Yutangchun

It's said that in the Ming Dynasty Wang Jinlong, the son of the Minister of Rites, made acquaintance with Yutangchun, a famous singsang girl in a whorehouse, when he was studying in the capital. The two pledged to love each other forever. After a year in the whorehouse, Wang Jinlong used up all his money. Then he was driven out of the whorehouse and reduced to live by begging on the street. Hearing of this, Yutangchun secretly sent someone to bring him her savings and treasures and persuade him to return home and devote himself to his studies.

After Wang Jinlong left, Yutangchun became a fidget, having no thought of eating or sleeping upon recalling the past days spent with Wang Jinlong. And Yutangchun refused to engage in sexual intercourse, thus the owner of the whorehouse sold Yutangchun to a rich married businessman surnamed Shen as a concubine. Yutangchun did everything she could do to resist being sold, but her defiance was futile. Indeed, Shen's wife, having an adulterous affair with a man, schemed to poison her husband and frame Yutangchun. The county magistrate, who had accepted the evil-minded woman's bribe, beat Yutangchun bitterly and indiscriminately. Yutangchun was coerced into confessions under severe torture, and finally sentenced to death.

Just at this time, Wang Jinlong, who had become a high-ranking official, came to make investigaions. When hearing that it was Yutangchun who was sentenced to death, he immediately disguised as a commoner to seek for the truth behind the case. Then he heard the case again, which is shown in the picture. In the end, Yutangchun was exonerated and the two eventually married.

刘备被曹操打败后，投靠荆州刺史刘表。刘表的夫人蔡氏和其兄蔡瑁怀疑刘备有吞并荆州之心，便伺机害他。有次打仗，刘备缴获一匹千里马，刘备见刘表喜欢此马，便将它送给了刘表。刘表手下有一人颇懂相马术，说此马对主人不利，劝刘表将马还给了刘备。

一次，刘表请刘备代替他到襄阳去会见百官，该城西门外有一条檀溪河，河宽水急，不易通过。蔡氏兄妹认为这是个好机会，就在东、南、北门派重兵把守，只留西门，等待下手。席间，一个叫伊籍的人向刘备暗示蔡氏兄妹要害他，让他从西门逃出。行数里刘备被檀溪河阻住去路，这时追兵赶来，刘备急忙打马过溪，没走几步，马失前蹄。刘备大惊，然马从水中一跃数丈，飞身上岸，摆脱了追兵。

马跃檀溪

A Horse Jumping over the Tanxi River

After Liu Bei was defeated by Cao Cao, he submitted to Liu Biao, the chief of Jingzhou. Cai Mao, a millitary official who gained his status after his sister married Liu Biao, suspected that Liu Bei had an intention to seize Jingzhou, so they planned to kill him. Once, after a battle, Liu Bei seized a swift horse (which it was rumored could cover a thousand miles in a day). He saw Liu Biao was fond of the horse, and gave it to him. One of Liu Biao's followers boasted that he knew well about the art of judging horses; he said the horse would bring misfortune to its master, and persuaded Liu Biao to return the horse to Liu Bei.

Once, Liu Biao asked Liu Bei to go to Xiangyang City to meet his fellow officials there in his stead. The Tanxi River, by the west gate of Xiangyang City, was broad and the water turbulent made it hard to cross over. Cai Mao and his sister thought it was a good opportunity to kill Liu Bei. They deployed a large number of troops to hold the city's east, south, and north gates, and left the west gate unguarded. During the meeting, a person hinted that Liu Bei should watch out in case Cai Mao hurt him, and suggested that he could escape through the west city gate. Liu Bei went out of the city, and after riding for a few miles, he was stopped by the Tanxi River. At this moment, the troops chasing him arrived. Liu Bei hurried to urge his horse to cross the river, but having walked for a few steps in the river, the horse lost its balance and fell down. Liu Bei was gravely shocked, but suddenly and magically, the horse jumped high above water, landed on the west shore of the river. Liu Bei eventually shook off the troops chasing him with the help of the horse that had been perceived as an ominous animal.

金兀术有一义子陆文龙，英勇过人，是岳家军的劲敌。一日，岳飞正在为陆文龙一事苦恼，部将王佐浑身是血地闯入帐内。原来王佐特来献“苦肉计”。他自断右臂，打算诈降金兵，伺机杀掉金兀术、策反陆文龙。岳飞忍痛答应，泪如泉涌。王佐连夜到金营，金兀术果然对他深信不疑，把他留在营中。王佐利用能在金营自由行动的机会，接近陆文龙的奶娘，说服奶娘向陆文龙讲述了他的身世。原来，陆文龙本是宋朝潞安州节度使陆登的儿子。金兵进犯中原时，陆登夫妇竭力御敌、为国捐躯。金兀术将当时还是婴儿的陆文龙掳走，收为义子。陆文龙得知真相后，恨得咬牙切齿，誓为父母报仇雪恨。金兵此时运来一批轰天大炮，准备深夜轰炸岳家军营。陆文龙闻讯后，当晚和王佐、奶娘投奔宋营，将实情禀报了岳飞，使岳军免受了损失。王佐断臂，使猛将陆文龙回到宋朝，立下了战功。

王佐断臂

Wang Zuo Cutting His Arm Off

Lu Wenlong, the adoptive son of Jin Wuzhu, was ferocious and capable, who continued to create trouble for the Song army and prevent them from achieving a decisive victory. Actually, Lu Wenlong was the son of Lu Deng, who was in the charge of Lu'an Prefecture during the Northern Song Dynasty. When Jin troops besieged Lu'an, he sacrificed his life for the Northern Song and his wife also hanged herself to secure her integrity. Jin Wuzhu caught Lu Wenlong, an infant then, and adopted him.

When the Commander General Yue Fei was troubled by being unable to design a counter plan to fight back, one day, his subordinate general, Wang Zuo, entered his camp, with blood all over his body. As a matter of fact, he planned to serve as a spy in the Jin army. In order to get Jin Wuzhu's trust, Wang Zuo amputated his right arm, so as to have a chance to kill Jin Wuzhu and tell Lu Wenlong his background. Yue Fei accepted it with tears.

Wang Zuo came to Jin Wuzhu and pretended to surrender himself to the Jin; the latter trusted him completely, and gave him the carte blanche in the encampment. He made acquaintance with Lu Wenlong's wet nurse, and persuaded her to tell Lu his real origin. When Lu Wenlong learned the truth, he decided to take revenge. By the time the Jin army had a number of giant canons which were going to be used to bomb the encampment of the Song army, Lu Wenlong and his wet nurse followed Wang Zuo to the Song army. He reported the ongoing deployment (the dangerous bombing) to Yue Fei, which helped to stave off the total annihilation of the Song army. Wang Zuo's self-torture finally paid off.

包拯是北宋时期的清官，以断狱英明刚直而著称于世。他秉公执法，不避亲党，被称为“包青天”。

正当陈世美准备杀害香莲母子，开封府尹包拯巡视各地回到京城。秦香莲抱着一线希望，告到开封府。包拯劝陈士美认下香莲母子，但是陈士美贪恋功名利禄，一口否认有香莲妻儿之事。包拯便升堂审案，令秦香莲与陈士美对簿公堂。陈士美见实情无法掩盖，恼羞成怒，拔出剑来，要杀香莲母子，包拯喝住，画中描绘的便是此情景。包拯命衙役捆绑陈士美，虽然皇姑、国太都跑来前来求情，然包拯还是铁面无私，斩杀了陈士美。

铡美案

The Execution of Chen Shimei

Bao Zheng (999-1062), an incorruptible official of the Northern Song Dynasty born into a scholar family in Heifei, Anhui, was a much-praised judge from the Song Dynasty. He was famous for his uncompromising stance against corruption among the government officials, upholding justice and refusing to yield to higher powers including imperial relatives. Because of his renowned fairness, he was popularly glorified “Blue-Sky Bao” or “Lord Bao”. In opera or drama, he is often portrayed with a black face and a white crescent shaped birthmark on his forehead.

A portrait of Bao Zheng

Just at the critical point when Chen Shimei was going to assassinate Qin Xianglian, Bao Zheng, who worked as the civil governor of the capital city Kaifeng then, returned after making his rounds around the country. Qin Xianglian, seeing a bit of hope, impeached Chen Shimei, who abandoned his previous wife in order to marry the princess. Bao Zheng tried to persuade Chen Shimei to take Qin and her child, but Chen, fearing that he would lose his wealth and honor, firmly denied that he and Qin were married and had given birth to a child. Then Bao Zheng had to hold a formal hearing. Qin and Chen debated in court, and being unable to cover the truth, Chen Shimei was ashamed and furious. He took out his sword, and intended to kill Qin and her children in public. Bao Zheng stopped him, which is well-described in this painting. Then Bao Zheng ordered civil servants of the court to bind down Chen Shimei and despite that the emperor’s aunt and mother came to beg forgiveness for Chen, Bao Zheng had Chen Shimei executed.

芒种是送花神的日子。一清早，大观园里的姑娘们都由丫环陪着走了出来，惟独不见黛玉。宝钗准备去潇湘馆找黛玉出来。正走着，她远远看见宝玉走进了潇湘馆。宝钗不由停住脚步，为了避免黛玉的猜疑，转身就往回走。没走几步，忽然看见一对大花蝴蝶，一上一下，迎风飞舞。宝钗觉得十分有趣，想捉住它们，就从袖中取出一把扇子，扑蝴蝶。那一对蝴蝶忽起忽落，来来往往，宝钗一路追赶，直到累得大汗淋漓，气喘吁吁时才罢手。

宝钗戏蝶

Xue Baochai Playing with Butterflies

Mangzhong, the ninth of the Twenty-Four Solar Terms from the traditional Chinese calendar (usually June 6), was supposed to be the day for seeing the flower elf off. On the early morning, girls lived in the Grand View Garden all went out with their maids, except Lin Daiyu. So Xue Baochai, Jia Baoyu's another cousin, went to the Bamboo Lodge to invite Daiyu.

A drawing of Xue Baochai Playing with Butterflies

As she approached the Bamboo Lodge, Baochai saw Baoyu entered Daiyu's residence, which made her slow down. Xue Baochai was a well-educated and reasonable girl. She knew Baoyu and Daiyu were used to behaving uninhibitedly when they were along together since they grew up under one roof. And Daiyu, at the best of times, was always jealous and petty-minded. If she followed Baoyu in, he would be embarrassed and she would be bothered. Then she turned back. After several steps, she saw a pair of big colorful butterflies dancing on air. Baochai thought it quite interesting, and intended to catch them. She took out a folding fan from her sleeve, and began to flap. However, the two butterflies were quite agile, and they shifted quickly from one position to another, which made the hunter breathe heavily and sweat. Learning it was a tough task, Baochai eventually gave up.

赤壁大战之前，因曹军不习水战，曹操命人将战舰用铁索相连，中间铺上木板，将士行走其上，如履平地。于是，周瑜和诸葛亮决定用火攻，烧掉曹操的连环战船、一举打垮曹兵，然而须有东南风方可放火。可正值隆冬季节，何来东南风？于是周瑜请诸葛亮帮忙。诸葛亮满口答应，让周瑜于南屏山建一座“七星坛”。这一日，诸葛亮上坛祭风。周瑜调兵遣将，只等东南风起，准备与曹兵厮杀。

果然近三更时分，旗幡转动，刮起了东南风。周瑜嫉妒诸葛亮如此神通广大，有夺天地造化之法、鬼神不测之术，唤来兵将往南屏山杀死诸葛亮。诸葛亮料定周瑜必会加害于他，预先派赵子龙来接应。待周瑜兵将到达七星坛时，他早已乘船离开。这幅画里就是诸葛亮“借”完东风，正走下坛去。哪里会“借风”呢？不过是诸葛亮通晓天文气象，再加上自己的聪明、智慧罢了。

七星坛孔明借东风

Zhuge Liang Sacrificing to the Wind from the Seven-Star Altar

Prior to the Battle at Chibi, Cao Cao ordered to chain his warships together to stabilise them and reduce sea-sickness among his soldiers. As a result, this gave the chance to Zhou Yu and Zhuge Liang to attack Cao's ships with fire, which could spread quickly to destroy Cao's entire fleet. However, Zhou Yu knew the fire would be effective only if the southeastern wind rose; it was a harsh winter (a time when the northwestern wind dominated in China), how could they summon the southeastern wind? He turned to Zhuge Liang. Zhuge Liang was delighted to give Zhou Yu a hand, and he asked Zhou to build the Seven-Star Altar on Nanping Mountain. After the altar had been erected, Zhuge Liang began to pray for the wind, and Zhou Yu deployed his army preparing to fight Cao Cao as long as the southeast wind blew.

At 1 am, the sound of the wind was heard and flags began to wave westwards. However, Zhuge Liang's extraordinary prominence excited Zhou Yu to jealousy. He said, "This man has power over the heavens and authority over the earth. He cannot be allowed to live to be a danger to us." Then he sent an army to kill Zhuge Liang. Actually, Zhuge Liang merely had some knowledge of astronomy and meteorology. He knew Zhou Yu was jealous of him and was always seeking opportunities to kill him, so he had informed Zhao Yun to pick him up, and had already left. The scene in this painting is that after calling upon the east wind, Zhuge Liang is leaving the altar. Zhuge Liang had simply made a prediction based on knowledge and wisdom.

春秋时，晋文公即位后，行赏有功之臣。家臣介子推跟随文公奔波流亡19年，文公无意中将他遗忘。介子推的邻居见他有功无赏，心怀不平。可介子推却功成身退，不愿贪图犒赏。老母见儿子有志气，决定和儿子一道隐居深山，不与世人争名利。介子推便背着老母进山。

晋文公得知后，觉得很对不起介子推，亲自上山寻找介子推母子，未果。晋文公想到介子推是个孝子，如果焚山烧林，他一定会背着母亲逃出来。于是，他下令放火烧山三天三夜。但介子推始终不肯出山，与老母相抱死于枯柳之下。晋文公见此情景，后悔莫及。为了纪念介子推，晋文公下令每年到了介子推烧死的这一天全国全吃冷饭冷菜。“寒食节”即由此而来。寒食节一般在清明的前一天或两天，过去人们在这时候要祭祀介子推，以后又扩大到祭祀各家的祖宗，逐渐与清明节合并。

Jie Zitui Carrying His Mother into a Mountain

During the Spring and Autumn Period, Duke Wen of Jin seized power and after he came to throne, he rewarded those who had helped and supported him. Jie Zitui was a personal minister to Duke Wen, following him for 19 years; on the way of his exile, Jie always accompanied him, going through all kinds of hardships and difficulties. However, the Duke forgot to put him on the reward list. Even Jie's neighbor felt the lack of justice for him, Jie Zitui was ignorant of fame and wealth. His mother learned of his intentions, and was willing to live in seclusion in the mountains with him. So Jie Zitui carried his old mother and entered the mountains.

On learning it, Duke Wen felt guilty and went to search for them, but in vain. Duke Wen thought Jie Zitui was a filial son, and if he burned the woods on the mountain, Jie might come out for his mother's safety. The fire burned for three days, but Jie Zitui still did not show up. Finally, he and his mother was found to be dead under a withered willow tree, holding onto each other. Duke Wen regretted and in memory of Jie Zitui, he decreed that every year, on the day when Jie Zitui died, people should not set fires, and everyone should eat cold food. This is the historic background of the Cold Food Festival. Usually the Festival is one or two days before or after Tomb-Sweeping Day (a national Chinese holiday, the fifth of the Twenty-Four Solar Terms on the traditional Chinese calendar, April 5). In the past, people used to sacrifice to Jie Zitui during that time, and later, the sacrifice extended to their ancestors; thus, Tomb-Sweeping Day has become a day of sacrifice.

这幅画取意于唐朝诗人李咸用的诗歌《独鹤吟》。李咸用，颇有才气，又重功名，然而他一生不得志，仕途无门，只在人家的聘请下当过一个小官。于是，他对仕途心灰意冷，对跻身宦海、随波逐流的人也很反感。他把自己科举考试的失败归于统治者的昏庸无能、不识人才。因此，诗作的主题多为离群索居、孤芳自赏的伤感情调。

《独鹤吟》通过具有高洁品性而不愿与尘世同流合污的仙鹤形象，表达诗人孤寂而高傲的真实感情，是诗人一生的自我写照。

独鹤吟

Song of a Lonely Crane

Li Xianyong was a prominent figure, and he used to attach great importance to wealth and fame. However, he was unlucky all throughout his life, and was never selected by the court as a formal official, which was about the only career open to well-educated men in those days. He was only hired to take a low position once. Thus, he was disappointed at politics, and grew disgusted toward those who wandered in the political arena and lost themselves. He blamed his failure on the imperial examinations and the ignorance of the ruling class and their incapability to pick the prominent, and seemed to be dominated by a desire to live in solitude and to be a lone soul admiring his own purity.The themes of his poem were mostly about solitude, seclusion, self-pity as well as self-appreciation, and were full of sentimentality.

This painting is based on one of Li's most famous poems, *Song of a Lonely Crane*. For its elegant form and its allness amongst the feathered throng, the crane has always been a symbol of ideal for the traditional scholar who liked to imagine himself as being much above the mundane world. It is also one of the symbols of longevity and is often represented with other symbols of long life, such as pine tree, bamboo and the tortoise.

In his poem, Li describes the bird with its jasper-like long bill and scarlet crown, pridely standing amongst the breeze-caressed pines. Its head held so high that if it stretches its black neck, it would touch the sky; while if it weaves its spotless white plumage, the clouds would be dispelled. However, it is there all alone, a placid and solitary form of elegance, statue-like in the forest or under the moon, mindless of the hubbub of the querulous crows and attracted solely by the musical murmurs of the mountain spirits. It is really a depiction of the poet's life as a whole.

香菱自幼失去父母，被人拐卖给了薛家，做了薛蟠的陪房丫环。一天，香菱和几个丫头各采了些花草，斗草取乐。这个说有观音柳，那个说有罗汉松。大家你一句，我一句，对得很热闹。这时豆官说："我有姐妹花。"大家难住了，过了一会儿，香菱说："我有夫妻蕙。"豆官见香菱答上了，不服气地说，从来没有什么夫妻蕙。香菱争辩道，一枝一个花叫兰，一枝几个花叫蕙；上下结花为兄弟蕙，并头结花叫夫妻蕙。她手里拿的是并头结花的，所以叫夫妻蕙。豆官争不过她，便笑着说道，只是香菱心里想着刚外出半年的薛蟠，便把花儿扯成夫妻，说得香菱满脸通红，笑着跑过来拧豆官的嘴。这时，宝玉也采了些草来凑热闹。

香菱斗草

Xiangling Playing the Grass Game

Xiangling lost her parents when she was very young, and was kidnapped and sold to the Xue Family. She served Xue Pan, Xue Baochai's elder brother, as a personal maid. One day, she and other maids collected some flowers and grass, and began to play the grass game, which was a sort of game where participants competed about the shapes of the flowers and grass in their hands, such as the bodhisattva-shaped willow and the arhat-shaped pine.

The scene was quite lively and noisy. A maid named Douguan said, "I've got a sister- flower." All the participants seemed to have nothing more magnificent to compete with, but after a while, Xiangling said, "I've got a husband-and-wife orchid." Douguan responded in contempt, and said there was no such a shape in the grass game. Xiangling explained that a branch which had one flower was called lan orchid, and a branch with several flowers was called hui orchid; when the flowers growing one above the other on the stem, it was called a brother-orchid; when two flowers growing side by side at the top, it was called a husband-and-wife orchid.

Douguan could not win the debate, and began to laugh at her, "It's because your husband has been away for half a year and you're longing for him, so you dream up a husband-and-wife orchid. Shame on you!", which made Xiangling's face shine with embarrassment. Xiangling laughed and went over to pinch Douguan. Then the two rolled over on the grass, while the others laughed and clapped their hands. At this moment, Jia Baoyu had collected some grass and flowers too and came to join them, but surprised to find the other girls running away leaving Xiangling there.

洛阳孙公子，婚后20天丧妻。一天天降大雨，少女吕无病卷帘而入，因仰慕公子是世家名士，怜公子年轻丧偶，愿意作婢女。公子见她虽然面貌丑陋，但朴实温柔，又通晓文字，就纳她为妾。此后，公子娶了许家小姐做正妻，许小姐和无病亲如姐妹，后来许小姐生下一男孩，取名阿坚。无病对阿坚十分疼爱，悉心照顾。

后来，许小姐病逝，公子按父母之命娶了王氏小姐。王氏虽容貌艳美，但性情骄横暴戾，对无病总是谩骂、欺侮，对阿坚也是非骂即打，吵得全家不得安宁，孙公子忍无可忍，离家出走。一次，阿坚生病卧床，王氏不照顾，还不让无病照顾。无病最后抱起阿坚逃走，找到公子后，便倒地死去，只见衣服不见人，公子方知无病是鬼。为了感谢她的仁义，孙公子亲手为无病立碑刻字，称其“鬼妻”。

吕无病

The Ghost Wife

There was a young aristocrat, Mr. Sun, whose wife passed away just 20 days after their wedding. One day, it rained torrentially. A young girl entered his chamber. She said her name was Lü Wubing, and since she admired his talent and lamented that he had lost his wife at such a young age, she wanted to serve him as a maid. Mr. Sun could tell the girl was innocent, gentle and literate, and took her as a concubine, in spite of her ugly appearance. Later, Mr. Sun married another lady, who got along quite well with Lü Wubing and gave birth to a boy A Jian. Lü took careful care of the boy very much. However, the lady died later. Before her death, she told Sun, “Lü loves A Jian. Please let her be your wife after I die.” In tears, Sun promised he would, however, he could not follow through on his promise because his family urged against it, since Lü wasn’t matched Sun in social or economic status. Actually, no one knew where she was from.

Then Mr. Sun married a girl surnamed Wang under his parents’ arrangement. His new wife was beautiful in appearance, but ferocious and selfish in character. She always abused and beat A Jian, and the family was by no means in peace any longer. Mr. Sun could not bear the trouble, and deserted his own family. Once, A Jian was ill in bed, while Mrs. Sun not only did not take care of him but also prevented Lü Wubing from doing so. Lü, carrying A Jian, had to escape, and after finding Mr. Sun, she dropped dead. There were, however, only clothes on the ground after she fell down, and no corpse was seen. Mr. Sun then realized that Lü was a ghost. To show his gratitude to her kindness and affection, Mr. Sun buried her clothes and carved a tombstone for her, which has gone on to become legendary - Ghost Wife.

曹操之父曹嵩行经徐州时被杀，曹操以报父仇之名，发兵攻打徐州、大肆杀戮平民百姓。徐州太守陶谦势单力薄，无力抵挡，派人四处搬救兵。刘备领兵前来解围，打败了曹操大将。此时，由于吕布也发起对曹操的攻击，曹操无暇顾及徐州，只好撤兵，徐州之围遂解。

陶谦年迈体衰，二子又不堪重任，听闻刘备德高望重，他有心将徐州让与刘备。两次劝说，刘备皆执意不受，认为这是不义之举，只是答应陶谦屯兵小沛、保护徐州。不久，陶谦病重，派人找来刘备再次商议，劝刘备以汉朝城池、天下百姓为重，接受徐州。刘备仍然不肯，陶谦以手指心而死。徐州的军民、百姓拜求刘备执掌州权，刘备才掌管徐州。

陶谦三让徐州

Tao Qian Remising Xuzhou Three Times

Cao Cao's father Cao Song was killed while travelling through Xuzhou (in present-day Jiangsu Province), which prompted Cao Cao to launch a campaign against Tao Qian, the governor of Xuzhou. A very large number of common people living there were massacred by Cao's army. Liu Bei sent his troops and defeated Cao's general. At this time, Lü Bu regrouped his forces for a new attack on Cao Cao, who was forced to withdraw. Thus, Liu Bei rescued Xuzhou.

Tao Qian was then an aging and ailing man. What's worse, his two sons were not capable enough to run the city. He knew Liu Bei was a virtuous and capable man, so he twice asked Liu to take over his position. Liu Bei did not accept the offer, because he thought it was inappropriate to take a position under such conditions. But Liu just promised Tao Qian that he would deploy his army in Xiaopei (a place near Xuzhou) to protect Xuzhou.

Soon after, Tao Qian, on his deathbed, had Liu Bei summoned and tried to persuade Liu for the third time to accept the position for the sake of the safety of Xuzhou and its people. Liu Bei still did not agree with him. Soon after, Tao Qian died with his hand pointing to his heart. The soldiers and residents of Xuzhou all knelt down and begged Liu Bei to lead them, thus Liu Bei accepted and became the new governor of the city.

太原有个读书人，姓王，一天早上出门，遇见一个漂亮的少女抱着一个大包袱独自行走。他过去询问，得知：她的父母贪财，将她买给富人家，每天从早到晚非打即骂；她受不了折磨，因此逃了出来。王生很是同情，便收留了她。女子嘱咐他千万不可告诉外人。从此二人朝夕相处，王生渐渐荒废了学业。后来，王生碰见一位道士。道士说，王生身上有妖气，而且他的血都快被妖精吸干了。王生有些怀疑女子，但一想到她的美貌，就放弃了这个念头。回到家中，他发现门已上锁，只好翻墙进入；走到窗口前，往里一瞧，没看到那女子，却见一个恶鬼手中正拿着笔在一张人皮上描画。听见有人来了，恶鬼忙把皮披在身上，又变作美女。王生拔腿就跑，可为时已晚。恶鬼抓住王生，掏走了他的心脏。王生妻子哀求道士救活王生。道士被她的诚心打动，铲除了恶鬼，又指引她救活了王生。

画皮

Painted Skin

There lived a scholar in Taiyuan named Wang. One morning, he went out and came across a beautiful young girl who carried a heavy bundle and difficultily hurried along by herslf. The girl told him that her avaricious parents sold her as a concubine into a rich family, where she had been beaten and abused every day; she could not stand and ran away. Mr. Wang felt much sympathy for her; most of all, he was drawn in by her beauty and hastened to invite her to live with him in his study. The girl agreed but told Mr. Wang, "If you really want to take me in, do not tell the others." Hearing Wang' promise, she remained there without anyone knowing anything about it. Wang was with the girl day and night, gradually being lured away from his studies.

One day, Wang met a Taoist, who asked surprisingly, "Have you had any peculiar encounters?" "No." "But an evil air is in your body, moreover your blood is about to be drained away." Half-believed, Wang went back home. When he found the door was locked inside, he sensed something was wrong. He climbed over the wall, and peering inside his window, Wang indeed saw a terrible devil spreading a human skin upon the bed and painting it with a paint brush. As soon as it heard the footsteps, the evil hurriedly draped the skin and changed into the girl. Being half dead with fright, Wang immediately ran, but it was too late. The devil caught him and ate his heart. Wang's wife grieved deeply from her husband's death. She then implored the Taoist to help save her husband. Moved by her sincerity, the Taoist killed the devil finally freeing Wang to regain his life.

索　引

INDEX